BIO DESIGN

BIO DESIGN

Nature • Science • Creativity

WILLIAM MYERS

Foreword by PAOLA ANTONELLI

with 467 illustrations, 436 color

To my teachers, especially Celeste Topazio,
Lisa Farber, Michael Rosenfeld, and Alice Twemlow

William Myers lives in Amsterdam where he writes and gives public lectures about the history of art and design. In 2013–14 he curated an exhibition based on this book, *Biodesign: On the Cross-Pollination of Nature, Science and Creativity*, at The New Institute in Rotterdam. William has worked in a variety of roles for the Solomon R. Guggenheim Museum, MoMA, Cooper-Hewitt, National Design Museum, Design Academy Eindhoven and Genspace, the first community biotech lab in the United States. His writing has appeared in *Domus*, *Metropolis*, *The Architect's Newspaper* and *Next City*. William is a graduate of the MFA program in Design Criticism at the School of Visual Arts in New York.

Occasionally project profiles are contributed by Barbara Eldredge and Andrew Gardner. Barbara is a design writer and researcher based in New York. Most recently she worked for the Museum of Modern Art organizing its new department of Research and Development. Her writing has been featured in *New York Magazine*, *Metropolis* and core77.com. Andrew is a Master's student in the History of Design at the Bard Graduate Center in New York City. His work focuses on urban design, technology and cultural landscapes. Barbara contributes text on pages 162, 211, and 226, while Andrew contributes text on pages 147 and 172.

First published in the United Kingdom in 2012
by Thames & Hudson Ltd, 181A High Holborn,
London WC1V 7QX

First paperback edition 2014

Bio Design © 2012 Thames & Hudson Ltd, London
Text © 2012 William Myers
Foreword text © 2012 Paola Antonelli

Designed by The Studio of Williamson Curran

British Library Cataloguing-in-Publication Data
A catalogue record for this book is available
from the British Library

ISBN 978-0-500-29150-4

Printed and bound in China by Toppan Leefung

To find out about all our publications,
please visit www.thamesandhudson.com.
There you can subscribe to our e-newsletter,
browse or download our current catalogue,
and buy any titles that are in print.

On the front cover:
Objectivity. Images courtesy of Dr Eshel Ben-Jacob

On the back cover:
(top left to top right)
Carnivorous Domestic Entertainment Robots.
    © Marcus Gaab Studio
BioCouture. © BioCouture 2011
Blood Lamp. Image courtesy of Mike Thompson
Lung-on-a-Chip. Image courtesy of the Wyss Institute for
    Biologically Inspired Engineering at Harvard University
(below left to below right)
Exploring The Invisible. Image courtesy of Anne Brodie
Dune. Image courtesy of the architect
Carnivorous Domestic Entertainment Robots. Image courtesy
    of the designers
Future Venice. Image courtesy of Rachel Armstrong

The quotation on the back cover is taken from *Steve Jobs*
    by Walter Isaacson, published by Little, Brown in 2011.

Frontispiece:
Algaerium. Image Courtesy of Marin Sawa

VITAL DESIGN

Paola Antonelli

Design is not what it used to be. In schools and in studios, in
corporations and in political institutions, designers are using their
skills to tackle issues that were previously out of their bounds, from
scientific visualization to interfaces, from sociological theories to
possible applications and consequences of nanotechnology. They
do so by teaming up for every case study with the right experts,
who often seek designers' help in order to connect their theories
with real people and the real world. In the late 1960s, Ettore Sottsass
famously declared that design 'is a way of discussing society, politics,
eroticism, food and even design. At the end, it is a way of building
up a possible figurative utopia or metaphor about life.'[1] Design
is indeed about life and, at a time of accelerated technological
evolution and dramatic political, environmental, demographic,
and economical concerns, designers' presence guarantees that
human beings are always kept at the center of the discussion.

Designers' fascination with science is today reciprocated
by a generation of scientists who are eager to get their brains dirty
with reality. As explored first in the 2008 exhibition 'Design and
the Elastic Mind' at the Museum of Modern Art, New York (full
disclosure: yours truly was the curator), these novel collaborations are
often joyous contaminations in which scientists feel, even if just for a
moment, liberated from the rigor of peer review and free to attempt

intuitive leaps. Indeed, physicists, mathematicians, computer scientists, engineers, chemists, and bioethicists have leaped at the opportunity, their contribution encouraged and celebrated in a few centers of 'irradiation,' such as London's Royal College of Art Design Interactions program or Le Laboratoire, an idea incubator in Paris. The results (based on current research) have the lyrical and demonstrative power of art and the realistic possibilities of design.

It is, however, the experiments with biologists that have garnered the strongest momentum, and a new form of organic design is rapidly evolving—the biodesign that William Myers explores in detail in this volume. Biodesign harnesses living materials, whether they are cultured tissues or plants, and embodies the dream of organic design: watching objects grow and, after the first impulse, letting nature, the best among all engineers and architects, run its course. It goes without saying that when the materials of design are not plastics, wood, ceramics, or glass, but rather living beings or living tissues, the implications of every project reach far beyond the form/function equation and any idea of comfort, modernity, or progress. Design transcends its traditional boundaries and aims straight at the core of the moral sphere, toying with our most deep-seated beliefs. In designers' ability to build scenarios and prototypes of behavior lies a power that they should protect and cherish, and that will become even more important in the future.

William Myers has collected an impressive variety and number of case studies that involve organisms at all scales, from plants and animals to bacteria and cells, to be used as architectural, graphic, or interior elements. Architects working on wet buildings that adapt to changing environmental conditions and levels of occupancy, almost as if they were living organisms; designers concocting new diagnostic and therapeutic tools that rely on animals and plants; engineers devising new, self-healing construction materials. If our relationship with nature is broken, this book makes us hope that perhaps we will be able to fix it from within.

1
As reported in Peter Dormer,
'What is a designer?', *Design Since 1945*
(London: Thames & Hudson, 1993) p.10.

THE HYBRID FRONTIER

William Myers

This book presents an emerging and often radical approach to design that draws on biological tenets and even incorporates the use of living materials into structures, objects, and tools. Each chapter introduces a different theme, from designing for ecological integration to the use of speculative design and art as a teaching tool. Taken together, several of the projects profiled here reflect a pervasive shift in societal priorities, toward sustainable approaches to building and manufacturing. This unifying purpose is driving increased collaboration between designers and biologists—an essential ingredient in many of the projects—and offers thrilling new possibilities for design, art, and architecture. This volume brings together the most recent and representative examples of biodesign: a rapidly emerging approach observable in this collection of works from around the world.

Biodesign goes further than other biology-inspired approaches to design and fabrication. Unlike biomimicry, cradle to cradle, and the popular but frustratingly vague 'green design,' biodesign refers specifically to the incorporation of living organisms as essential components, enhancing the function of the finished work. It goes beyond mimicry to integration, dissolving boundaries and synthesizing new hybrid typologies. The label is also used to highlight experiments that replace industrial or mechanical systems with biological processes. The final chapter ventures beyond functional or speculative design into the realm of fine art, presenting a range of recent work that incorporates living matter.

The structures, prototypes, and concepts chronicled here, including proposals that employ new technologies and impose principles observed only in nature, prompt several questions. What are the implications and likely outcomes of these speculative projects? Does the sum of these experiments, including an embrace of natural systems and collaboration with the life sciences, amount to a paradigm shift in design practice? If so, how does it compare with other field-changing shifts in the trajectory of technological developments, from industrialization to the invention of computers?

As answers to these questions unfold over time, the space for cross-disciplinary collaboration and creativity prompted by scientific research will only expand, propelled by global imperatives such as the urgency to develop and implement cleaner technologies and the rise of do-it-yourself 'homebrew' biology. This convergence of fields, as well as of the expert with the amateur, is ultimately necessary to support the ongoing effort to alleviate the negative impacts of the legacies of the Industrial Revolution. And it will lead to the reconception of the primary design principles of value generation, growth, and sustainability. This book sets out to accelerate this effort by highlighting achievements in, and new approaches to, design with biology, encouraging collaborations and providing historical context for this growing field in design.

BEYOND BIOMIMICRY

ABOVE 1

In contrast with traditional architecture that is in combat with the environment, **Fab Tree Hab** is a housing concept that embraces and enhances the surrounding ecosystem. Living trees are integrated into the structures.

A NEW URGENCY

'It will be soft and hairy.' [1]

Salvador Dalí on the future of architecture, in response to Le Corbusier

Designers face an unprecedented urgency to alter their methods and reprioritize their goals to address the accelerating degradation of the environment. This new pressure—intellectual, ethical, and regulatory—demands recognition of the fragility of nature and our responsibility to preserve it for future generations. Under such shifting and intensifying constraints, designers are beginning to go beyond emulation to harness processes observed in the living world, where systems achieve perfect economies of energy and materials. Within this pursuit, working to achieve enhanced ecological performance through integration with natural systems, designers are turning to biologists for their expertise and guidance. This contrasts markedly with the design approach that characterized the 20th century: the mechanization of functions in order to overpower, isolate, and control forces of nature, usually by utilizing advances in chemistry and physics. The examples explored here illustrate how this new approach—designing with biology—lends itself to collaborations with life scientists and foreshadows what kind of consilience, or cooperation across fields, we can expect in the future.

The integration of life into design is not a magic bullet to solve these pressing issues. Nor will it be free from harmful missteps, deliberate misuses, or controversy. Dystopian visions of the future awash in biodesign gone awry are credible possibilities, and they are included in this book. Beyond growing structures with trees or integrating objects with algae bioreactors, biodesign includes the use of synthetic biology and thereby invites the danger of

disrupting natural ecosystems. These technologies will be wielded by people—the same biased and frail creatures who designed the world into a desperate mess in the first place. But the potential benefits, and the need to reform current practices toward an approach more in tune with biological systems, far outweigh these risks. Ultimately, design's embrace of nature—even coupled with the inevitable hubris that we can redesign and outdo it—is long overdue and the most promising way forward.

The focus of cross-disciplinary collaborations and their outcomes will, as always, depend on societal priorities and an array of market signals. Today there is a notable absence of the kind of regulation or system of incentives and disincentives that might lead to the eventual design and creation of environmentally remedial or zero-carbon objects and structures. The use of taxes and subsidies to spark such changes, for example, is still in its infancy. While Germany and Norway have made early and effective steps with policies that prioritize ecologically effective design, most of the industrialized world lags behind, especially the United States, where even the legitimacy of the federal agency to protect the environment is vulgarly challenged in political discourse.

Yet the costs of carbon emissions and climate change mount, and they will need to be addressed if a modern way of life, as we've come to know it, is to endure. Examples of biodesign profiled here anticipate this change: an accounting for, and eventual minimization of, what economists call negative externalities to the environment—the degradation of the air, soil, water, and life that does not figure into the end cost of manufacturing and building today. Only under new and sensibly designed constraints, such as a carbon tax on manufacturing, or incentives, such as a subsidy for structures that promote biodiversity, would projects such as 'Fab Tree Hab' (page 58) or 'BioConcrete' (page 80) become scalable.

ABOVE 2

Researchers at Delft University of Technology have developed **BioConcrete**, which is embedded with limestone-making microorganisms that allow the material to repair itself.

ABOVE   3

A modular system of algae-filled tubes absorbs solar energy for electricity generation and shades interior spaces in **Process Zero**, a proposed retrofit for a General Services Administration building in Los Angeles (page 52).

The imitation of nature in the design of objects and structures is an old phenomenon, recalling stylistic developments such as iron-enabled Art Nouveau in the 19th century through to the more recent titanium-clad fish shapes in the computer-aided designs of architect Frank Gehry. Yet this design approach is form driven and offers only a superficial likeness to the natural world for decorative, symbolic, or metaphorical effect. Design that sets out to deliberately achieve the qualities that actually generate these forms—adaptability, efficiency, and interdependence—is infinitely more complex, demanding the observational tools and experimental methods of the life sciences. The effort to master this complexity is well under way; it's been more than 30 years since scientists first altered a bacterium's DNA so that it could serve as a tiny factory producing an inexpensive and reliable source of human insulin.[2] At the beginning of the 21st century, the DNA-modifying techniques to reproduce such a feat and reconfigure the activity of a cell have become widely accessible. We have even reached the milestone of synthesizing an entirely artificial

DNA molecule that has successfully replicated and formed new cells.[3] The affordability of the basic tools of biotechnology has put them within reach of engineers and designers who may now consider basic life forms as potential fabrication and form-giving mechanisms. Indeed, that is precisely the intention of architects such as David Benjamin, who is teaching and practicing how to wield life as a design tool and insists that 'This is the century of biology.'[4]

In the 19th century the combination of standardization of measurements, the Bessemer steel-making process, and the steam engine converged to enable the Industrial Revolution, answering the call of democratic, capitalistic nation-states seeking market growth. Facilitating this development was the increasing quality and plummeting price of steel, which rapidly fell from $170 per ton in 1867 to $14 per ton before the end of the century.[5] Similarly, and following what has become known as Moore's Law, the computing power of microchips has roughly doubled every two years since the 1990s. This phenomenon, amplified by the rise of the Internet and the worldwide adoption of standards like HTML, has supported a Digital Revolution.[6] Computer technology exponentially spread and intensified the practices and effects of the Industrial Revolution, and they addressed the demands of a rapidly globalizing economy. These demands include pressure to compete in foreign markets, to coordinate increasingly complex supply chains, and to achieve continual economic expansion through productivity gains. In fulfilling these needs, digital technology lubricates the gears of civilization as we know it, supporting economic growth and maintaining relatively low unemployment and stable governments across most of the developed world.

In the first decade of the 21st century and beyond, the forces that prompted industrialization and digitization persist, but a new, more urgent, and arguably longer-term need has arisen that calls for a new revolution—the requirement for ecologically sound practices in design that guide scarce resource management, particularly in manufacturing and building. Abundant evidence makes plain that the pace of world economic development in its current form, relying on the rapid consumption of natural resources (including fossil fuels), cannot be maintained.[7] The scale and scope of human activity and projected changes in climate, economic demand, urbanization, and access to resources over the next several decades will necessitate new standards of energy efficiency, waste elimination, and biodiversity protection.

Models that meet such rigorous demands have been found only in nature, the emulation of which is now moving beyond stylistic choice to survival necessity. Driven by research in the life sciences, the mechanisms of natural systems—from swamps to unicellular yeasts—are quickly being decoded, analyzed, and understood. The architectural program of many of these systems is DNA, the sequencing and synthesis of which are quickly becoming financially viable, following what has become known as the Carlson Curve: the costs of sequencing and synthesizing base pairs of DNA have fallen dramatically over the last 10 years, just as steel and computing power became inexpensive commodities in previous centuries.[8] The possibilities arising from this new accessibility of the basic ingredient of living systems will surely multiply, particularly given the pace of capital investment and the proliferation of entrepreneurial ventures poised to exploit its potential. Although these technologies are still new and require much more research before they can easily be applied to complex organisms, the pace of investment and growth is significant: more than 2 percent of United States GDP is now attributable to products that rely on genetic modification.[9] As the expertise to manipulate and wield the machinery of life spreads, it will impact numerous fields and lead to several collaborations; biodesign, as I have defined it, is an opportunity that designers will not miss and that is already attracting tinkerers of all stripes.

As it often does, art illuminated the path forward. Bioart of the last decade, including works by Eduardo Kac, such as the living, glowing 'GFP Bunny' in 2000 and the numerous projects that have emerged from

Art Nouveau attempted to mimic natural forms displaced by industrialization. The movement emerged in France but then spread swiftly around the world. The Hôtel Tassel in Brussels is a masterwork of Victor Horta, and it was completed in 1894 for the scientist Émile Tassel.

SymbioticA, foreshadowed the now burgeoning do-it-yourself biology (DIY bio) movement. Facilitated by the availability of inexpensive equipment and emboldened by like-minded enthusiasts through instant communication over the web, amateur biologists are now creating transgenic organisms and even inventing novel equipment on their own. These new creators, some of them with design experience, also follow in the footsteps of tech entrepreneurs working out of garages in California in the 1970s and 1980s, and they bring an ethos of independence that is unlinked from the agendas or conventions of universities and corporations.

PHYSICAL SCIENCE TO LIFE SCIENCE: A HISTORY OF NATURE IN DESIGN

'The Stone Age did not end because humans ran out of stones. It ended because it was time for a re-think about how we live.'[10]

Architect William McDonough

The desire to follow nature, to adhere to its underlying forms in the pursuit of harmony, can be traced back to antiquity, to the writings of Vitruvius, as well as to Goethe's work on morphology and the Romantic notion that certain truths were observable in nature and unknowable to reason. The close examination and formal mimicry of nature by designers reached a height in the late 19th century, in the Art Nouveau style in France and in its iterations across Europe, coinciding with the work of naturalists and pioneers of biology, like Ernst Haeckel, who meticulously described, named, and illustrated thousands of new

SymbioticA is a pioneering research laboratory at the University of Western Australia that enables artists and researchers to engage in wet biology practices. It hosts residents, workshops, and symposia to support the exploration as well as the critical evaluation of scientific developments.

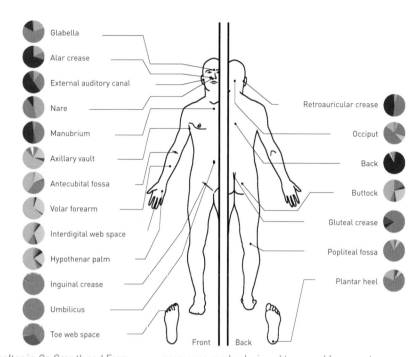

Actinobacteria
■ Corynebacterineae
■ Propionibacterineae
■ Micrococcineae
■ Other actinobacteria
▨ Bacteroidetes
■ Cyanobacteria

Firmicutes
■ Other firmicutes
▨ Staphylococcaceae

■ Proteobacteria

■ Divisions < 1%

☐ Unclassified

Glabella
Alar crease
External auditory canal
Nare
Manubrium
Axillary vault
Antecubital fossa
Volar forearm
Interdigital web space
Hypothenar palm
Inguinal crease
Umbilicus
Toe web space

Retroauricular crease
Occiput
Back
Buttock
Gluteal crease
Popliteal fossa
Plantar heel

Front | Back

ABOVE 7

Illustrations of shells from a variety of gastropod mollusks, reproduced from Ernst Haeckel's influential *Kunstformen der Natur* ('Artforms of Nature'), which was published in 1904.

ABOVE 8

BioBE Center researchers at the University of Oregon at Eugene are working to map the microbiome (microorganism population) of the built environment, collecting samples from a variety of spaces and analyzing how these different groups impact human health.

species. Shortly thereafter in *On Growth and Form* (1917), D'Arcy Thompson described numerous links among biological form, physics, and mechanics, and highlighted how optimization was frequently achieved in nature. This also coincided with the First World War, and the rapid rise of mechanized industry as a dominant feature of economic, aesthetic, and political life in Europe and the United States.

Interest in nature as a model or tool for design remained a consistent, if minor, current in architecture of the early 20th century. This was particularly so in the work of figures such as Frank Lloyd Wright, Alvar Aalto, and even Mies van der Rohe, for their focus on integration of indoor and outdoor spaces, use of natural materials, expression of structure, and consideration of architecture as a component of a larger whole—at least its immediate built surroundings. The idea of emulating nature on a larger scale emerged decades later in post-war Japan, articulated by the built and theoretical megastructures of the Metabolist movement that embraced impermanence, citing the fluctuations of nature as a logical guiding principle for buildings and cities, which themselves undergo massive transformations that can be considered in terms of cycles, including destruction and rebirth.

The more familiar contemporary understanding of the built environment and industrial manufacturing as systems affecting their natural surroundings matured in the wake of the environmental movement and the energy crisis of the 1960s and 1970s, as expressed through the works of Richard Buckminster Fuller, Rachel Carson, and Victor Papanek.[11] Perhaps the best representation of the ideas they espoused is the concept of industrial ecology, explained first and with cogent precision in 1989 by Robert Frosch and Nicholas Gallopoulos, two scientists working for General Electric.[12] Their thesis can be summarized: industrial

processes can be designed to resemble ecosystems wherein every waste product becomes a raw material for another process. This idea was explored further, with a naturalist view, by Janine Benyus in her seminal book *Biomimicry: Innovation Inspired by Nature* (1997), and her continuing work through the Biomimicry Guild and Institute. Following similar principles, in *Cradle to Cradle: Remaking the Way We Make Things* (2002), architect William McDonough and chemist Michael Braungart retold the history of Western architecture and industrial design to highlight their inherently destructive relationship with the people and environments from which they had risen. These authors also demonstrated the sort of cross-disciplinary partnership necessary to connect scientific research and rigor to industrial and building technologies for improved ecological performance. In a sense, they symbolized a return to the type of consilience that characterized the sciences and applied arts from the Renaissance, when leading artists and architects were also scientists, until about the 18th century, when the effects of the Scientific Revolution took hold and led to dramatically specialized fields of study.

Today, this rift between fields is narrowing by necessity. We recognize that designers do not simply create things like teapots and office towers but instead act as initiators of systems of resource collecting, labor application, manufacturing, marketing, distribution, consumption, and disposal. These activities, all oversimplified by the tendency to consider the object as an end in itself, present a uniquely complex set of problems and support the assertion that from an ecological standpoint, there are no such things as things: there are only *systems*. This realization mirrors new research in biomedicine that suggests the human body hosts approximately ten foreign cells for every one of its own making. We depend on all this microscopic life—trillions of cells—for essential functions, like digestion and resistance to infection, making us all ecosystems in miniature.

The built environment is no different: as research by the BioBE Center (page 248) suggests, a better understanding of microbial life in indoor spaces—a vast and undiscovered realm we interface with all the time—may inform a probiotic design approach that reduces reliance on mechanical ventilation. These realizations arise in part from new access to the nanoscale, the ability to manipulate matter on the cellular and molecular levels. Just as standardization and manufacturing tolerances to the millimeter scale were crucial to the move from craft to the Industrial Revolution, as well as to the practices and goals of the Bauhaus school, the ability to change the inner functioning of a cell exponentially increases designers' reach, and is enabling a move from the industrial to the biotechnological. This in turn is becoming the medium of choice for a new Bauhaus school to emerge, perhaps in the form of the One Lab School for Urban Ecology (page 247).

This new access in scale also offers new vocabulary to the language of form, and may satisfy a larger need to bring the living world closer to our everyday lives. Perhaps in the recent past the mere mimicry of forms displaced by industrialization and globalization was sufficient as a symbol, but that time has past. In *Complexity and Contradiction in Architecture* (1966), which laid the intellectual foundation for postmodernism in architecture, Robert Venturi argued that the labored rectilinear style of the modernists was in fact a dishonest representation of functionalism and that both greater visual harmony and expression of function was achieved through formal conflict: shapes, lines, and textures that disrupt one another. Echoing that critique, one can see nature-inspired design and its iterations, often posturing under the banner of biomimicry as a labored style for its own sake that does not represent biodesign, for its intention strays from the priority of delivering enhanced ecological performance.

It is primarily by cooperation, communication, and debate that effective approaches to biodesign will be developed and implemented, and a legible formal language will emerge. As progress is made, however, and as designers and scientists work together more frequently, it's essential to recognize the challenges along with the opportunities. As shown in a recent study at the University of Cambridge, which examined such collaborations, obstacles often arise, such as disagreement about how to share intellectual property rights, a lack of shared vocabulary, and conflicting working styles and standards.[13] These and other issues will be at the forefront as society acknowledges that the consumption of irreplaceable resources and the loss of biodiversity driven by economic activity cannot be sustained. Consequently, systems of nature and the biologists who work to understand them will be integral to new systems for designing and creating. Only this type of consilience might help to bring the material existence of artificial environments and objects into a sustainable harmony with nature, a state upon which everything ultimately depends.

LEFT 9

To the present day the Pantheon remains the largest unreinforced dome in the world. Its stable structure was made possible by concrete that was poured in sections and supported by a wood scaffold until it dried, combined with clever engineering to reduce the weight of the rock substrate with increasing height.

THE EVOLVING GOALS AND DESIGN OF CONCRETE: A TRAJECTORY TOWARDS BIODESIGN

'Our objective is to use bio-based materials and processes for civil engineering to reduce environmental pressure.' [14]

Henk Jonkers, Researcher and Instructor, Bio-based Geo- and Civil Engineering Program, Technology University of Delft

Concrete's 2,400-year history offers an insightful example of the shift over time to biodesign, from some of civilization's earliest structures to new

LEFT 10

An early example of iron-reinforced concrete, the Lighthouse of Port Said was completed in 1869, just a week prior to the opening of the Suez Canal. The building was an important asset in facilitating global trade and had come under British imperial control by 1882.

methods of using bacteria as an ecological means of reinforcement. Concrete has served designers and engineers as the spine of infrastructure and the foundational material of structures since antiquity. First widely used in the 4th century BC, it was integral to the Roman Architectural Revolution, which spanned several hundred years and generated structures—including domes, arches, and aqueducts—that still stand today.[15] Soon after the fall of Rome, the formula for concrete, calling for particular proportions of calcium oxide, pulverized rock, clay, ash, and water, was lost for thirteen centuries. It is useful to pause for a moment to ponder how builders for so long looked at ancient monuments that bested their own engineering ability. This age without concrete ended with its rediscovery in 1756 in England, the precise time and place of the dawn of the Industrial Revolution.

Approximately a century later, reinforced concrete was developed in France by François Coigent and was deployed to create several structural typologies that are common today.[16] The utility and historical significance of the material is well illustrated by many of his projects, from the sea wall in Saint-Jean-de-Luz, to the lighthouse in Port Said, Egypt, and the Aqueduc de La Vanne in Paris. All of these projects met infrastructure needs arising from the forces brought to bear by widespread industrialization and the rise of global capitalism in the form of colonialism: constructing ports to facilitate the movement of freight to support commerce, and infrastructure to facilitate rapid growth in urban populations. Similarly, the first structure in Britain to feature a reinforced concrete frame was a factory: a flourmill built in Swansea in 1897.[17]

With the benefit of centuries of hindsight, it is possible to see concrete's evolution—from its discovery, loss, and rediscovery to its current widespread use in reinforced form—as closely intertwined with the evolving needs and priorities of the societies that used it. In the centuries during which its formula was unknown, much building occurred, but the forces driving it apparently did not create a strong enough imperative for the material's rediscovery to occur. The needs of an empire—roads, bridges, ports, barracks, and aqueducts—demanded such a material from the Roman builders who, through experimentation and discovery, found a way to deliver it. With the dissolution of the empire, the need for a material like concrete was likewise diminished, although many builders, mocked by the splendid monuments in their midst, would be in want of its formula.[18] Similarly, one can see the needs of the industrial age to maximize land use—by means of factories, bridges, ports, and ever-taller buildings—as driving the deliberate search for a leap in material technology, one that was answered by iron and, eventually, steel-reinforced concrete

Today, a new and powerful need is emerging to reduce the environmental impact of human activities, including building: use fewer materials and less energy, and consider the entire design life cycle, from conception through manufacture to disposal. Understood as part of the continuum of developments in material technology, this need introduces a new dimension to how performance is evaluated: the degree of sustainability. Design in the 21st century is expected to perform in new ways that take into account its impact on worldwide energy and material cycles. The effects of the rapid development of the global economy and the rising prosperity of hundreds of millions of people—particularly in India and China—are exacerbating scarcities of natural resources and demanding that systems of design, manufacture, and consumption evolve. The poor example set by the United States and Western Europe, in terms of environmental degradation and waste of material resources throughout the 19th and 20th centuries, simply cannot be followed by all the world's citizens, now numbering more than seven billion—the environment cannot endure it.[19]

The urgency of this demand for material sustainability and ecological preservation grows even as the world recovers from an economic downturn. At current rates of production and consumption, carbon emissions would lead to an uninhabitable climate for much of the planet within 300 years.[20] Developing strategies to respond to this bleak outlook results in exercises such as considering how to build in a desert with precious few resources, as shown by the architect Magnus Larsson in his proposal 'Dune' (page 62), which would harness bacteria to build walls that halt the spread of the Sahara. Ultimately, the constraints of extreme environments force designers to examine and replicate life: the only resource-management system that is known to function within conditions as harsh as those of a desert.

It is with such a view that a new type of concrete is being developed at Delft University of Technology in the Netherlands. There, Henk Jonkers has adopted the use of bacteria to create a living, self-healing concrete that might outlast, and be cheaper to maintain than, the conventional variety (page 80).[21] The bacteria offer a means of reinforcement, infusing the material and lying dormant for years or decades until a crack appears, weakening the concrete, whether in a road or structural support. By admitting oxygen and moisture, the crack prompts these bacteria to secrete limestone, effectively sealing it naturally. If perfected and widely adopted, such biointegrated material technology could have an enormous impact: a full 5 percent of human-generated carbon emissions result from the manufacture of concrete, so even a marginal increase in the material's service life would amount to a breakthrough. It is precisely this type of research, led by a biologist focused on making civil engineering more ecologically sound through integration with a living process, that heralds a new approach to designing with biology.

For much of history, performance and quality were measured by the degree to which a designed material, object, or structure addressed a set of needs only once it was completed and handed off to the user. This primacy and narrow definition of function is no longer valid. In the 21st century it is being replaced by a new, more sophisticated understanding of factors, such as the impact of carbon emissions, product life cycle, and resource scarcity. In addition, new dimensions of function have become increasingly important, such as an object's ability to restore a sense of human connectivity, enable new forms of interaction, or make critical observations about the future trajectory of technologies and behaviors. As a result, as this examination of concrete illustrates, the performance of a design has come to be judged by a much larger set of criteria.

THE PROMISES AND PERILS OF PARADIGM SHIFT

'If we were incapable of handling nature as we found it without causing lasting damage, why would we handle its manipulation any better?' [22]

Angeli Sachs, Curator, Museum of Design, Zurich

The demand to design differently—to bring production and construction into a more integrated relationship with natural processes—is growing and will accelerate collaborations between designers and biologists. This phenomenon is being encouraged by educators like Maria Aiolova, organizer of the One Lab; Alberto T. Estévez, who heads the program in genetic-biodigital architecture at the International University of Catalonia; and David Benjamin, who introduces architecture students at Columbia University to the emerging field of synthetic biology. Simultaneously, regulatory action to combat climate change by enforcing ecological performance standards and preserving what remains of natural resources gains ground, albeit slowly. Promising advances in synthetic biology and the availability of tools for genetic engineering also multiply the possible benefits of harnessing nature, much like HTML standards helped lay the groundwork for the web.

Beyond stylistic consideration or symbolic meaning, biodesign pioneers collaborate with the greatest urgency and potential for positive impact, propelled by societal forces and new research. A major difference between a proposal like Le Corbusier's *The Radiant City* (1935) and Magnus Larsson's 'Dune' (2008) is that the latter is a response to a new conception of necessity. Lewis Mumford, criticizing Le Corbusier, wrote: '[his] skyscrapers had no reason for existence apart from the fact that they had become technological possibilities.'[23] In contrast, Larsson's proposal both addresses and harnesses elements of nature in a struggle more consequential than those that Le Corbusier pondered, his declarations of 'architecture or revolution' notwithstanding.[24] The 20th century did

By harnessing bacteria to form rigid structures from a mixture of sand and nutrients, Magnus Larsson's project **Dune** proposes the formation of habitable oases in the desert that will also help to protect endangered arable soil.

Resembling the first digitally created typeface, Digi-Grotesk S, **Symbiosis** utilizes bacterial cultures in petri dishes to shape letters, with variations created by elements in the growing environment (page 142).

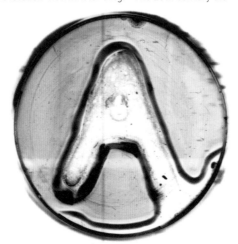

not demand as dramatic a transformation as that which the 21st century appears to require. Building with bacteria and other organisms is simultaneously becoming a technological possibility and a *necessity*.

An analysis of the history of technology and design rightly prompts skepticism about the embrace of new design that uses living matter, regardless of how extreme the conditions of climate change or other pressures might become. Evidence strongly suggests that designers could misuse the new powers they are obtaining with the help of biology. Designers and architects are still people bound to their cultural

ABOVE   19

A dark future may await a world awash in biological innovation. In the fictional narrative of **E.Chromi** (page 142), a Dutch terrorist organization (Orange Liberation Front) is compelled to threaten the world's biologically generated and patented colors with antibiotics.

ABOVE   20

According to **Synthetic Kingdom** (page 168), unintended yet horrifying possibilities could result from biological alterations set loose upon the environment, such as lungs within a smoker that are crystallized by carbon monoxide biosensors.

biases and personal frailties. Aspects of inherited, dysfunctional impulses, such as neo-colonialism, a rush to change for its own sake, myopic pursuit of profit, and media-savvy theatricality out of proportion with practical potential, will persist as design develops new intersections with the life sciences. Designers and artists are also responding to these looming dangers and have created numerous objects and narratives to articulate dark potential futures that we may unwittingly bring into being. Alexandra Daisy Ginsberg has envisioned such futures in critical projects like 'E.Chromi' (page 167) and 'The Synthetic Kingdom' (page 168), and—disturbingly—has found them frequently misinterpreted as literal, earnest proposals for new technologies. One goal of this book is to incite discussion and careful consideration of the potential unintended consequences of biodesign, something that is too often overlooked in the breathless optimism that characterizes discussion of this field today.

Should biodesign be the next design paradigm, as foreshadowed throughout this book, in which biological and biomimetic processes replace those that are mechanized and digitized today, we can expect a host of benefits and burdens. The spread of biodesign promises to be much like mechanization in the 20th century, as described by historians such as Sigfried Giedion in *Mechanization Takes Command* (1948): upending accepted practices, extinguishing traditions, attenuating natural beauties, and shaping an alien way of life. How we manage this change is yet to be observed, but Giedion struck a prescient, cautionary note when examining how mechanization had infiltrated agriculture and the raising of livestock: 'A new outlook must prevail if nature is to be mastered rather than degraded. The utmost caution is imperative. This calls for an attitude turning radically away from the idolatry of production.'[25] As vast, unsustainably managed agribusinesses attest, his vision was accurate. Fixation on economic growth through unfettered markets may be our undoing: disaster looms if new biological inventions simply accelerate the current cycles of environmentally destructive design and building in the relentless pursuit of short-term gains.

NOTES

1
Salvador Dalí, *The Unspeakable Confessions of Salvador Dalí* (New York: HarperCollins, 1981) p. 230.

2
Using recombinant DNA to alter *Escherichia coli* bacteria to create human insulin, the first synthetic insulin was produced and distributed by Genetech in 1978.

3
J. Craig Venter et al., 'Creation of a bacterial cell controlled by a chemically synthesized genome' *Science*, July 2, 2010: 329 (5987), 52–56.

4
David Benjamin, 'Bio fever' *Domus*, published online on March 30, 2011 (http://www.domusweb.it/en/op-ed/bio-fever/).

5
Andrew Carnegie, *The Empire of Business* (New York: Doubleday, Page & Co., 1902) (see especially 'Steel Manufacture in the United States in the Nineteenth Century' pp. 229–242).

6
As measured by the number of transistors fitting onto an integrated circuit.

7
Corinne Le Quere, Michael R. Raupach, Josep G. Canadell, and Gregg Marland 'Trends in the sources and sinks of carbon dioxide' *Nature Geoscience*, November 17, 2009: 2(12) 831–836.

8
Rob Carlson, *Biology Is Technology: The Promise, Peril, and New Business of Engineering Life* (Cambridge: Harvard University Press, 2010) pp. 63–79.

9
This measure includes pharmaceuticals, industrial applications and genetically modified crops; ibid pp. 150–178.

10
As quoted in 'Eco-designs on future cities' BBC News, June 14, 2005 (http://news.bbc.co.uk/1/hi/sci/tech/4682011.stm).

11
See R. Buckminster Fuller and Kiyoshi Kuromiya, *Critical Path* 2nd edn (New York: St. Martin's Griffin, 1982); Rachel Carson, *Silent Spring* (Boston: Houghton Mifflin,1962); Victor Papanek, *Design for the Real World: Human Ecology and Social Change* (New York: Pantheon Books,1971).

12
R.A. Frosch and N.E Galloupolos, 'Strategies for manufacturing' *Scientific American*, 1989: 261(3) 144–152.

13
Alex Driver, Carlos Peralta, and James Moultrie, 'Exploring how industrial designers can contribute to scientific research' *International Journal of Design*, April 30, 2011: 5(1) 17–28.

14
Interview with the author, January 18, 2010.

15
William MacDonald, *The Architecture of the Roman Empire*, Vol. 1 (New Haven: Yale University Press, 1982) pp. 18–22.

16
Sigfried Giedion, *Building in France, Building in Iron, Building in Ferroconcrete*, ed. Sokratis Georgiadis (Santa Monica: Getty Center, 1995) pp. 150–151.

17
Patricia Cusack, *Early Reinforced Concrete*, ed. Frank Newby (Surrey: Ashgate Publishing, 2001) p. 82.

18
Masterworks, such as those of Filippo Brunelleschi in the 14th and 15th centuries, were exceptional examples of engineering achievement that rivaled those of the Roman Empire, without the benefit of concrete.

19
Thomas Friedman, *Hot, Flat, and Crowded* (New York: Farrar, Straus and Giroux, 2008) pp. 53–76.

20
Anthony J. McMichael and Keith B. G. Dear, 'Climate change: Heat, health, and longer horizons' *Proceedings of the National Academy of Sciences*, May 25, 2010: 107(21) 9483–9484.

21
Henk Jonkers et al., 'Application of bacteria as self-healing agent for the development of sustainable concrete' *Ecological Engineering*, 2010: 36, 230–235.

22
Angeli Sachs, 'Paradise lost? Contemporary strategies of nature design' *Nature Design* (Zurich: Museum für Gestaltung Zürich, 2007) p. 273.

23
Lewis Mumford, 'Yesterday's city of tomorrow' *The Lewis Mumford Reader* (New York: Pantheon, 1986) p. 212.

24
The more complete quote is 'Architecture or revolution. Revolution can be avoided.' Le Corbusier, *The Radiant City* (New York: Orion Press, 1933, republished 1964) p. 289.

25
Sigfried Giedion, *Mechanization Takes Command* (New York: Oxford University Press, 1948) p. 256.

1.

THE ARCHITECTURAL HYBRID

Living Structures and New Ecological Integrations

OPPOSITE   21
See 'Baubotanik Tower', page 36.

Here we examine projects on architectural and urban scales that incorporate biological processes. Spanning several countries and a variety of approaches, these works originate from a deep respect for and fascination with the power and elegance of natural phenomena. The designs deliberately embrace the energy flows, complexities, and uncertainties of the outer, unbuilt environment and explore ways in which architects can exploit advances in biology, including synthetic biology, to build more ecologically. They apply both new technologies (such as algae bioreactors in 'Filene's Eco Pods') and ancient methods (for example, building with living trees by directing their branch and root growth in 'Root Bridges of Meghalaya'). A unique aspect of this approach is its inherent uncertainty— the builder relinquishes the control and predictability that characterize conventional processes of designing and building.

In 'Oyster-techture,' the common oyster is deployed to simultaneously build wave-attenuating reefs to protect the shore from storm surges, filter pollutants from the water, and help foster local community by creating opportunities for seaside recreation and commerce. This mollusk is fantastically fecund and, in sufficient numbers, can clean entire bays in a single day while acting as a cornerstone for several other forms of sea life. A waterfront city's planners might consider such a scheme as providing useful infrastructure and a partner to help reach specific, long-term goals beyond the aesthetic.

'Baubotanik Tower' and 'Lake Constance Footbridge' use willow trees, which root aggressively, even into ground that may be insufficiently firm to support conventional foundations, to buttress experimental structures. Such creative, dynamic architecture offers a multitude of benefits: exposing designers to the complexities of working with, rather than against, environmental conditions; providing a foothold for other animals so as to maintain biodiversity; and creating an incentive for the owners of the structures to protect local water, soil, and air quality.

These projects also delve into the fanciful for the sake of challenging accepted limits of architectural practice and technology. While it might seem imprudent to genetically modify trees to glow at night with bioluminescence, as in 'Genetic Barcelona Project,' the rapid growth of cities around the world, combined with a lack of imagination in finding low-cost, low-energy solutions to simple problems, such as the illumination of public spaces, suggests that far-reaching ideation is absolutely necessary.

'Fab Tree Hab,' a proposal to construct sustainable homes with trees at their core, is immediately realizable using existing technologies and offers enormous potential benefits to communities. However, despite successful test structures and a thorough business plan, growing time requirements have so far made it untenable for developers. Should new regulations or incentives favor such ecologically integrated structures, the potential of such architecture could finally be realized. Obstacles to adoption closely resemble the difficulties that other available cleaner technologies, such as electric cars, experience. As Thomas Friedman argues, a baseline cost assigned to pollution, such as a carbon tax, is a necessary green light to spur industry into action. Until then, the tremendous benefits of conscripting life—such as trees, oysters, and bacteria—to enhance both the built and the natural environments will require extraordinary imagination and risk.

Taken together, these projects represent an effort to better understand local ecosystems in order to align built and living structures for improved function. By creating hybrids of animate and inanimate material, these designers also challenge the modernist precept that clear boundaries separate the built and natural worlds, that these spaces are inherently at odds with one another. These pioneering architects and urban planners, and the life scientists with whom they collaborate, demonstrate how beautiful, vigorous hybrids might benefit and ultimately preserve one another.

HARMONIA 57

By resembling a living organism, can a building limit
its harmful effects on its surroundings?

Porous organic concrete, irrigation system, living plants, glass, metal.

Greg Bousquet (French) / Carolina Bueno (Brazilian) / Guillaume Sibaud (French) / Olivier Raffaelli
(French)—Triptyque, São Paulo, Brazil

COMPLETED

Water is the central feature of this project to create
flexible office space in west São Paulo. Rainfall
and wastewater are collected, treated, and reused,
thereby creating continuous cycles much like in
nature. Rather than try to conceal exchanges of
moisture and heat, processes are visible through
a relatively low-tech network of tubes, plumbing
tanks, sprinklers, and pipes, which sometimes
double as guardrails. The irrigation conduits that
serve the whole building, along with the pumps
and the water-treatment system, embrace the
outer walls almost like veins and arteries.

Harmonia 57 comprises a pair of blocks
connected by a metallic footbridge and punctuated
by several terraces and windows with functioning
wooden shutters. Between the two main structures,
a plaza offers an outdoor space from which to view
the multicolored and ever-changing exterior of the
building. The walls are made of porous concrete, with
pore-like openings interspersed throughout for plants
to take hold. The water system envelops the whole
edifice in a light mist, utilizing internal resources to
maintain a healthy exterior, like sweat cooling the skin.

In contrast to the rough vegetation protruding
from the outer walls, the internal spaces have
smooth, monochromatic surfaces, with decks
and patios framed by concrete shapes that echo
the skyline of Vila Madalena, a neighborhood
of galleries and artists' studios.

OPPOSITE 22

Natural light and fresh air are in abundance
throughout the interior space, thereby allowing
the embedded plantings to flourish.

ABOVE   23

A water circulatory system nourishes the plants on the façades of the building with graywater and rainwater that are collected on site.

LEFT / ABOVE   25, 26

Indoor and outdoor spaces are integrated with walkways and a plaza, highlighting the theme of harmony between structure and surroundings.

LEFT   24

Colorful tubes and tanks provide inexpensive and functional decoration for the structure's exterior.

LEFT / ABOVE   27, 28, 29

Native plants are cultivated in a low-maintenance living roof that does not need to be watered.

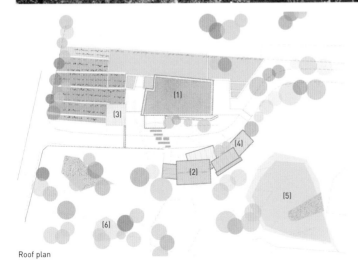

BELOW   30

Ground plan and roof plan, the latter showing:
(1) visitor center, (2) bird-ringing facility,
(3) open-air classroom, (4) bird observation point,
(5) large pond and, (6) biological treatment pond.

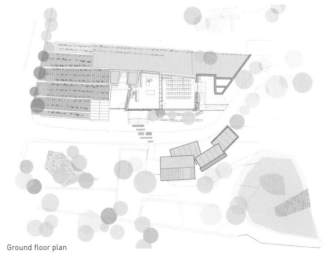

Roof plan

Ground floor plan

GUTMAN VISITOR CENTER

Blurring the boundary between the built and natural environments.

Wood, recycled plastics, stone, local plants, soil.

Weinstein Vaadia Architects, Tel Aviv, Israel; commissioned by the Society for the Protection of Nature in Israel

COMPLETED

ABOVE 31

As the weather cools in Europe, migrating birds face increasing difficulty in finding safe stopovers as regions in the Middle East become more urban.

This structure is located in a wooded area of Jerusalem that is a favorite for bird-watching and where the Society for the Protection of Nature operates a research center. It sits among a cluster of habitats that serve as the stopover for thousands of birds on their migration from Europe. Many of their routes have been attenuated over time by urban development that creates conditions hostile to wildlife.

To help address this situation, the building features several small spaces and compartments that are optimized to allow plants and animals to sprout and burrow. In particular, crevices and recesses were designed with the nesting behavior of local birds in mind so that they might take up residence in the walls. The aim was to integrate the construction with the surrounding environment and enhance it with spaces for life to take hold and flourish, much like a coral reef in the sea.

The **Gutman Visitor Center** is equipped with a graywater recycling system and a living roof adapted to the local arid climate. All the species planted here are native and do not require watering or labor-intensive maintenance. In sharp contrast to most architecture, which has a combative relationship with local forms of life, the center's design follows the principle of integration and is well aligned with the priorities of the commissioning client.

ROOT BRIDGES OF MEGHALAYA

Living constructions that last for centuries.

Rubber tree (Ficus elastica), betel nut palm (Areca catechu).

Numerous designers, Khasi tribespeople, within present-day India

IN PRODUCTION

The northeastern Indian state of Meghalaya includes some of the wettest places on the planet, with up to 1,200 cm (470 in.) of rain annually. In the Khasi and Jaintia hills, the water creates numerous swift-flowing rivers that are dangerous to cross and require bridges to afford basic mobility to the local people. In a predominately agrarian economy made up of tribes that have lived in the area for centuries, a natural and effective solution has been developed: bridges grown from the roots of rubber trees.

Without the need for specialized training and equipment that other types of bioengineering require, the **Root Bridges of Meghalaya** are coaxed from the natural, albeit slow, growth of *Ficus elastica*—a rubber tree within the banyan group of figs. These trees thrive on the slopes of hills and have strong rooting systems. The growth of their many secondary roots, which would normally fan out in all directions, can be guided using a betel nut trunk that has been sliced down the middle and then hollowed out into a half-cylinder. Placed across a river, these trunks ensure that the thin, tender roots grow straight and eventually reach the opposite bank, where locals encourage them to take hold in the soil. Given enough time and repeated with several trees in each part of the river, this process ensures that sturdy, ever-evolving living structures are created, the form of which adjusts over time and is never fully complete.

Some of these root bridges, which take approximately 15 years to become functional, are more than 30 m (100 ft) long. The stresses of use and weather can strengthen them over time, allowing them to last for hundreds of years. Although precise dating is difficult, it is widely accepted that many are in excess of 500 years old (the practice is thought to have begun in the 1500s). One example, partly named after the river that it spans, is known as the Umshiang Double-Decker Root Bridge and is a remarkable testament to the engineering possibilities of living structures.

Sadly, many of the region's rivers have in recent years been poisoned by the runoff from nearby illegal mines. If the disruption to local ecosystems continues unabated, these ingenious works of design that are engineered to live indefinitely will shrivel and die.

OPPOSITE   32

Over time, bridges are shaped from the roots of several trees. These natural structures are capable of lasting for hundreds of years.

ABOVE   33

The bridges are ever changing in form and they are strengthened by the addition of branch and grass clippings, which nourish the roots.

ABOVE   34

The Double-Decker Root Bridge: a dramatic two-storey structure that spans the Umshiang River.

LEFT   35

As with all living structures, the bridges rely on a healthy environment for their maintenance. Abundant clean air, water, and soil are essential.

CATTEDRALE VEGETALE

How far can the interrelationship between construction
and spontaneous growth in nature be taken?

Firs, chestnuts, hazel, hornbeams, nails, string.

Giuliano Mauri (Italian)—artist; commissioned by Arte Sella, Trenito

IN PRODUCTION

Outside of Bergamo, northern Italy, on the slopes
of Mount Arera, is a structure that is the last work
of the late Italian designer Giuliano Mauri, which
he designed for the Arte Sella, Art and Nature
International Meeting exhibition in 2001. It is roughly
the size of a Gothic cathedral, with three naves
made up of 80 columns of intertwined branches.
It stands approximately 21 m (69 ft) tall and consists
of 1,800 firs, 600 chestnut branches, and 6,000 m
(20,000 ft) of hazel branch weaved throughout.

Inside the perimeter, 42 hornbeams have
been planted. These are expected to grow over
time to provide the roof to the 'building.' As the
years pass, the protective wooden scaffolding placed
around the trees to assist and direct their growth
will rot and fall away, giving their nutrients back
to the soil to support the construction still further.

Cattedrale Vegetale (vegetal cathedral)
is a living, ever-changing edifice that adapts
to its surroundings while supporting them,
providing shelter and nutrients for countless
species, from mammals to microorganisms. It
was inaugurated in 2010 as a part of Bergamo's
observance of the United Nations' International
Year of Biodiversity and in tribute to its designer.

OPPOSITE   36

The form of this living ecclesiastic architecture
echoes the conventions of a Gothic cathedral.

ABOVE 37

With the shifting seasons come some dramatic changes to the appearance and visitor experience of the structure, which will develop over many years as plant growth fills out the roof and walls.

BELOW 38, 39

The supportive wood scaffolding will eventually rot and fall away, to be absorbed by the soil as nutrients for the structure's continued growth.

ABOVE / LEFT   40, 41

The living cathedral enhances the surrounding
environment, not simply visually but also by
providing a foothold for many species, in contrast
with the inertness of a dead or artificial structure.

BAUBOTANIK TOWER

Can architects relinquish control of form and allow
nature to grow and shape their structures?

Silver willow (Salix alba), steel-tube scaffold, zinc-coated steel grating.

Ferdinand Ludwig (German) / Cornelius Hackenbracht (German)—Institute of Modern Architecture and
Design, University of Stuttgart, Germany

PROTOTYPE

The art of designing constructions that are made
using living trees has been dubbed *Baubotanik*
('building botany') by a group of architects at the
University of Stuttgart, Germany. This demonstration
project explores engineering with living plants
to integrate a small tower into its immediate
environment. It also blends research and application
by uniting architects, engineers, and natural
scientists in an endeavor to create a structure
and test new possibilities, offering insight from
the perspectives of their individual disciplines.

The main feature of **Baubotanik Tower** is its
utilization of plants as load-bearing systems, taking
advantage of what the architects call the 'constructive
intelligence' of trees: like human muscles, tree
branches naturally strengthen in response to stress
or increased loads. At the same time, this practice
exposes researchers to the biodynamics and
uncontrollability of natural growth. The conflicts that
this lack of control creates in building inspires a form
of architecture that is characterized by accidental
processes, hope, and risk. The architects also take
a critical stance by embracing an 'aesthetic of
uncertainty' in the use of living materials. Building
botany undermines the implicit claims of traditional
architecture as stable, permanent, and self-sufficient.

The tower has a footprint of 8 sq. m (86 sq. ft)
and a height of 9 m (29 ft), and it incorporates three
walkable levels. It is the first *Baubotanik* project
using the plant-addition method, which involves
grafting trees together. These create a timber-framed
support structure that is bolstered by scaffolding.
As soon as the living structure is stable enough
to support the ingrown levels and take over the
loading capacity, the scaffold is removed. As it is
dependent over time on natural factors, such as
rain and temperature, the duration of the process is
hard to predict, but a period of between 5–10 years is
expected for the design to become fully functional.

OPPOSITE   42

Exploiting the robust and aggressive willow,
these experiments utilize the load-bearing
capacity of living trees. In a few years they will
support the weight of the grown structures and
the metal scaffolding will be removed.

LAKE CONSTANCE FOOTBRIDGE

Arbo-architecture combines trees and man-made materials.

Common osier (Salix viminalis), stainless steel, zinc-coated steel grating.

Ferdinand Ludwig (German) / Oliver Storz (German) / Hannes Schwertfeger (German)—
Institute of Modern Architecture and Design, University of Stuttgart, Germany

COMPLETED

An early project from the *Baubotanik* team, this simple botanical-technical structure is used to demonstrate tree-integrated architecture. Built on a low-lying wetland where a conventional support structure would not be possible, the **Lake Constance Footbridge** is constructed from thickly planted willow—a tree that roots aggressively, grows rapidly and can be readily cultivated from small cuttings. These trees also grow high and crosswise, which can help in forming a stable meshwork. There is no foundation in the usual sense of the word; instead, the trees absorb the entire load and redirect it into the ground through their roots.

The structure is made from 64 vertical and 16 diagonal bundle struts, each comprising approximately a dozen plants. The bundles form the base for a walkable steel grating 2.5 m (8 ft) high and 22 m (72 ft) long, which also has a stainless-steel tube handrail and can be entered through two cross paths by ladder. The living supporting structure is engineered using the willow *Salix viminalis*, which can regenerate and root into the earth independently.

The site's moist reed meadow offers excellent conditions for the continual growth of the trees. Only a few weeks after construction was completed, leaves sprouted from them, demonstrating the vitality of the local soil. Dense green walls emerged in the first growing season, enveloping the sides of the bridge. During each autumn and winter, however, the trees drop their leaves to reveal the structures within, allowing the steel elements and geometrical shape to dominate.

The bridge illustrates how integration with living processes creates an incentive for the designer, builder, and user to maintain conditions that are conducive to life. Such dynamic, ever-changing structures require clean air, soil, and water to maintain their functionality. This is analogous to proven aquaculture schemes in which the business interests of farmers of fish and shellfish align neatly with the preservationist goal of maintaining and improving water quality.

These architects continue to build new experimental structures and have been instrumental in organizing a new specialization at the university in engineering with living plants.

ABOVE   43

The trees eventually intertwine with the steel railings to create a living/non-living hybrid.

ABOVE 44

The footbridge is anchored in a saturated meadow where constructing a traditional foundation would be problematic. The trees are well adapted and thrive in such an environment.

ABOVE 45

Like human muscle, branches and trunks strengthen in response to stress over time and have the capacity to self-repair when damaged.

ABOVE 46

The footbridge, just like other living structures,
relies on a healthy environment and actively
helps to support a diverse local ecosystem.

ABOVE   47

Care must be taken in the first stages of 'building botany' projects to direct and restrict growth.

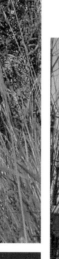

RIGHT   48

The uncertainty and impermanence of living materials are key to this form of architecture.

BIO MILANO

Can a new approach to urban planning for Milan serve as a model for cities to forge a more integrated relationship with nature?

Various media and materials, including graphics, models, architectural diagrams.

Stefano Boeri (Italian)—Boeri Studio, Milan, Italy

IN PRODUCTION

Bio Milano is a six-part plan aimed at reforesting and rehabilitating sections of Milan, forming symbiotic relationships between natural and built environments. The goal of the architect is to create a biodiverse metropolis emphasizing an increase in biologically active spaces, including new types of agriculture. The project also aims to facilitate the germination of new business and jobs for thousands of people in sustainable industries, such as renewable-energy generation.

One component, **Bosco Verticale** (vertical forest), is a residential project in the center of Milan. Its dual towers are a bold experiment to combine housing and dense forest in a single, compact footprint. Reaching 110 m (360 ft) and 76 m (249 ft) high, the towers' external walls will host more than 900 trees of a variety of species as well as several hundred shrubs. Achieving a similarly verdant tract of land would probably require either 10,000 sq. m (110,000 sq. ft) of uninterrupted forest or 50,000 sq. m (538,000 sq. ft) in a conventional residential setting. The potential benefits of the towers are many: in addition to the aesthetic appeal of so much dense foliage, the plants will offer footholds for a multitude of species, including birds and insects.

Boxes, integrated into terraces that cover the structures, will be planted with trees of varying size and root strength, taking into consideration the greater wind force with increasing height. For the building's residents, the trees will dampen noise and generate newly cleaned air. As their dense vertical arrangement

deprives them of sufficient rain, the trees rely on the building's graywater circulation system for water.

Wood House is a proposed social housing project that taps into the cycle of tree growth and clearance taking place along the Ticino River. The low-density structures would rely on prefabricated forms of construction to control costs, but also allow for a high degree of customization to suit individuals' needs.

Courtyard Farms calls for the restoration of 60 publicly owned and abandoned courtyard farms around Milan to provide a new source of locally grown food. The renovated structures would serve as a base for biomass growth for clean energy and, potentially, as a testing area for research and development in biotechnology.

Expo 2015, designed for the next Universal Exposition, to be held in Milan in 2015, will create a vast 'global kitchen' in the northwest of the city. Instead of the traditional natural pavilions, each country taking part will have a section of land to cultivate in order to display forms of biodiversity protection and remediation, new technologies, and possible solutions to food-production problems. Following the event the area will be used as a scientific park for agricultural research.

OPPOSITE   49

Bosco Verticale is currently under construction in Milan and will eventually include more than nine hundred trees and plants in a compact footprint.

ABOVE / RIGHT   50, 51

The two towers will play host to hundreds of
trees and shrubs in a compact footprint, utilizing
terrace space to create a vertical forest.

Metrobosco will be a circle of forests around
the city to support several species of animals that
live in or pass through the Milanese plain. The
project will combine existing parks and farmland,
and will be only partially accessible to people. It
includes the planting of three million trees, of which
10 percent have been planted in the last two years.

Alongside these five distinct efforts, the
BioMilano plan seeks to cultivate remedial plants and
microorganisms on polluted land in order to eventually
reintegrate these spaces into the wider ecosystem.
This effort is part of a research project by Chiara
Gerolldi that uses biological cleanup methods around
Porta Romana. A long, unfortunate history of industrial
pollution and eventual abandonment in the area is
giving way to decontamination and slow healing.

RIGHT   53, 54

A global kitchen will be created at **Expo 2015**, where pavilions will offer displays of biodiversity and strategies to enhance food production.

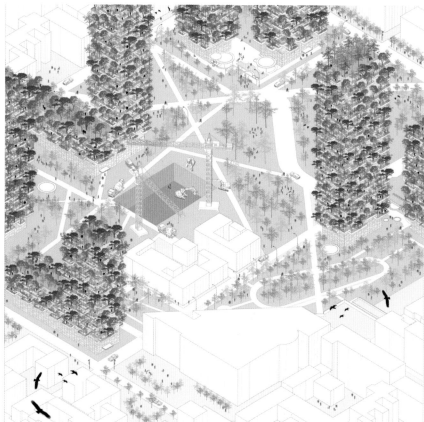

OPPOSITE   52

In **Metrobosco**, forests will surround Milan and provide a habitat for several local animal species while allowing only limited access to people.

EDITT TOWER

Combining street-level activity and green spaces in
a skyscraper to foster community building.

*Mechanically jointed components, integrated photovoltaics, various trees
and vegetation.*

**T. R. Hamzah & Yeang, Malaysia / Urban Redevelopment Authority, Kuala Lumpur, Singapore; sponsored
by the National University of Singapore**

CONSTRUCTION PENDING

OPPOSITE / ABOVE   55, 56

Biodiversity protection and enhancement are
prioritized in this tower, which allows for natural
growth in more than half of its total area.

This project in Singapore demonstrates an ecological
approach to the design of a high-rise construction
that will provide spaces for a variety of uses, from
retail units to auditoriums. Starting with a detailed
survey of the site's ecosystems, the architects found
an essentially devastated environment with little
topsoil, flora, or fauna. To address this absence of
life and attempt to rehabilitate the site, **EDITT Tower**
(which takes its name from 'ecological design in the
tropics') will incorporate heavily planted façades
and terraces, which will form a continuous spiral
from the ground to the uppermost 26th floor. The
resulting total planted area should be in excess
of 3,800 sq. m (41,000 sq. ft)—more than half the
total gross area of the building. The species to be
cultivated will be chosen from local native varieties.

To complement the greening of the exterior of
the edifice will be systems to catch rainwater, recycle
graywater, and utilize solar energy collected from
photovoltaics. To enhance its versatility, there is a
deliberate effort at placemaking through the creation
of wide, publicly accessible ramps around the first
six floors. These will be lined with shops, cafés,
performance spaces, and viewing decks in an attempt
to bring street life to the lower levels of the skyscraper.

The design takes into account potential future
use, anticipating different functions over the course
of the tower's 100–150 year service life. Partitions
and floors will be removable, and many materials
will be mechanically rather than chemically bonded,
thus facilitating their future recovery and reuse.

Solid Waste Recycling

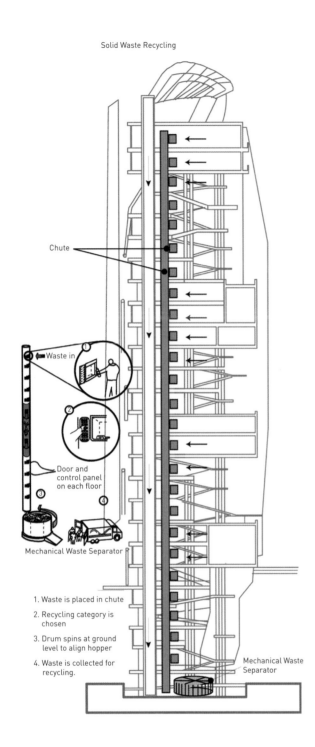

Chute

1. Waste in

2.

Door and
control panel
on each floor

3.

4.

Mechanical Waste Separator

1. Waste is placed in chute

2. Recycling category is
   chosen

3. Drum spins at ground
   level to align hopper

4. Waste is collected for
   recycling.

Mechanical Waste
Separator

Planting Concept

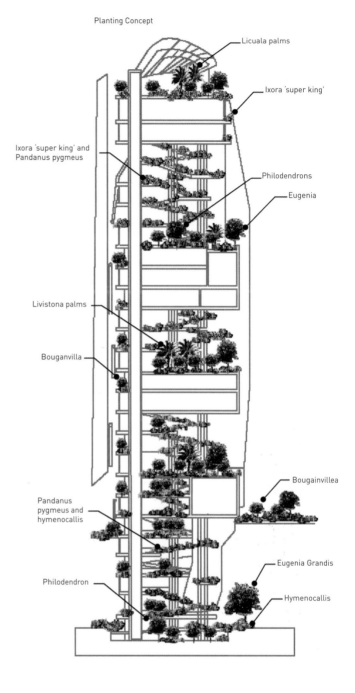

Licuala palms

Ixora 'super king'

Ixora 'super king' and
Pandanus pygmeus

Philodendrons

Eugenia

Livistona palms

Bouganvilla

Bougainvillea

Pandanus
pygmeus and
hymenocallis

Philodendron

Eugenia Grandis

Hymenocallis

ABOVE / RIGHT   57, 58

Cycles of resource collection and reuse are
integrated into the design, along with specific
plans for the introduction of plant species.

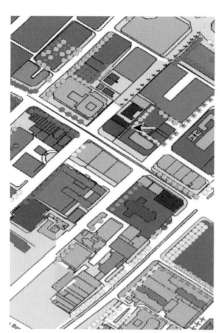

This plan shows a survey of the existing vegetation species located within the area surrounding the site.

- ● Cassia fistula
- ◉ Khaya senegalensis
- ✳ Angsana
- ◎ Ficus religiosa
- ● Eugenia polyantha
- ◉ Swietenia macrophylla
- ◉ Yellow flame
- ● Lagerstroemia speciosa

- ● Eugenia grandis
- ◎ Cerbera odollam
- ◉ Plumeria rubra
- ● Ficus Benjamina
- ◡ Cassia spp.
- ◎ Erythrina variegata
- ✦ Ravenala madagascariensis

- ✳ Roystonea regia
- ✤ Veitchia merrillii
- ✿ Ptychosperma macarthurii

- ✦ Livistona chinensis
- ▲ Neodypsis decaryi

An examination of the local area highlighted the dearth of biodiversity in the urbanized setting.

LEFT / ABOVE 60, 61

Public spaces are planned throughout several of the structure's upper floors, inviting opportunities for social interaction and economic activity, and supporting a sense of both community and place that more normally occur only at street level.

FILENE'S ECO PODS

Conversion of an abandoned urban development into a temporary mobile bioreactor-cum-botanic garden.

Algae bioreactor, algae, prefabricated modules, various plants.

Eric Höweler (Dutch) / Meejin Yoon (American) / Franco Vairani (Argentinean) / Joshua Barandon (American)—Höweler + Yoon Architecture, Boston, USA / Squared Design Lab, Los Angeles, USA

CONCEPT

The objectives of this proposal are to stimulate the local economy and ecology of downtown Boston through the integration of energy production and architecture, while taking advantage of a stalled construction site known as Filene's Development. The architects propose prefabricated modules that can be used as incubators in which to grow algae for biofuel. Individual units could also be rented out to scientists for use in algae-based research. The ability of these 'pods' to interlock and be moved around allows them to fill different types of space. For example, they can be affixed to vacant buildings or lots, and any voids between them can be planted with productive gardens.

Microalgae are a robust potential energy source that can be grown vertically and on non-arable land. Algae farming uses sugar and cellulose to create biofuel while functioning as a carbon sink, thereby also concentrating the benefits of photosynthesis. The kind of bioreactor process envisioned here does not yet exist, but recent research on single-step algae oil extraction and low-energy, high-efficiency light-emitting diodes make the technology an intriguing possibility.

The proposed location of **Filene's Eco Pods** and their highly visible nature are intended to introduce the public to important energy-production processes on which they depend. The project also hopes to spark heightened ecological awareness. The architects see this as anticipatory architecture that is capable of generating a new micro-urbanism that is adaptable, inexpensive, and environmentally beneficial.

ABOVE   62

Over time, modular units can be combined and recombined in almost unlimited iterations to meet the needs of both the users and the site.

ABOVE / OPPOSITE   63, 64, 65

A mechanical armature lifts and stacks the pods, arranging them in rows and columns. The spaces in between can be used as public gardens.

PROCESS ZERO: RETROFIT RESOLUTION

The challenge of making a 1960s construction energy self-sufficient.

Modular microalgae bioreactors, thin-film photovoltaic panels, graywater recycling system.

HOK (worldwide) / Vanderweil (USA) / HOK team (Colin Benson, Jarek Bieda, Alesia Call, Ming Hu, John Jackson, Monika Kumor, Anica Landreneau, Sean Quinn, Scott Walzak, Sean Williams, Antony Yen) / Vanderweil Engineers (Brandon Harwick, Stephen Lahti, Iyabo Lawal, Patrick Murphy)

CONCEPT

This team proposes a visionary retrofit for a government General Services Administration block located in downtown Los Angeles. This would reduce the current overall energy demand by 84 percent while generating the remaining 16 percent on-site, resulting in a net zero-energy building.

The design includes a 2,300 sq. m (25,000 sq. ft) web of pipework that contains natural microalgae and envelops the south façade. This network of bioreactors performs various functions: here the algae reproduce; extracting nutrients from the building's graywater, helped by energy from the sun, they photosynthesize, thereby producing lipids for on-site conversion into fuel and oxygen to enhance the office atmosphere; they absorb harmful emissions from the adjacent freeway; and they provide shade to parts of the interior.

The architects of **Process Zero: Retrofit Resolution**, based in Washington, have also incorporated proven energy-conservation and renewal strategies into their design. Three angled atria in the roof and eight light wells maximize the amount of daylight that enters the block and ensure that all workspaces are well lit; integrated louvers allow natural ventilation; a new façade wrapped in 3,250 sq. m (35,000 sq. ft) of photovoltaic film generates solar power; 2,790 sq. m (30,000 sq. ft) of rooftop solar collectors circulate recycled water to aid climate control; and office equipment is operated by a centralized computing system.

OPPOSITE TOP   66

Algae filled tubes cover the exterior walls, capturing solar energy for fuel production while also shading and cooling the interior spaces.

OPPOSITE   67

Proven resource conservation and renewal strategies are combined with still-developing photobioreactor technology to create a self-sustaining and energy-neutral structure.

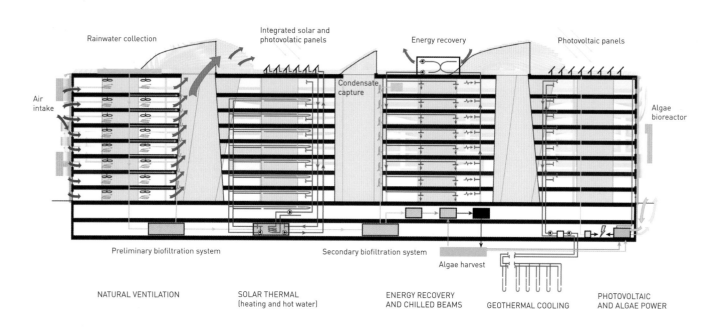

Rainwater collection

Integrated solar and photovolatic panels

Energy recovery

Photovoltaic panels

Air intake

Condensate capture

Algae bioreactor

Preliminary biofiltration system

Secondary biofiltration system

Algae harvest

NATURAL VENTILATION

SOLAR THERMAL
(heating and hot water)

ENERGY RECOVERY
AND CHILLED BEAMS

GEOTHERMAL COOLING

PHOTOVOLTAIC
AND ALGAE POWER

Radiant
floor heating

Chilled beams

Energy recovery

Phase change ceiling

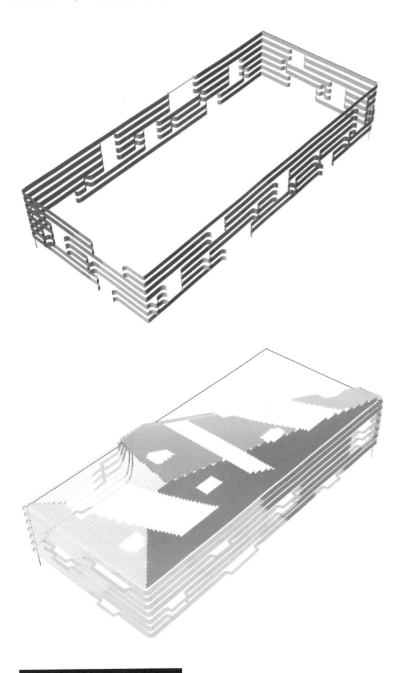

ABOVE 68

Inspired by the functions of a living cell, dual membranes cover the façade of the building carrying photovoltaics and algae-filled tubing.

ABOVE 69

This modernist, 1960s building in Los Angeles is the subject of the proposed self-sufficient retrofit.

ABOVE 70

The 25,000 sq. ft microalgae bioreactor could generate 9 percent of the building's energy needs.

LEFT 71

The microalgae can synthesize wastewater and absorb carbon dioxide generated by nearby traffic to produce oils, which can be extracted for fuel.

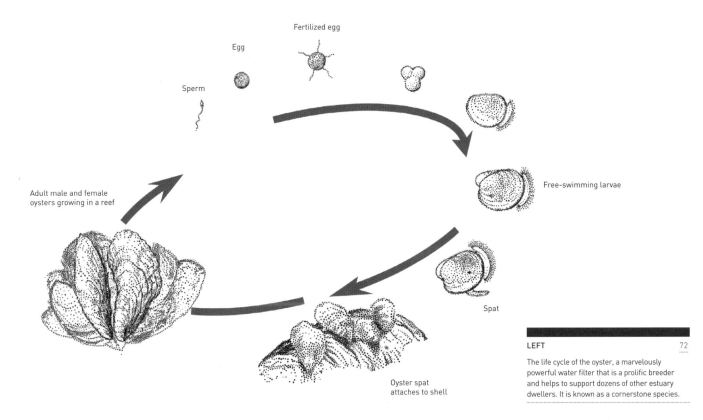

Fertilized egg

Egg

Sperm

Adult male and female
oysters growing in a reef

Free-swimming larvae

Spat

Oyster spat
attaches to shell

LEFT   72

The life cycle of the oyster, a marvelously
powerful water filter that is a prolific breeder
and helps to support dozens of other estuary
dwellers. It is known as a cornerstone species.

2050

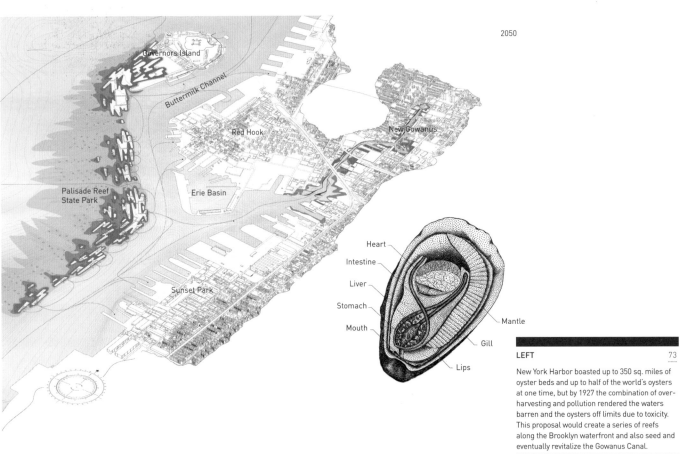

Governors Island

Buttermilk Channel

Red Hook

New Gowanus

Palisade Reef
State Park

Erie Basin

Sunset Park

Heart
Intestine
Liver
Stomach
Mouth

Mantle

Gill

Lips

LEFT   73

New York Harbor boasted up to 350 sq. miles of
oyster beds and up to half of the world's oysters
at one time, but by 1927 the combination of over-
harvesting and pollution rendered the waters
barren and the oysters off limits due to toxicity.
This proposal would create a series of reefs
along the Brooklyn waterfront and also seed and
eventually revitalize the Gowanus Canal.

OYSTER-TECHTURE

Can New York—former oyster capital of the world—remodel
part of its harbor by resurrecting the humble mollusk?

*Marine piles, fuzzy rope, wooden platforms, artificial reefs, oysters
(Crassostrea virginica).*

Kate Orff (American)—Scape/Landscape Architecture PLLC, New York, USA

CONCEPT

ABOVE 74, 75, 76

Resurrecting the oyster in these waters would
unleash a virtuous cycle of habitat formation and
local economic growth. Combined with thoughtful
urban planning, the city waterfronts could at last
become both accessible and enjoyable again.

With oyster reefs as the building blocks of a
reincarnated ecosystem, largely intended to protect
against storm surges and the rising tides expected
in New York Harbor in the coming decades, this
project demonstrates the potential of biology to
enhance the urban environment beyond conventional,
aesthetic effects. The plan is to resurrect the thriving
oyster habitat that existed there until the early 20th
century but was destroyed by over-harvesting and
pollution. If realized, it would significantly improve
water quality through the biofiltration of the oyster
beds, and support economic growth and community
development in stubbornly depressed portions
of Brooklyn by creating a new regional park.

Oyster-techture includes spaces dedicated
to spawning and farming the oyster—a cornerstone
species that enables other marine life to thrive—in
the shallow waters of the Bay Ridge Flats, south of
Red Hook, Brooklyn. The architects have designed
an armature of marine piles connected by a mesh of
'fuzzy rope' that provides a support structure for young
oysters, raising them above the harbor floor to prevent
them from being silted up. Over time, a new reef will
develop, with agglomerations of oysters and other
sea life creating a watery urban landscape that will
include navigational channels, diving platforms, and
recreational boardwalks. While it would take decades
for the mollusks to be safe for human consumption,
this project could prepare the way for the eventual
return of oyster carts to the streets of Manhattan,
as well as reconnect New Yorkers with their harbor.

The scheme was part of a special exhibition
organized by MoMA PS1—a contemporary art
center—to address one of the most urgent challenges
facing the Unites States' largest city: sea-level
rise resulting from global climate change. The
exhibition was the culmination of an architects-
in-residence program that brought together five
interdisciplinary teams to re-envision the coastlines
of New York and New Jersey, and to imagine new
ways of occupying the harbor with adaptive 'soft'
infrastructures that are sympathetic to the needs
of a vibrant ecology. The resulting proposals are
intended to help change residents' relationships
with the city's vast but underutilized waterfront.

FAB TREE HAB

Can we draw on ancient methods of construction to create homes that truly work with, rather than against, nature?

Computer numerical controlled produced scaffolds, a variety of native trees.

Mitchell Joachim (American) / Lara Greden (American) / Javier Arbona (American)—Massachusetts Institute of Technology, Cambridge, USA

CONCEPT

This concept suggests an alternative to the sterile, stand-alone homes that are at odds with their immediate environment. It offers a method for growing residential accommodation from native trees that remain living and integrated with the ecosystem. Here, a growing structure is grafted into shape with prefabricated computer numerical controlled reusable scaffolds. Depending on the weather conditions and location, it should take approximately seven years to grow.

The creation of **Fab Tree Hab** relies heavily on 'pleaching', the ancient process of tree shaping in which tree branches are woven together so that as they continue to grow they form archways, lattices, or screens. The trunks of inosculating (self-grafting) trees, such as elm, oak, and dogwood, form the load-bearing elements, while the branches provide a continuous crisscross frame for the walls and roof. Interlaced throughout the exterior is a dense protective layer of vines, which is interspersed with soil pockets that support growing plants.

During the slow process of construction, the trees and plants are allowed to grow over a computer-designed removable plywood frame. Once the living elements are interconnected and stable, the wood is removed and can be reused. Research at the Massachusetts Institute of Technology, where the designers undertook their studies, has explored the potential of woody plants that grow quickly and develop an interwoven root system that is soft enough to 'train' over a scaffold but then

hardens to be very durable. The inside walls would be made from conventional clay and plaster.

Technical demonstration and innovation is still required for some components—principally the bioplastic windows that can adapt to growth of the house, and the management of nutrient flows across the walls to ensure that the interior remains dry and free from insects. The time required for it to be habitable is approximately 5 years—far longer than for a more 'traditional' construction, but its health and longevity should be far greater. Above all, the 'growth' of such a home should be achievable for a minimal price, requiring little labor or fabricated materials. The realization of these structures will begin as an experiment but thereafter it is envisioned that the concept of renewal will take on a new architectural form—one of interdependency between nature and people.

OPPOSITE   77

By directing their growth, trees and woody plants can be integrated into built structures. This slow construction method creates living architecture integrated with—and enhancing— the environment.

ABOVE / BELOW / OPPOSITE   79

After the structure is grafted into shape a variety of plants fill in the gaps in the façade, encouraged by the use of perforated scaffolding through which stems and leaves can intertwine.

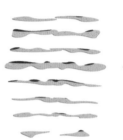

1. Rainwater harvested
2. Thermal fill (clay- and straw-based)
3. Vine surface lattice
4. Bioplastic windows
5. Buoyancy driven ventilation
6. Cool air intake
7. Packed-earth and tile flooring
8. Solar-heated water pipes under floor

ABOVE   78

Energy and nutrient flows are connected with the natural cycles of the surrounding ecosystem, thereby harnessing both cool air and rainwater.

BELOW   80

A living structure is slowly grafted into shape with the help of prefabricated and reusable scaffolding. Organic processes and time together become the essential construction materials. Depending on the climate, it takes about 5 years of guided tree growth before the house is functional.

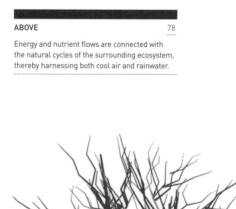

RIGHT   81

The interdependency between architecture and the environment that underpins this home is an incentive to preserve clean air, water, and soil.

DUNE

Could microorganisms help to build the equivalent of the Great Wall
of China across the Sahara to prevent the spread of the desert?

Sand, bacteria (Sporosarcina pasteurii), water, urea, calcium chloride.

Magnus Larsson (Swedish)—Architectural Association, London, UK / Magnus Larsson Studio, London, UK

CONCEPT

This architect envisions building structures out of sand in the Sahara and forming a 6,000 km (3728 mile) barrier to protect against the spread of the desert. This speculative, audacious plan would harness the ability of a particular bacterium to perform construction by naturally converting dunes into sandstone (based on work by Jason De Jong's team at the Soil Interactions Laboratory, University of California, Davis). During the process, the stone would be shaped to collect moisture, protect trees, and shelter thousands of people at relatively little cost.

The urgency of the problem that this project attempts to address cannot be overstated. A United Nations study (Adeel et al., 2007) concludes that 'Desertification has emerged as an environmental crisis of global proportions, currently affecting an estimated 100 to 200 million people, and threatening the lives and livelihoods of a much larger number.' The displacement of communities that is often generated by the spread of the desert regularly aggravates political instability in several of the affected countries, such as Sudan, Chad, and Nigeria.

Dune was inspired by the ongoing project in the same area to plant trees and vegetation across a dozen countries in the region, the goal of which is to protect the Sahel Belt—a stretch of dry savanna just south of the desert. Funds for this Great Green Wall are still being raised, but there has been progress in Senegal, where some 500 km (311 miles) of trees have been planted.

Bacteria, water, urea, and calcium chloride would be injected into the sandscape and would—via a process called microbial-induced calcite precipitation—produce calcite, a natural cement, that would cause the sand to solidify within 24 hours. By choosing where to apply the microorganism, the architect would have a degree of control over the process, but the final form would be heavily influenced by the environment. While the principal aim would be to produce a barrier against sand moved by the wind, the structure's formation would be augmented by wind action. Thus the design elegantly harnesses the energy embodied in the problem to propose its solution.

ABOVE 82

Sand solidified by bacteria and shaped by the wind eventually allows water to accumulate and forms a barrier against the spread of the desert.

RIGHT 83, 84

The wind and sand that result in expansion of the desert, threatening settlements and arable land, are exploited in biological construction.

ABOVE   85

A dune cross-section with rigid chambers where precious moisture and soil might be preserved.

ABOVE   86

The shape of the structure here is shown in a tafoni pattern—characteristic of rock that has been eroded by wind or moisture for many years.

ABOVE 87

Resisting the spread of the desert becomes ever more difficult and yet important as the climate warms. The vast savanna of the Sahel Belt is one of many areas that are currently under threat.

ABOVE 88, 89

Microbially induced cementation is a natural process that can be observed in swamps and lakes. It is not harmful to humans and will cease once available nutrients have been depleted.

ABOVE 90

The architect's proposal stemmed from an examination of extreme environments, such as desert, ocean, and tundra, where traditional approaches to building are simply unfeasible.

HYDRONET SF 2108

How do you envision an ecologically sound city that still serves the needs of an enlarged population a century into the future?

Computer renderings.

Lisa Iwamoto (American) / Craig Scott (American)—IwamotoScott Architecture, San Francisco, USA

CONCEPT

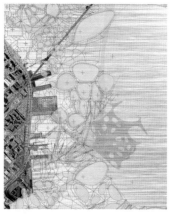

ABOVE   92

Large ponds of algae intended for biofuel production and zones devoted to aquaculture would characterize the city's waterfronts.

ABOVE   93

A forest of towers containing algae would store water and hydrogen, while an array of mechanical water collectors would open on a daily basis to absorb water from the fog.

OPPOSITE   91

A geothermal plant resembling a mushroom would channel energy from beneath the earth's surface into a citywide distribution system.

This scheme was developed as the architects' entry into the City of the Future design competition, organized by the History Channel, to imagine San Francisco in 100 years' time. Its grand prize-winning project sees a future in which circulation networks in the city are more interconnected but also more self-sufficient. It proposes a citywide, multiscale transportation network that collects, distributes, and stores natural resources and energy, creating exchanges that work in concert and thereby resemble an ecosystem.

To accommodate a projected doubling of population by 2108 while resisting continued outward sprawl, **Hydro-Net SF 2108** incorporates high-density housing that is interspersed around an extensive aquaculture zone. The projected 3–5 m (10–16 ft) rise in sea level would be leveraged as an opportunity to grow algae in large ponds and in forests of sinuous towers for biofuel production.

The planned underground infrastructure would tap vast reserves of water and power from aquifers and geothermal energy below the city. It would provide a transportation network within which hydrogen-fueled hovercars could travel safely at high speeds. In addition, the scheme would link to an array of mechanical 'flowers' that harvest freshwater from the city's daily fog cover.

GENETIC BARCELONA PROJECT

Might a gene from a jellyfish provide more natural urban light sources?

Genetically modified bioluminescent trees, batteries, jellyfish (Aequorea victoria).

Alberto T. Estévez (Spanish)—Genetic Architectures Office, International University of Catalonia, Barcelona, Spain

CONCEPT

Looking to nature for inspiration, this proposal is a reassessment of how we illuminate urban areas and a search for alternative approaches. Based on interdisciplinary research, it explores the creation of plants with natural light-emitting abilities for use in public spaces. Specifically, **Genetic Barcelona Project** involves introducing the gene for luminescent protein production from the jellyfish *Aequorea victoria* into the DNA of several trees to impart bioluminescence. The architect emphasizes the potential of this natural process to begin replacing conventional lighting, with its ecologically burdensome reliance on metals, fossil fuels, and industrial fabrication.

Bioluminescence, the ability of living organisms—such as much marine life—to produce and emit light, is made possible by certain proteins. The potential applications of this natural phenomenon for industrial and commercial uses are many and, unlike the kind of light on which we're most reliant after the sun has set, the chemical reaction that generates it consumes little energy and produces no harmful waste. The project's vision for Barcelona anticipates both increased access to bioluminescence and a more conscious accounting of how conventional illumination incurs cost and produces waste.

ABOVE   94

Artistic rendering of genetically modified, bioluminescent trees illuminating the street and sidewalk in front of Antoni Gaudí's Casa Milà.

ABOVE   95

Bioluminescent plants might be deployed to reduce the costs of building and maintaining infrastructure, such as roads with heavy traffic.

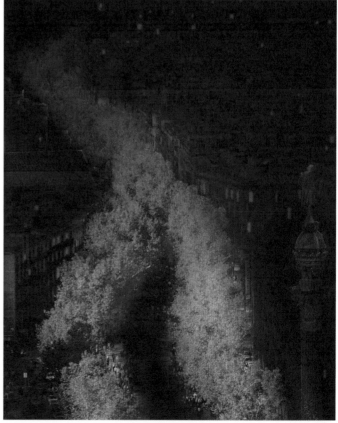

ABOVE   96

The natural process of generating light within organisms is well understood and occurs in several types of fungi and in numerous sea creatures. The gene that codes for the light reaction can be inserted into host organisms.

RIGHT   97

The urban scene could be transformed by these living lights, using the efficiency of organisms and their internal reactions—phenomena that offer superb economies of material and energy.

KINDERGARTEN

Incorporating vines and trees into an unconventional school inspired by the microscopic structure of plant cells.

Wood, iron, glass, computer numerical controlled milled scaffolding, native trees and vines.

Alberto T. Estévez (Spanish) / Diego Navarro (Spanish)—Genetic Architectures Office, International University of Catalonia, Barcelona, Spain

CONCEPT

Here the architects propose integrating nature and computer numerical controlled- (CNC-) milled scaffolding to create an enchanting learning space for children. The proposed site is in Vilobí del Penedès, an area west of Barcelona that is dense with vineyards and interspersed with woods against the backdrop of nearby Montserrat.

A square grid of wooden beams provides both the base and a magnificent pergola-like cover for the construction, which is easy to both digitalize and build. Beneath the canopy is a magical world for children, including hills, trees, several types of suspended vine, a pool, gardens, and classroom spaces.

Kindergarten aims to foreground the natural environment within the built space while finding formal inspiration from electron microscope imagery of plant structures at the cellular level. The architect translated these pictures into high-ceilinged, tent-like classroom spaces.

BELOW   98

CNC-milled, undulating tent shapes provide a surface area for plants and vines as well as creating high-ceilinged classroom spaces.

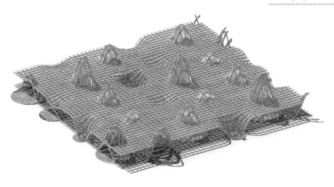

ABOVE 99

The vines provide a link to the local agricultural tradition while helping to create a comfortable environment that is reminiscent of the outdoors and is conducive to both learning and play.

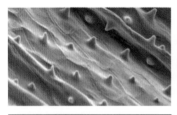

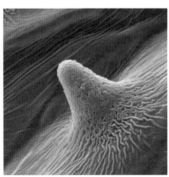

ABOVE / RIGHT 100, 101, 102

Electron microscope images of cellular structures growing, differentiating, and organizing inspired the architect, who identified a link between these phenomena and early education.

BELOW 103

Mount Montserrat is the ever-present backdrop to Vilobí del Penedès as well as being the formal inspiration for the design of the kindergarten.

ABOVE   104

A vision of Venice stabilized by the work of
'programmed' protocells that are able to coat
structural supports with layers of limestone.

ABOVE   105

The narrow woodpiles beneath the structures of
Venice. Protocells would work to broaden these
supports, slowing down the process of sinking.

LEFT   106

Along the Venice canals, clams, mussels,
and barnacles routinely fix carbon from
the surrounding environment to produce a
limestone-like material for their own needs.

FUTURE VENICE

Can we harness natural processes to prevent Venice from being swallowed up by the soft mud on which it was built?

Protocells, models, renderings.

Rachel Armstrong (British)—University of Greenwich, London, UK / Advanced Virtual and Technological Architectural Research Laboratory, Bartlett School of Architecture, University College London, UK

CONCEPT

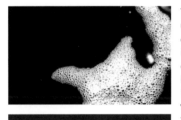

ABOVE   107

Protocell behavior could be directed to resemble a metabolism that uses light energy and fixes carbon to eventually form reef-like structures.

This proposal aims to help reclaim Italy's 'Floating City' in a sustainable way. It anticipates a new form of architecture that is self-repairing and closely integrated with changes in the surrounding natural environment, effectively metabolizing a product of human activity (carbon dioxide) into components (calcium carbonate) for construction. The architect's vision is a response to the fact that building technology has remained largely unchanged for hundreds of years—relying on blueprints, industrial manufacture, and teams of workers to create an inert object that is ecologically isolated and unsound.

Future Venice proposes using cell-like droplets of oil and organic material that exhibit behaviors similar to those of living organisms to reinforce the pylons on which much of Venice rests. These 'protocells' could be programmed to perform functions that replicate biological processes, such as microbial cementation (the slow process by which corals and coralline algae build a reef).

Collaborating architect Philip Beesley (from the University of Waterloo, Toronto, Canada) has already shown (in his work 'Hylozoic Ground,' exhibited at the Venice Biennale of Architecture 2010) that they can form micro-building blocks of limestone from the carbon dioxide dissolved in water. By leaving this deposit on the weak, wooden framework that underpins the Venetian city, the protocells would thicken and strengthen the existing supports, distributing their loads over a larger area to slow, or even stop, the current rate of sinking, which is expected to accelerate due to climate change.

This artificial reef would be an alternative to the plan to install a series of steel floodgates to control tidal movement in the lagoon surrounding Venice.

2.
ECOLOGICAL OBJECT ENGINEERING

Replacing Industrial and Mechanical Processes

OPPOSITE · · · 108
See 'Microbial Home', page 96.

This section focuses on how biological processes, both natural and engineered, are being considered as viable alternatives to those of more conventional technologies. The examples given here include contained systems, as well as experiments in localizing fabrication with organic processes, in order to achieve material and energy savings while reducing their environmental impact. These designs have broad implications but are realized on a human scale, smaller than the architectural or urban context. Much of this work responds to concerns about the damaging legacy of the Industrial Revolution, which has resulted in the current standards of manufacture, consumption, and disposal that we now recognize are in need of urgent reform.

The proliferation of the design approach profiled here is linked to the rise of biofuels and the rapidly growing biotechnology economy. As described by Rob Carlson in *Biology is Technology: The Promise, Peril, and New Business of Engineering Life* (2010), this sector of the United States' economy is responsible for more than 2 percent of GDP. Within this area, which is defined as including products that rely on genetic modification, the major components are biologics (pharmaceutical applications) at $75 billion, agriculture at $110 billion, and industrial (including fuels, enzymes, and materials) at $115 billion. Notably, the growth rate in these categories reliably outpaces that of other areas of activity.

For designers, the category of industrial applications is particularly enticing relative to the others given that food and drug products are highly regulated and that the barrier to entry for industrial applications can be low. As discussed in *Nature* (2010), a garage biologist might spend just $10,000 or less on equipment to get up and running, and that cost is falling. If spread between a few participants—a biologist, a designer, and a marketer, for example—the cost of launching a biotech startup becomes even less than purchasing an automobile.

As the financial outlay required to tinker with biological systems decreases, there is a growing desire—

fueled by greater awareness of environmental issues, as well as potential financial rewards, bolstered by the ever-rising expense of commodities such as oil and labor—to replace the inefficient, traditional industrial reliance on machines with the processes of microorganisms and plants. This shift, which is seen in varying degrees, crosses fields of study and professions, from biochemistry and economics to civil engineering and industrial design.

In parallel with this change is a new conception of value creation that has begun to emerge that accounts for the renewability of energy and more holistic thinking about the impacts of an object's entire life cycle. The growing base of knowledge in biology about the functioning of cells, as well as large investments in the commercialization of related technologies, are also important factors.

The paths taken by designers toward these efforts are many, but their role as mediators between scientific research and the public is well established, as described by Paola Antonelli in *Design and The Elastic Mind* (2008). Knowledge and innovation must be integrated with usability if a product is ever to materialize as successful: Google's restrained homepage, an iPad's touch-screen gesture system, and the seemingly obvious but brilliant Facebook 'like' button all attest to the importance of intuitiveness to widespread adoption. The creativity of the projects described in this section suggest that we may stand on the brink of similar virtuoso design achievements in the expanding intersection of biology and technology.

BIOBRICK

Can the humble brick be turned from an environmental menace into the building block of a more sustainable future?

Sand aggregate, bacteria (Sporosarcina pasteurii).

Ginger Krieg Dosier (American)—American University of Sharjah, United Arab Emirates / Vergelabs

PROTOTYPE

The brick is a ubiquitous and effective construction component that has endured for thousands of years, relatively unchanged. Its inherent simplicity—it demands few skills, materials, or technologies, is durable, and is sized to fit the human hand—can be much admired. But while its form and function have been mastered, its standard method of production requires reform: intense heat energy, usually applied in kilns that burn coal, with a requirement for large quantities of agricultural soil, leaves a significant ecological footprint.

In contrast, the **BioBrick** utilizes a natural process found in common bacteria to fuse sand particles and thereby create a rigid shape with strength and durability comparable to those of conventional bricks. Here, the architect combines the microorganisms with sand and a solution of calcium chloride and urea to initiate microbial-induced calcite precipitation (MICP), whereby the bacteria glue the grains of the sand together to form stone.

As with all life processes, this one is sensitive to environmental conditions and doesn't yet align with the demanding pace of industry. Factors such as temperature, density of nutrients, and pH levels must all be maintained within particular ranges for it to work, and it can take a full week to form a single brick, instead of the usual two days.

Another challenge of biologically grown bricks is their toxic by-product: ammonia. Production on a large scale would require supplementary processes to contend with this potentially dangerous gas. While

this represents a considerable obstacle, alternatives to traditional brick making are sorely needed. The sheer scale of world production is daunting: more than 1.23 trillion bricks are made every year, many in developing countries and at great ecological expense—they produce more pollution than the world's airplanes during the same period. So alternatives must be explored as resource depletion accelerates. In nature, MICP has been slowly creating rock formations on earth for billions of years and has only recently captured the interest of scientists and engineers who are motivated to harness it for human ends.

ABOVE   109

A comparison of a microbially formed BioBrick (left) and a standard concrete brick (right).

BELOW   110

A prototype of a full-scale 3D printer that precisely deposits bacteria, urea, and calcium ions onto a bed of sand in successive layers.

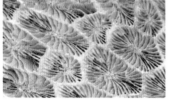

ABOVE 111

A scanning electron microscope image of bacterially cemented aggregate. With increasing magnification, the rhombohedral geometry of the calcite is revealed. Bacterial 'fossils' appear within the cement as rod-shaped voids.

ABOVE / RIGHT 112, 113

Some 75 percent of brick production worldwide takes place in India, China, and Pakistan, where energy-intensive, traditional methods dominate. In contrast, the reactions involved in forming the BioBrick can occur at room temperature.

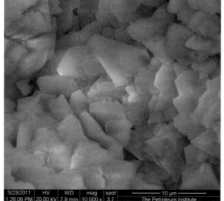
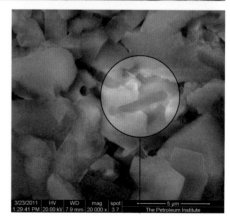

ABOVE 114, 115, 115

Sections of *Leptastrea transversa* coral, taken from a vernacular fort wall in Sharjah in the United Arab Emirates, revealing patterns of natural calcium carbonate formation.

BIOCONCRETE

By 'healing' the cracks in concrete, can bacteria increase
the lifespan of our buildings—both current and future?

Concrete, bacteria (Sporosarcina pasteurii), calcium lactate.

Henk Jonkers (Dutch)—CiTG Microlab, Delft University of Technology, the Netherlands

PROTOTYPE

ABOVE 117

Conventional concrete is eroded and weakens
over time, allowing moisture to enter through
cracks and to rust the reinforcing metals within.

Traditional concrete is key to the construction
industry and is found in all kinds of building. However,
its drawbacks include its serious environmental
impact and the fact that it is prone to cracking. The
brainchild of a microbiologist, an alternative material
has been developed that is capable of automatically
filling any fissures that appear over time. It is
made by adding specialized bacteria to concrete.

An endless variety of bacteria occur in nature
and many are well adapted to artificial environments,
some of which are extreme, so these microorganisms
have been called 'extremophiles.' From a human
perspective, concrete may appear to be a supremely
inhospitable environment for life—dry and rock-
solid within. However, to these bacteria it poses
few challenges. A select group of extremophiles not
only thrive in barren conditions but also naturally
produce limestone. This ability can be harnessed
to seal holes and strengthen weak areas.

Concrete incorporating these hardy bacteria,
known as **BioConcrete,** could benefit both the
economy and the environment because the traditional
building material is ubiquitous, it is expensive to
maintain, and it creates a tremendous carbon footprint
through the burning of limestone to obtain calcium
oxide, which is an essential component of cement.
The self-healing material would lower the cost of
remediation work and delay the requirement for
rebuilding, as well as reduce the demand for cement,
which currently contributes more than 5 percent to the
world's human-generated carbon dioxide emissions.

The major goal of current research is
to find the right bacterium that can, when
integrated into concrete, actively repair a structure
throughout its 50–100 year service life.

ABOVE 118

Biological concrete containing microorganisms
and deposits of nutrients. Samples are created to
test the material's properties in the laboratory.

ABOVE   119, 120, 121, 122

Microbially induced cementation (shown here at the microscopic level) occurs in nature.

LEFT   123

Several species of bacteria have adaptations that allow them to live in extreme environments, such as in the interior of mineral rock formations.

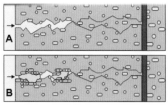

ABOVE   124

Two cross-sections of concrete showing the structure before and after the bacteria become active and secrete limestone inside the material, thereby sealing the crack before moisture and air can penetrate deeper and create further damage.

FAR LEFT   125

Henk Jonkers with concrete samples at Delft University of Technology in the Netherlands.

LEFT   126

Samples of *Sporosarcina pasteurii* in the laboratory.

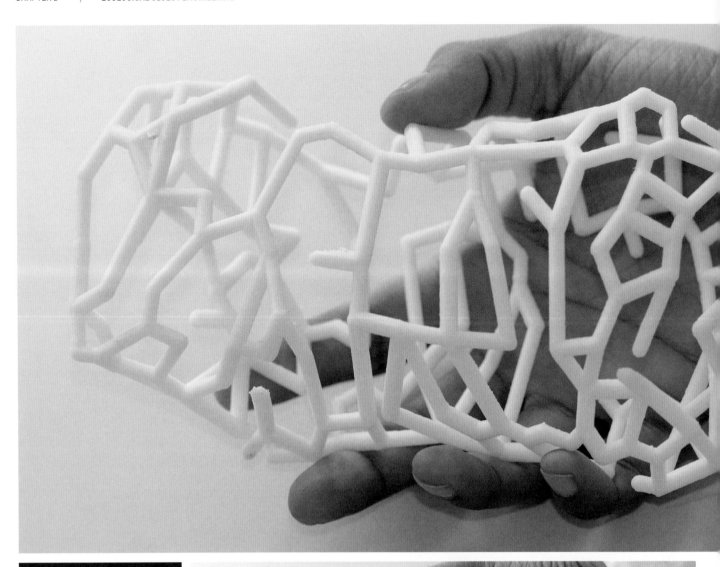

ABOVE 127

A physical model of an exoskeleton that has been designed using evolutionary computation. (See the workflow example at the top of pages 84–85.)

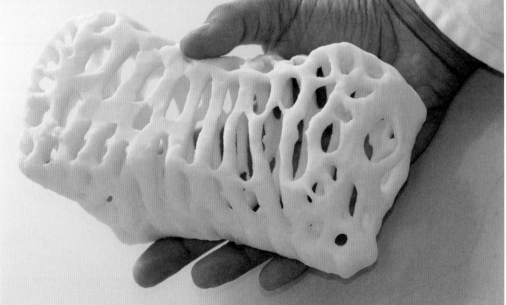

RIGHT 128

A physical model of an exoskeleton designed using an equation derived from observations of xylem cell growth.

BIO-PROCESSING

An exploration using plant cells as design tools.

*Xylem cells from artichoke plants, Autodesk IDEA Studio,
Eureqa software.*

David Benjamin (American) / Fernan Federici (Argentinean)—Columbia University Graduate School of
Architecture, Planning and Preservation, New York, USA / University of Cambridge, UK / Creative
Machines Lab, Cornell University, New York, USA

PROTOTYPE

This joint project brings together a synthetic biologist and an architect as part of the Synthetic Aesthetics program, supported by the National Science Foundation. It explores new ways of applying biological systems as design tools, with a focus on using cells as bioprocessors.

While there may be numerous examples of identifying and using the form of nature in design and architecture, the team seeks to identify and utilize the logic of nature. Echoing investigations first made by D'Arcy Wentworth Thompson and outlined in his seminal *On Growth and Form* (1917), this exploration digs beneath outward appearance to harness the underlying processes of optimization found in plants.

Bio-processing uses patterns in xylem cell growth to solve architectural structural design problems. One goal is to extract the complex behaviors of these cells at the micrometer scale and to apply them to architecture at the scale of meters.

In the course of this collaboration, the team studied the physical constraints of a cell in order to see how its exoskeleton might offer material-distribution solutions for architectural forms. To do this, it generated data sets corresponding to the growth of the xylem cell exoskeletons, then fed this data into an application developed by Hod Lipson (a robotics engineer at Cornell University, Ithaca, New York), called Eureqa. This software then derived a mathematical equation approximating the data. This in turn becomes a tool to create new cell-like forms for potential applications.

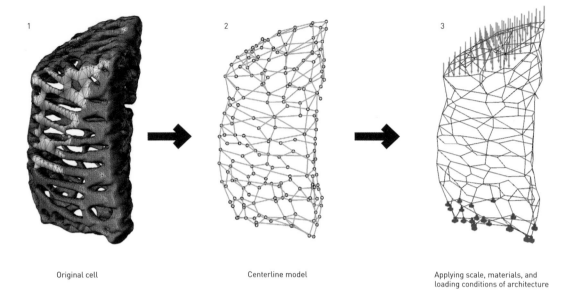

1

Original cell

2

Centerline model

3

Applying scale, materials, and
loading conditions of architecture

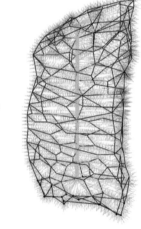

Field of vectors and
blue control line

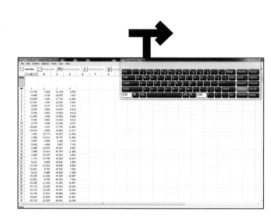

Dataset generated from vector and control line

ABOVE   129

These workflows exhibit the logic of a xylem
cell's growth using computational tools. The first
workflow starts with a xylem cell scan, converts
it to a digital model, applies structural forces
in a computer simulation, then uses a genetic
algorithm to generate and evaluate various
possible configurations to find the form with
maximum strength and minimum material.
In the second workflow, an equation for xylem
cell formation is derived by analyzing data
relating to the distances, thicknesses, and angles
of the natural cell. This equation is then used to
calculate how the natural system might create
exoskeletons in more complex shapes.

OPPOSITE   130

In this last workflow, xylem cells are induced to
fill a custom void (such as the U-shaped space
shown here), allowing for the observation of how
xylem cells 'solve' a variety of spatial problems.

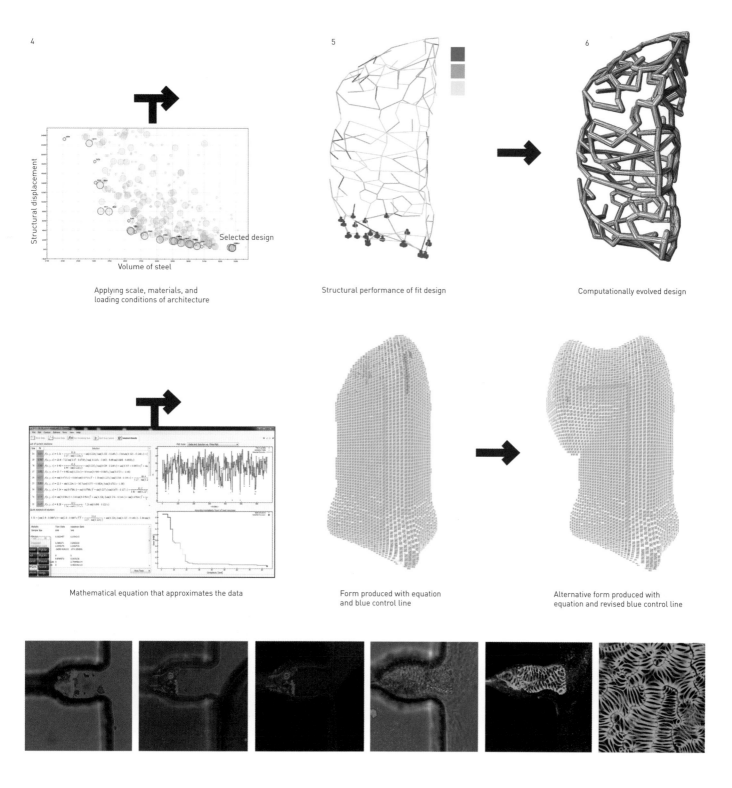

4

Applying scale, materials, and
loading conditions of architecture

5

Structural performance of fit design

6

Computationally evolved design

Mathematical equation that approximates the data

Form produced with equation
and blue control line

Alternative form produced with
equation and revised blue control line

A RADICAL MEANS

Using the ability of microorganisms to turn sand into stone challenges the conventions of industrial design and manufacture.

Bacteria (Sporosarcina pasteurii), sand, water, calcium chloride, urea.

Damian Palin (Irish)—Royal College of Art, London, UK / Imperial College, London, UK / Delft University of Technology, the Netherlands

PROTOTYPE

Here the artist/biominerologist utilizes a natural cementation process of bacteria (microbially induced calcite precipitation) to cast an everyday object in a new form of sandstone. The microorganisms (*Sporosarcina pasteurii*) form calcium carbonate crystals when dissolved in calcium and urea, which then form bonds between loose grains of sand and result in a material that can be shaped in a mold before hardening.

A Radical Means—'a radical departure from current means of human production'—offers a system of manufacturing that, if it can be scaled and mastered, could occur at temperatures considerably lower than current industrial methods, such as injection molding. The greatest challenge has been producing the right conditions for the bacteria to live homogeneously within a mold during casting.

If unevenly distributed and grown, the microorganisms create noticeable discrepancies between cast and final form. Thus an 'imperfect' technique produces an uneven result, but one that mirrors an organic form and is more sustainable and thought-provoking than one created using standard methods of fabrication.

ABOVE   131

The mold for a basic stool into which a mixture of aggregate, nutrients, and bacteria are poured.

ABOVE 132

The finished stool, formed naturally by countless microorganisms over time and without the need of high temperatures or mechanical intervention.

ABOVE 133

The stool mold with nutrients and bacteria being added, in contrast to injection molding processes requiring synthetic materials and intense heat.

ABOVE 134

Irregularities emerge in the finished piece, shown here being removed from the mold.

ABOVE 135

The designer, Damian Palin, aims to develop bio-inspired materials and production processes. At Nanyang Technical University in Singapore he is working to extract key minerals from the brine produced as a result of the desalination process.

ALGAERIUM

Can simple algae bring both biofuel production
and colorful design into our homes?

*Glass, water, marine algae (including Tetraselmis sp., Dunaliella sp.,
Pyrocystis lunula), freshwater algae (including Hydrodictyon sp.).*

Marin Sawa (Japanese)—Central Saint Martins College of Art and Design, London, UK

PROTOTYPE

This textile-inspired project proposes bringing algae
into built environments to generate living light as
an ever-changing decorative element. The plants'
processes of photosynthesis and bioluminescence
are exploited to find design solutions that work
in the contemporary home and outdoor urban
spaces. The designer leverages simple yet powerful
microorganisms to produce dynamic color systems
that react to their immediate surroundings.

Crafted in a home biology lab, **Algaerium**
was created with knowledge adapted from biology
and molecular gastronomy (a subdiscipline of food
science) in order to cultivate strains of algae that are
adapted to the design's environment and can serve
as a source of green energy. Algae are grown and
then encapsulated in a sphere of 'biological skin'
that allows them to photosynthesize normally—
absorbing carbon dioxide and producing oxygen.

A modular arrangement of clear, flexible
tubing circulates a cocktail of algae capsules
and carefully prepared water containing artificial
color-changing elements that respond to carbon
dioxide levels. In addition, some of the algae
are bioluminescent, so with shifting levels of
photosynthesis-promoting sunlight, the color
of the system changes; and with the movement
of the water, some of the microorganisms glow.

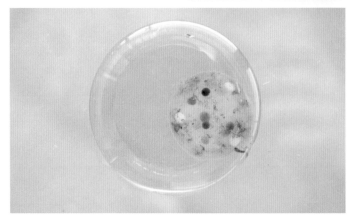

TOP   136, 137

Different algae species are monocultured and
then brought together within one biological
sphere. They are immobilized and sustained
within an in vitro environment of light, water,
carbon dioxide, and sterilized conditions to
prevent contamination from external factors.

ABOVE / OPPOSITE   138, 139

The inner and outer membranes are made of
alginate and glass, respectively. The latter allows
the algae to be contained and integrated into our
urban environment. This 'pod of algae' suggests
a futuristic alternative to the traditional pot plant.

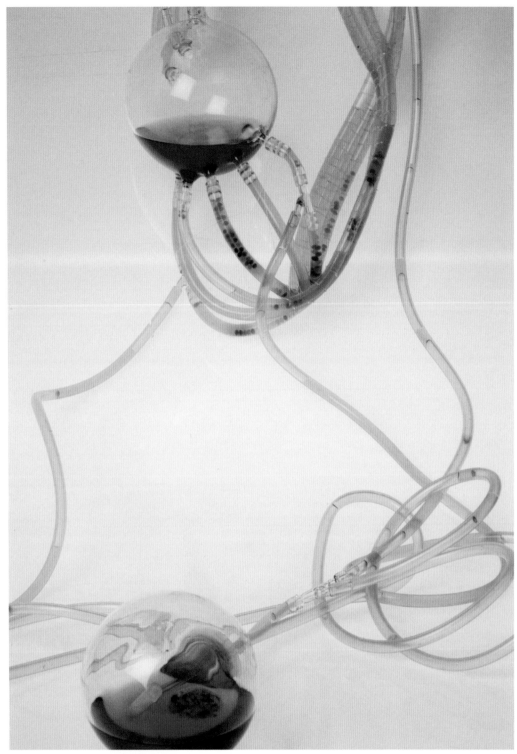

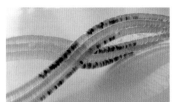

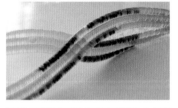

ABOVE 141, 142

The algae photosynthesize as normal within the second skin and their consumption of carbon dioxide is made visible as the color of the fluid within the system changes from yellow to purple.

ABOVE 140

Four vessels are connected by tubes containing living microalgae enveloped in an organic second skin and fluid that reacts to their photosynthesis.

ABOVE   143

The prototype is an exploration of the aesthetics of algae, biochemistry, and textile weaving for use in spatial installations, as an alternative to conventional vertical greenery, such as ivy.

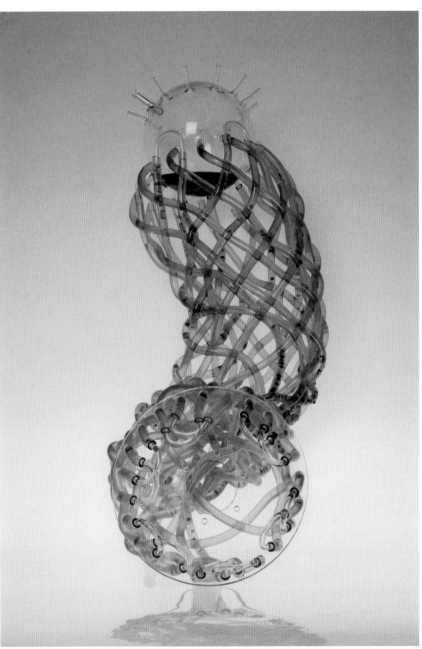

ABOVE   144

The globe vessel here acts as a joint to connect numerous individual modular systems.

LUNG-ON-A-CHIP

By replicating organs outside of the human body, could we reduce the substantial time and costs involved in clinical trials?

Microfluidic channels etched into transparent polymer, human alveolus and endothelial cells.

Donald E. Ingber (American) / Dongeun Huh (South Korean)—Wyss Institute for Biologically Inspired Engineering, Harvard Medical School, Harvard School of Engineering and Applied Sciences, Boston, USA / Children's Hospital Boston, USA

PROTOTYPE

This biomedical application incorporates live human cells in a tiny testing device that mimics the functioning of the human lung. It allows researchers to monitor the behavior of cells at the margin between the air sacs and the capillaries, a critically important area in which the body interacts with the environment. It is at this boundary that inhaled particles and pathogens are passed into the bloodstream. The advantage in recreating this interface outside the body is its potential to replace human and animal subjects for numerous types of drug testing and toxicity screening.

Lung-on-a-chip consists of a series of microfluidic channels etched into a flexible, transparent polymer casing. A central conduit houses two layers of human cells with a porous membrane in between. The upper layer comprises cells from the alveoli (the air sacs deep within the lungs that resemble miniature bunches of grapes, where gases pass between the lungs and the blood). The lower layer is made up of endothelial cells from the capillaries, which convey blood that is rich in oxygen to the rest of the body.

The flexible channels expand and contract as the controlled air pressure fluctuates. This stretches the cells and very closely replicates the conditions of breathing. The unit's transparency facilitates real-time observations of inflammation or other responses to foreign bodies being introduced into the airflow chamber.

So far the behavior of the cells replicates that in live subjects, suggesting that in the near future this coin-sized device might help to dramatically reduce the cost of certain medical testing procedures while addressing ethical concerns. The team is also developing other 'organs' on chips, such as a beating heart and a gut undergoing peristalsis, as well as bone marrow and cancer models.

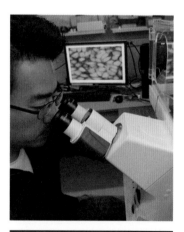

ABOVE   145

This 'on-a-chip' technology permits the real-time observation of how human tissues and organs respond to drugs, pathogens, and other agents.

ABOVE   146

This chip contains live human cells in a system of
channels in a way that replicates the region of the
lungs where inhaled particles, organisms, and
gasses pass into the bloodstream. Air pressure,
temperature, and moisture levels are all carefully
controlled so as to mimic human breathing.

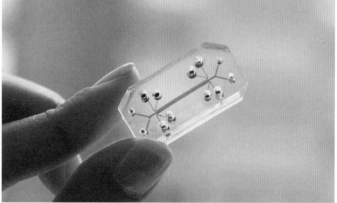

ABOVE   147

Observations have shown that the cells in the
device respond in the same way as those in live
subjects. The technology may help to accelerate
medical research while also cutting costs and
tackling ethical concerns about animal testing.

ACTIVE MODULAR PHYTOREMEDIATION

Using plants to reduce the need for power-hungry mechanical ventilation.

Hybrid hydroponic plants (including English Ivy, Golden Pothos, Boston Fern), organic plant media mix, rhizosphere microbial communities.

Anna Dyson (Canadian) / Jason Vollen (American) / Ted Ngai (Canadian) / Matt Gindlesparger (American) / Peter Stark (American) (with research assistants Ahu Aydogan (Turkish) and EmilyRae Brayton (American))—Center for Architecture Science and Ecology, New York, USA

PROTOTYPE

This team has created a prototype to help improve indoor air quality while reducing pressure on energy-hungry heating, ventilation, and air-conditioning systems. It is well understood that contemporary construction materials and designs negatively impact the internal environment of buildings, thereby contributing to health problems for many people. This situation is often worsened by the high levels of pollution in urban spaces that typically surround these edifices. The **active modular phytoremediation system** works to address this issue with a design that is both elegant and low energy.

Modular pods that contain a variety of hydroponic plants are mounted to a wall. The growing method used for the plants has the advantage of exposing their roots, resulting in three to four times the efficiency compared with potted plants, in which air filtration occurs through the leaves. In this scenario, air is directed across the roots, which absorb airborne toxins, including volatile organic compounds and particulate matter, which are harmful to people. Since these particles are taken in at the root level and not through the leaves, the plant does not become toxic. The air-cleaning system is scheduled to be installed and tested in the Public Safety Answering Center II, a Bronx emergency response center in New York.

ABOVE   148

By exposing the plants' roots and channeling air over them, the system exploits the air-cleaning ability of microorganisms that digest toxins and thus prevent their harmful effects on humans.

ABOVE   149

A variety of hydroponically grown plant species can be wall mounted in modular, plastic pods.

Refreshed air

Contaminated room air

ABOVE   150

Rather than draw in and circulate air from the immediate surrounding environment, which may be polluted, the system 'scrubs' the air with both natural and low-energy mechanical processes.

ABOVE   151

Modularity allows the arrangement to be scaled up where space and light are available, helping to reduce the need for energy-intensive heating, ventilation, and air-conditioning solutions.

ABOVE 152

A design concept for a series of biological devices
for the home, aimed at creating an ecosystem
capable of filtering, processing, and recycling
sewage, effluent, garbage, and wastewater.

RIGHT 153

Larder is a dining table with terracotta boxes at
its heart for storing food at different temperatures.

MICROBIAL HOME

With bio-digestion at its center, can the home become more self-sufficient and less wasteful of natural resources?

Mixed media, including wood, ceramics, methane digester, various bacteria.

Jack Mama (British), Clive van Heerdan (British, born South Africa)—Philips Design, Eindhoven, the Netherlands

PROTOTYPES

Microbial Home is a concept that comprises several integrated appliances that heat, refrigerate, and generate food, as well as digest waste products. The units are designed to work in a cyclical way that resembles an ecosystem, the aim being to maximize the use of the mass and embodied energy that normally moves through our domestic spaces. The designers adopt a view of the home as a biological machine for filtering, processing, and recycling what we conventionally view as waste.

The **Methane Bio-digester** is central to the idea. Embedded in a kitchen island that includes a chopping surface, a waste grinder, and a gas cooking range, it generates methane from the work of bacteria digesting organic matter in the waste-disposal unit. The gas powers the range, as well as lights and water-heating components in other parts of the system.

The **Larder** is a combined dining-room table and food storage unit. Terracotta boxes set into the table's center are warmed by the hot water pipes from the bio-digester and are of varying thicknesses and volumes to provide a range of temperatures.

The **Paternoster** is a device for 'up-cycling' plastics (provided they are free from toxic chemicals). They are ground into small pieces that can be digested naturally by fungi, which can, in turn, be harvested and eaten. The mushrooms grow in a removable wheel-shaped holder for easy access.

The **Bio-light** is an array of glass cells that can be hung or wall mounted and are connected via silicon tubes to a food reservoir at the base.

Illumination is provided either by bioluminescent bacteria—maintained by methane from the bio-digester—or by chemically charged liquid florescent proteins. Both methods produce light at low temperatures, as opposed to incandescence, which involves significant heat waste.

The **Urban Beehive** is designed to allow domestic beekeeping. It can be installed in an exterior wall, with the outside portion fitted with an opening that allows the bees to enter and exit. On the inside, contained in a glass vessel, is a chamber that can be viewed, similar to an ant farm, from inside the home. The insects find a preexisting honeycomb structure on which they can begin to build their wax cells, while the interior glass permits the entry of orange light, which they need to see. The device includes a system for pacifying the occupants with smoke in order to facilitate harvesting of the honey from the inside.

The concept of the **Filtering Squatting Toilet** recognizes waste as a necessary component of a domestic ecosystem and highlights the essential shift from utility-dependent sanitation to regenerative, localized solutions. An array of charcoal, sand, and ceramic filters diverts solids to the bio-digester and generates graywater for other uses. It aims to show the energy value of human waste and raise awareness about wasting water—the flush mechanism is based on the one liter flush toilet technique developed by the Sulabh Foundation in India.

RIGHT   154

Containing charcoal, sand, and ceramic filters, the **Filtering Squatting Toilet** draws out nutrients that can be used to cultivate plants, thereby highlighting the value of what we consider waste.

RIGHT   155

Mounted on a window and open to the outside, the **Urban Beehive** offers an updated version of the ant farm concept. Viewers from indoors can watch bees construct and maintain their hive.

ABOVE / BELOW   156, 157, 158

The **Larder** uses energy from the **Bio-digester** to alter the temperature of its food-storage boxes.

ABOVE   159

The **Bio-digester** is a kitchen waste-disposal system. It houses bacteria that consume unwanted organic matter and produce methane to power the cooking range and water heater.

ABOVE 160

Named after the old passenger lift system that moved people in a looping conveyor, this hand-powered appliance—the **Paternoster**—breaks down certain plastics so that they can be digested by fungi that, in turn, can be harvested and eaten.

RIGHT 161

Detail of the internal grinding mechanism of the **Paternoster**. Plastics must be free from toxic inks and finishes to safely grow mushrooms.

ABOVE / LEFT   162, 163

The **Bio-light** comprises glass chambers filled
with either bioluminescent bacteria and nutrients
or the enzymes and proteins needed to sustain
illumination, which works at lower temperatures
than those required for incandescent lighting.

BIOPLASTIC

Is the production of biodegradable plastic from a bountiful
non-petroleum source—human waste—now within our reach?

Various natural and genetically modified microorganisms, wastewater.

Ryan L. Smith (American) / John Bissell (American)—Micromidas, Davis, USA

PROTOTYPE

This endeavor relies on a newly developed process that utilizes wastewater streams, with their dense organic content, to manufacture polyhydroxyalkanoate (PHA) plastic. Recycling sewage that would otherwise require further treatment before reentering the water cycle, it uses a variety of specialized microorganisms to consume and convert the organic matter to a highly versatile material that can be used in packaging and injection molding, for example.

The technology is currently being tested in a pilot plant in northern California. If it can be scaled successfully then it may offer an ecologically sound and cost-competitive alternative to plastics derived from either traditional petroleum processing or the more recent biotechnical sugar fermentation, which still relies on fossil fuels.

The research approach in developing **BioPlastic** involved prospecting for bacteria and other microorganisms with special characteristics that could support PHA production, then applying intensive selective pressures and performing genetic screening to arrive at highly specialized strains that essentially function as plastics factories, with little more than human waste for fuel. Selective breeding is supplemented with genetic alterations to turn on or off particular, beneficial microbial traits.

The amount of oil currently used for plastic production is significant—approximately two million barrels a day in the United States, accounting for about 10 percent of oil consumption. While PHA production via microorganisms would not account

for all of this, it represents a sensible approach of recognizing and utilizing energy and nutrient flows that are readily available but being ignored. The process also recalls the words of Victor Hugo, who lamented in *Les Misérables* how the flow of the Paris sewer, a potential source of fertilizer, was thoughtlessly wasted: 'the incalculable element of wealth under our own hand, we send to the sea.'

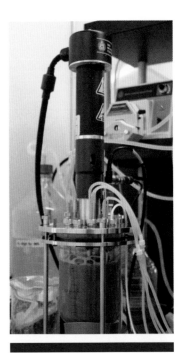

ABOVE   164

A cocktail of microorganisms—both natural and genetically enhanced—filter and digest nutrients from wastewater and thus produce organic matter that can be converted into polyhydroxyalkanoate.

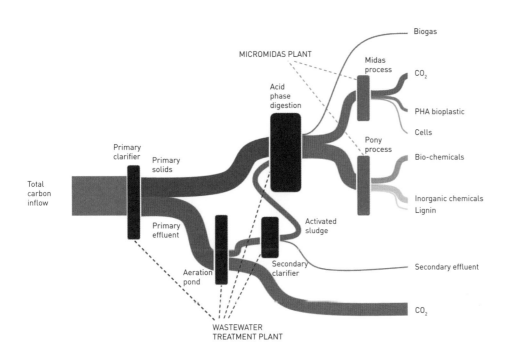

MICROMIDAS PLANT

Biogas

Midas
process

CO_2

Acid
phase
digestion

PHA bioplastic

Cells

Pony
process

Bio-chemicals

Primary
clarifier

Primary
solids

Inorganic chemicals
Lignin

Total
carbon
inflow

Primary
effluent

Activated
sludge

Secondary effluent

Aeration
pond

Secondary
clarifier

CO_2

WASTEWATER
TREATMENT PLANT

ABOVE   166

Extracted compounds can be processed into
biodegradable plastic that has a variety of uses.

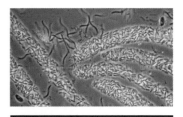

ABOVE   167

Microorganisms are the planet's first and still
most effective filtering mechanism, and they
have adapted (or been altered) to consume and
convert nutrients in virtually any environment.

ABOVE   165

The numerous stages of waste treatment
highlight the potential useful end products of
a system integrated with Micromidas plants.

ABOVE   168

The use of small treatment chambers helps
researchers to determine how combinations of
microorganisms perform in different conditions.

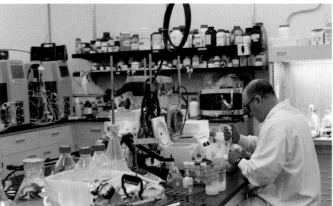

ABOVE   169

An important goal of the research is to find better
ways to manage our current carbon and nutrient
cycles while also competing with conventional,
petroleum-dependant material production.

AQUADYNE LIVING WALL

Is growing plants on vertical walls moving from a design statement to an earnest effort to reap ecological benefits?

Recycled mixed polymer waste, low-grade plastics, plants, stainless steel.

Cityroofs Ltd, Leighton Buzzard, UK, in conjunction with Halfen, Dunstable, UK

COMPLETED

ABOVE / RIGHT   171, 172, 173

Plants are cultivated directly onto a lightweight, capillary substrate. This material is porous yet rigid enough to hold the plants in place.

This technology uses a lightweight permeable slab manufactured from recycled plastic as the substrate for plant growth. The material allows water to flow through it easily while avoiding any risk of negative environmental impacts through leaching. Numerous plant species grow on the boards, which are fitted within a lightweight stainless-steel frame for attachment to the façades of structures. The resulting screen of living plants offers the interior protection from solar gain to reduce the reliance on air-conditioning and energy use.

Aquadyne Living Wall can be used on roofs and walls, and it serves both to minimize the effect of water ingress on the building's fabric and as a capillary growing medium, with no requirement for soil. The porous surface is sprayed with a variety of plant seeds, which are allowed to grow for some weeks prior to installation. Following installation, a hydroponic system powered by photovoltaics delivers water and nutrients, which can be augmented with harvested rainwater and graywater.

OPPOSITE   170

The aesthetic enhancement of a green wall is coupled with building performance benefits, such as reducing surface weathering and modulating temperature to cleaning the surrounding air.

ECOCRADLE

Are mushrooms the answer when it comes to finding a versatile and sustainable alternative to plastics?

Fungal mycelia, local agricultural waste (including seed husks).

Eben Bayer (American) / Gavin McIntyre (American)—Ecovative Design LLC, New York, USA

IN PRODUCTION

Ecovative Design has created an organic replacement for traditional petroleum polymer foam—material that typically lasts for hundreds or thousands of years, represents 25 percent of the volume of waste in landfill sites, and often contains harmful compounds, such as benzene. Called MycoBond, it has potential for use in many kinds of products, from building materials through packaging to automotive components. The low-energy composite is heat-resistant and completely biodegradable.

EcoCradle is a packaging solution made from MycoBond that offers a viable and preferable alternative to polystyrene. The production process relies on the the natural growth of mushrooms—specifically the mycelium, which is the vegetative structure of a fungus. This provides a living framework for the material as it grows. The other main ingredient is crop waste (such as seed husks). This is mixed in a feedstock medium for the mycelium and placed in molds that determine the form of the end product. The mycelium grows to fill whatever space is available and creates a rigid polymer matrix. The result is a lightweight, non-compressible structure that is as durable as the competition while kept in dry conditions but will begin to degrade when discarded on the compost heap.

The material is competitive, in terms of price and production time, with petroleum-based products. It grows in the dark and is ready in less than two weeks. Fungal strains can be adapted to feed on local crop and biomass waste in virtually any region of the world.

ABOVE   174, 175

This all-natural material can be grown to fill custom shapes, making it useful for packaging.

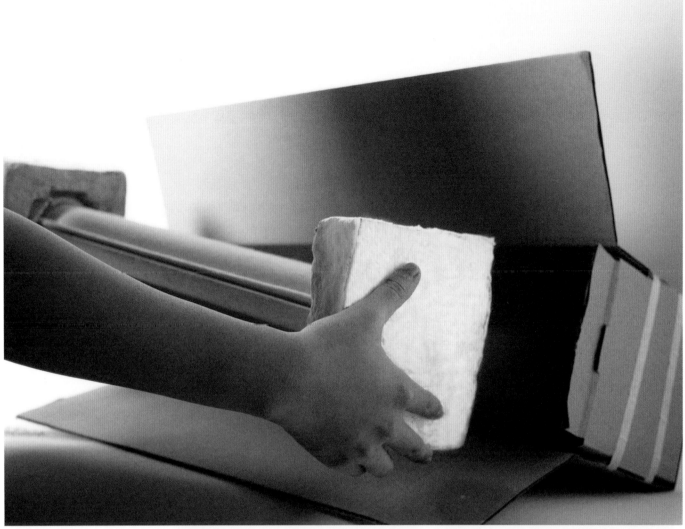

ABOVE   176

Unlike polystyrene, which has a brief useful life
but lasts for hundreds of years in landfill, this
material can be returned to the soil immediately
after use, where it will decompose harmlessly.

ABOVE / RIGHT   177, 178

Early adopters of the packaging material include
Dell Computers, Steelcase and the US National
Oceanic and Atmospheric Administration.

BIOCOUTURE

Bacteria-grown clothes with reduced environmental impact recast a fashion statement as an ecological stance.

Green tea, sugar, yeast, grown microbial-cellulose, natural dyes.

Suzanne Lee (British)—Central Saint Martins College of Art and Design, London, UK

PROTOTYPE

Many textiles rely on plant material or petrochemicals for their raw materials. This project looks at how microorganisms might be used to grow biomaterials for use not only in the fashion industry but also in other areas of manufacturing where fabrics are required.

During the fermentation of sugar, a process by which bacteria gain energy (and one that we exploit in yoghurt production, for example), some strains spin microfibrils of pure cellulose. These adhere to each other, eventually forming a dense but flexible layer. In **BioCouture**, bacteria are added to a sugary green tea solution that also contains yeasts and other microorganisms. After two to three weeks, a 'skin' of around 1.5 cm (0.5 in.) thickness forms on the surface of the liquid that can be removed and used in different ways. Still wet, it can be shaped around three-dimensional forms, whereas if allowed to dry flat, it can be cut and sewn in the manner of more traditional textiles. The material dyes easily with natural colorants.

The product feels similar to artificial leather but, just like vegetable waste, it is safe to compost at the end of its useful life. The designer is now planning to develop the process so that the bacteria can be directed to produce cellulose in a particular shape while retaining its flexibility. She is also looking to control biodegradation so that the products do not decay unexpectedly, as well as to make the material water resistant.

Conventional textile production, consumption and disposal have a serious impact on the environment. However, this new technology promises a more sustainable option. Once implemented on a large scale, it could also exploit waste streams from the food and drink industry.

OPPOSITE   179

Bacteria in a nutrient medium feed on the sugar and produce thin strands of flexible cellulose, eventually forming a skin on the liquid's surface.

ABOVE　　　　　　　　　　180

Shaped like a denim jacket, this garment is
entirely hand stitched from grown bacterial
cellulose and is then treated with indigo dye.

ABOVE   181

A bomber jacket with a stenciled fruit print, using
a mix of blackberries, blueberries, and beetroot.

LOCAL RIVER

Is increased home production and storage of food a way to allow fish stocks and other natural resources to recover from overexploitation?

Blown glass, water pump, joints, various fish and plants.

Mathieu Lehanneur (French)—Studio Mathieu Lehanneur, Paris, France; commissioned by Artists Space, USA

COMPLETED

In response to the rise in 'locavorism' (a preference for locally sourced food), this project represents a miniature fish-farm-cum-kitchen-garden that combines aquaponics with a symbiotic relationship between fish and plants. The plants are able to derive nitrate-rich nutrients from the waste of the fish housed in a tank beneath them. At the same time they filter impurities from the water and help to oxygenate it, thereby optimizing the fishes' environment. This balance is like a miniature ecosystem and mirrors methods used by large-scale fish farms that grow lettuce on trays on the surfaces of ponds containing growing tilapia.

The design of **Local River** is an acknowledgement of the increasing desire for fresh food that can be traced to a local source. As well as anticipating a rise in demand for farm-raised freshwater fish in the shadow of overfishing in our seas, the project offers an equally appealing but more functional alternative to the 'TV aquarium.' Here, the elements of a meal cohabit for a short period in the equivalent of a refrigerator before being served up to their keepers.

OPPOSITE   182

This aquatic home garden has both functional and decorative aspects—freshwater eels and other fish cohabit with an herb garden.

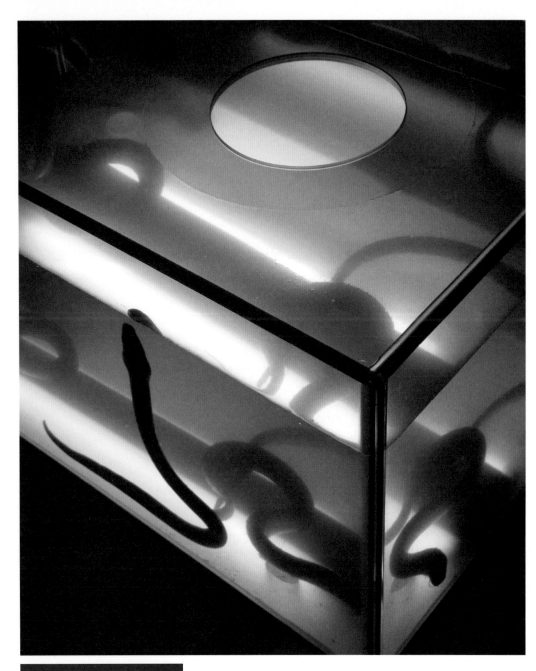

ABOVE   183

The refrigerator aquarium not only stores food
but also encourages the owner to gain a deeper
understanding of the cycles within the food chain.

ABOVE / RIGHT   184, 185

Freshwater trout, eel, and perch are appealing
given that many saltwater varieties of fish favored
by diners are now in decline all over the world.

MOSS TABLE

Instead of treating it as a troublesome weed, should we encourage moss as a renewable source of energy?

ABS plastic, acrylic, carbon fiber, carbon paper with platinum microparticles, neoprene, moss, soil.

Carlos Peralta (British, born Colombia) / Alex Driver (British) / Paolo Bombelli (Italian)—Department of Chemical Engineering and Biotechnology, Department of Biochemistry, Department of Plant Sciences, Institute for Manufacturing, University of Cambridge, UK / Department of Chemistry, University of Bath, UK

PROTOTYPE

Humble mosses might not generally be welcome in the suburban lawn, but their potential to provide cheap electricity may cast them in a new light. This team of designers and scientists views these plants as viable candidates for use in an emerging technology called biophotovoltaics.

With **Moss Table**, they show how such organisms could be used in the near future to power small devices, such as lamps and clocks, by harnessing the energy of the sun. During photosynthesis, moss creates a range of organic compounds, some of which are released into the soil. Symbiotic bacteria, in turn, feed on these compounds and, when breaking them down for their own use, liberate a steady flow of electrons into the soil. Using ribbons of carbon fiber to absorb them, the charged particles can be channeled into a usable electric current.

In presenting an everyday object—a table—the team offers a visual shorthand for the potential of their research to a broad audience. By exhibiting their work they hope to spread interest in both the technology and the potential benefits of future cross-discipline collaborations like their own.

OPPOSITE 186

To demonstrate the utility of harnessing the activity of soil microorganisms, the designers chose an everyday object that both requires a source of electricity and benefits aesthetically from including a living component.

ABOVE / ABOVE RIGHT   187, 188, 189, 190

Planters containing both moss and rich soil are arranged in repeating vessels within the table.

ABOVE   191

Each planter is fitted with a carbon fiber, which captures and channels the flow of electrons that results from the organic activity within the soil.

ABOVE   192

Energy transferred from the moss powers a light.

ABOVE   193

The robust nature of moss makes it an excellent choice for a design that highlights the theme of symbiosis: a portion of the light energy produced is reabsorbed by the photosynthesizing cells.

RIGHT   194

Some early sketches of the design concept.

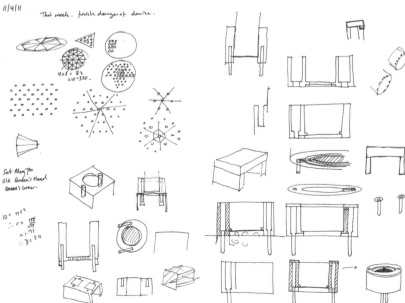

BIODIGITAL CHAIR

Can a grassy field and a public bench be combined in an effective hybrid with the help of computer modeling?

Wood, polystyrene, grasses, computer numerical controlled milled components.

Alberto T. Estévez (Spanish) / Alejandro Muiño (Spanish)/ Diego Navarro (Spanish) Genetic Architectures Office, International University of Catalonia, Barcelona, Spain

COMPLETED

Inspired by Salvador Dalí's quip that the future of architecture 'will be soft and hairy,' this team sought to create designs for public spaces that represent new fabrication standards and require neither models nor molds. In **Biodigital Chair**, the optimal shape for the seating was determined using parametric design tools (software that suggests precise shapes and materials when supplied with a set of inputs). The structure was then produced from wood by a computer numerical controlled milling machine. Finally it was allowed to become 'furry' by growing a layer of grass over the form. This living component of the work both enhances its function—making a more enjoyable outdoor seat—and reflects its 'organic' design origins.

RIGHT 195

Public seating and a park area are combined in this elongated, living bench in Barcelona.

ABOVE   198

Organic and disposable components containing populations of bioluminescent bacteria are fixed to the façades of several downtown buildings.

ABOVE   196

Lighting devices and billboards that are powered by bacteria can be used in cities (this artistic rendering shows Times Square in New York).

RIGHT   197

Glowing bars containing *Pyrocystis fusiformis* are excited by the wind to light outdoor public spaces.

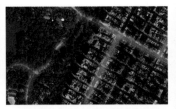

ABOVE / RIGHT   199, 200

Ambient public space lighting for streets and parks within cities, and a natural environment illuminated with populations of bioluminescent bacteria, also used to light wayfinding signs.

BIOLUMINESCENT DEVICES

Living lighting that can be configured for different public spaces.

Algae (Pyrocystis fusiformis), bacteria (Vibrio fischeri), mycelia, various types of agricultural waste.

Eduardo Mayoral González (Spanish) University of Seville, Spain / Graduate School of Architecture, Planning and Preservation, Columbia University, New York, USA

CONCEPT

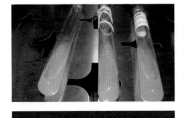

ABOVE   201

A culture of the bacterium *Vibrio fisheri* in nutrient-rich agar at the One Lab in Brooklyn, New York.

This project involves the design and fabrication of architecturally integrated glowing devices that employ the bioluminescence of populations of microorganisms. The result is organic illumination that requires no metals, industrial manufacture, or electricity, and that produces no artificial waste. The proposal envisions several applications of bioluminescence on streets, in public parks, on highway posts, on signs, and on shelters. Integrating a natural, chemical reaction generated by an organism into the built environment serves to challenge the conventional divide between fabricated and natural spaces while addressing the urgent need to increase architecture's ecological performance.

Bioluminescent Devices for Zero-Electricity Lighting utilizes a species of bacterium, *Vibrio fischeri*, that naturally glows pale green in the dark, and a species of alga, *Pyrocystis fusiformis*, that emits blue light when excited by movement. Notably, both microorganisms produce bioluminescence in a circadian rhythm, meaning that they are more active and thus produce more light at night.

The microorganisms can be grown on agar and will continue multiplying for as long as nutrients are available. The architect tested them in laboratory environments (in collaboration with One Lab in Brooklyn, New York) to determine how best to encase and preserve them in controlled habitats. Different populations were placed inside transparent containers of different shapes to determine what devices might be possible—from simple lights through to billboard images.

Both are natural microorganisms that thrive in sea habitats all over the world and they may prove to be useful for genetic alteration to support different design applications in the future.

BIOENCRYPTION

Bacterial DNA offers digital storage in a system that could hold approximately 900 terabytes within a single gram of *E. coli.*

Modified bacteria (Escherichia coli), encryption methods.

Yu Chi-Shing (Chinese) / Yim Kay-Yuen (Chinese) / Li Jing-Woei (Chinese) / Wong In-Chun (Chinese) / Wong Kit-Ying (Chinese) / Chan Ting-Fung (Chinese)—2010 iGEM (International Generally Engineered Machine Foundation competition) Team, School of Life Sciences, Chinese University of Hong Kong; gold medal winners at the International Genetically Engineered Machine Competition in 2010

PROTOTYPE

Building on previous work (Bancroft, et al., 2001), and an experimental exercise carried out in 2007 at Keio University, Japan, in which researchers encoded a simple string of letters (Einstein's $E = mc^2$) into the DNA of a common soil bacterium, this student project takes this DNA encoding concept further. The iGEM team created a digital storage system that uses the combination of molecules used in the DNA base pairs: guanine, cytosine, adenine, and thymine.

Bioencryption involveds a method of breaking data up into small strings of code, not unlike the way in which a hard drive splits information into sectors for easy storage and recovery. With chunks of information sprinkled among the five million or so different base pairs in a single molecule of DNA, information can be compressed to a fantastic level, given the minuscule size of a bacterium: 40 million or more can inhabit a gram of soil.

The team also created an elaborate three-tiered security encryption and series of checks so that the stored strings of data are scrambled and do not interfere with cell function. Any natural mutation that might corrupt the information is detected and addressed. If the technology can be developed fully, it could be used to protect and store vast amounts of data, thanks to the natural redundancy of such prolific and robust species. As a new blank slate for information, such a system might be useful for encoding data on the provenance of genetically modified organisms, such as food crops.

ABOVE   202

Petri dishes, flask and burner used by the iGEM team at the Chinese University of Hong Kong.

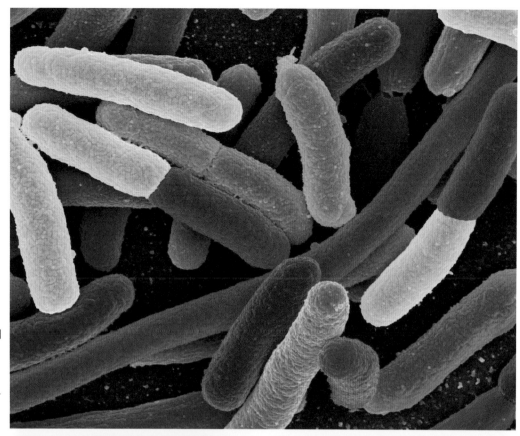

RIGHT 203

Artistic rendering of multicolored bacteria as a representation of genetic manipulation at the cellular level to store the 1s and 0s of binary code.

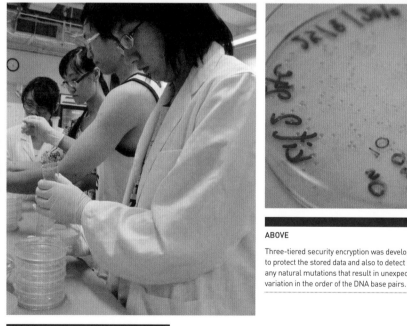

ABOVE 204

The team devised a system to split digital data into sectors and spread it across the five million different base pairs in a single DNA molecule.

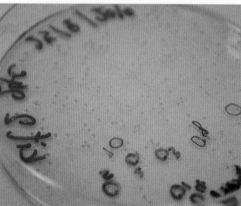

ABOVE 206

Three-tiered security encryption was developed to protect the stored data and also to detect any natural mutations that result in unexpected variation in the order of the DNA base pairs.

ABOVE 205

The student researchers received a gold medal at the annual iGEM competition for their efforts.

ALGAL FILTER MACHINE

Can we gradually adapt our power grid using algae that not only feed on carbon dioxide outputs but also can be turned into fuel?

Renderings using Grasshopper, Rhino, Adobe Creative Suite.

Nathan William Smith (American)—Columbia University Graduate School of Architecture, Planning and Preservation, New York, USA; BIO:OIL Landscape Futures Workshop with David Benjamin, Geoff Manaugh, Mark Smout, and Laura Allen

CONCEPT

In this proposal, developed in the Graduate School of Architecture, Planning and Preservation at Columbia University, the architect imagines systems on three different scales: the car, a coal-burning power plant, and a robotic mechanism that combs the Los Angeles River. These would capture existing streams of carbon dioxide output to feed algae for biofuel generation, thereby acting as engines and filters for the environment simultaneously.

The architect takes the position that fossil fuels are undeniably effective as energy sources but that their unintended toxic outputs and scarcity call for remediation. Other energy-producing systems that rely on corn or sugar still fall short because they continually need fossil-fuel input, such as the nitrogen-fixing reaction used to generate fertilizers.

Algae offer an appealing alternative because they grow readily and robustly with little more than abundant sunlight and nutrients such as carbon dioxide. They are comprised of around 50 percent lipid oil, which can be converted to biodiesel. **Algal Filter Machine** (AFM) would rely on advancements in synthetic biology to create algae that can be harvested for energy more effectively than is possible today. One goal is to choreograph a system with a recursive nature—one that repeats cyclically using the same components. The result would resemble the energy and nutrient flows that characterize natural ecosystems, but on an industrial scale.

Recursive Car: Growing Gasoline: here the automobile becomes an autonomous system that fuels its own propulsion. The AFM works in a range of phases in order to smooth the transition from a fossil fuel to a biofuel. In this instance, both types of fuel work symbiotically.

Algal Power Plant: Growing Electricity: using an existing fossil-fuel-burning power plant, the AFM harnesses carbon dioxide and nitrogen to feed algae, in effect sequestering these outputs as inputs for supplementary biofuel generation.

Los Angeles River Stations: Growing Fuel for an Entire City: the proposed system acquires carbon dioxide and nitrogen from smog and embeds them into a newly created open algal system within the Los Angeles River. The AFM works within a mechanism that moves along the water, cycling the input of carbon dioxide and nitrogen while removing the algal cells. The algal cells are circulated within the skin of these dynamic structures where they are processed for fuel, as water flows back into the river.

ABOVE / OPPOSITE 207, 208

Abundant heat and carbon dioxide generated by a conventional combustion engine is harnessed in the **Recursive Car** to feed algae and thereby create biofuel that powers the vehicle further.

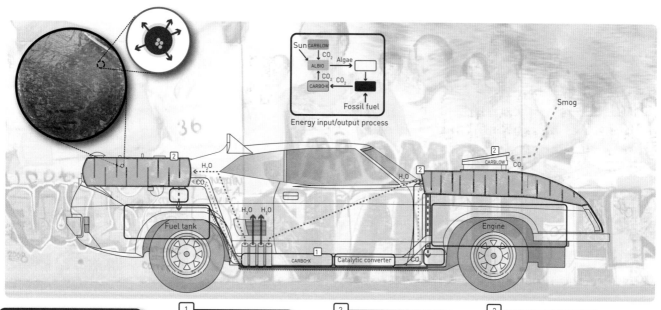

Energy input/output process

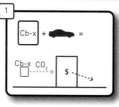

1 - Carbon Dioxide and Nitrogen output collected by the Carbo-x (Cb-x) can be taken to an algael processing plant to be used in the creation of biofuel (with incentives).

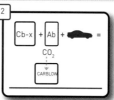

2 - Carbon Dioxide and Nitrogen output, collected by the Carbo-x can be used in local-mobile algael growth (Ab) for instant biofuel. Adding the Carblow allow the vehicle to work use the free CO2 currently exiting in the atmosphere, therefore cleaning the air and feeding the algae.

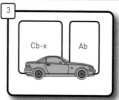

3 - Newer vehicles will already be equipped with this technology in order to reduce (and eventually eliminate) carbon emissions.

RIGHT 209

Smog from a traditional fossil-fuel burning power plant is captured and used to fuel the growth of algae in the alternative biofuel **Algal Power Plant**.

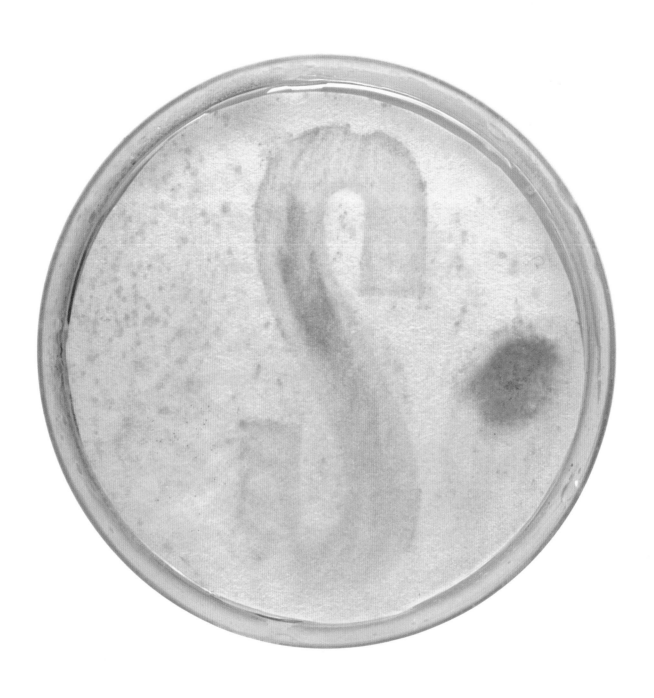

3.

EXPERIMENTAL FUNCTIONS

Speculative Objects, Teaching Tools, and Provocations

OPPOSITE 210
See 'Symbiosis', page 142.

This section introduces cautionary tales, critical commentary, and experimental technologies meant to spark discussion about potential—and often surprising—future functions of design. The unifying approach among them, although with differing objectives, is to hack life into new machines. Some of these endeavors demonstrate how technology will likely corner us into uncomfortable ethical dilemmas or invite unintended disasters, while others are literal teaching tools, intended to illustrate what has become possible with biology rather than simply to comment on it. Many of the works emerge from close collaboration between designers and biologists, and foreshadow how exchanges among disciplines are set to multiply over the coming years.

       This collection of work emphasizes the importance of experimentation in design, and of continually evaluating and expanding what's possible, however improbable. Despite its ever-deepening connection to the sciences, design of this kind takes a decidedly different approach than scientific experimentation, which is characterized by reductionism, a necessary strategy for eliminating potential possibilities and arriving at experimentally demonstrated knowledge. In contrast, design can remain indefinitely in a concept stage and be effective even when imaginary, as in the cases of 'Synthetic Kingdom' or 'Pigeon d'Or', which help non-experts to understand the possible implications of the march of technology propelled by scientific research. These projects explore the significant and diverse potential of this growing intersection of disciplines to enable designers to impact both the mundane and the intimate aspects of our lives, from methods of medical diagnosis to how we clean our cities. In many ways they explain what we don't yet have language to express or responsibly evaluate. Some exist in the broadening space between student thesis and work of art, an incubation zone increasingly supported by design, art, and science museums as much as online media's appetite for new projects that are imaginative and somewhat controversial.

The emergence of synthetic biology and the do-it-yourself biology (DIY bio) movement are important developments influencing the creators of these speculative projects. As an engineering approach, synthetic biology is a burgeoning field that reduces subcellular mechanisms—particularly protein synthesis—to series of DNA sequences that can be made artificially and introduced into host organisms. The implications of this are vast across disciplines, but for design especially, since one goal of synthetic biologists is to 'black box' all these codes and processes so that one can eventually work with organisms and genes as we do today with software that allows users to drag and drop buttons, links, and graphics without having to know anything about the underlying HTML code.

Imagining designers with the power to tailor organisms in virtually limitless ways is cause for both breathless optimism and frightening dystopian visions. In parallel, DIY bio welcomes to biology curious tinkerers who may lack formal science instruction. Enabled by newly inexpensive laboratory equipment and the support of thriving online communities, the rogue DIY ethos lends itself to research unrelated to the agendas of industry or the conventional focus of the academy on publishing. Such an environment is fertile ground for designers creating work to question the direction of biotechnological development and to provoke debate.

Interest in speculative design is heightened by exhibitions such as 'What If ...' at the Science Gallery in Dublin, 'Synthetic: Art and Synthetic Biology' at the Natural History Museum in Vienna, and 'Design and the Elastic Mind' and 'Talk To Me' at the Museum of Modern Art, New York. It has also been frequently observed in the work of students, particularly from the Design Interactions program at the Royal College of Art in London and SymbioticA at the University of Western Australia. Many of these projects also imply a generational shift, as they are the work of young talents and foretell a thrilling future for design that reaches into unexplored fields and areas of culture.

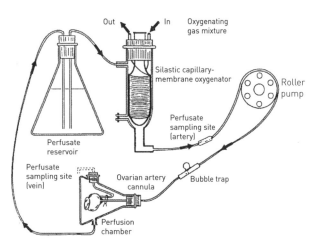

Figure 2-5. *In vitro* perfusion system (Dharmarajan *et al.* 1993).

ABOVE   212

Original profusion system developed by
Professor Arunasalam Dharmarajan, School
of Anatomy & Human Biology, University of
Western Australia, used as inspiration for the
Victimless Leather technoscientific body, 2004.

RIGHT   213

Installation view of the first showing of the work
at the John Curtin Gallery in Perth, Australia,
in 2004.

VICTIMLESS LEATHER

Living objects shaped for human use are a near-future possibility. What responsibilities do we have toward them, and why?

Biodegradable polymer, connective, skin, and bone cells, nutrient media, glassware, peristaltic pump, tubes.

Oron Catts (Australian, born Finland) / Ionat Zurr (Australian, born UK)—Tissue Culture & Art Project, hosted by SymbioticA, Art and Science Collaborative Research Laboratory, School of Anatomy and Human Biology, University of Western Australia, Australia

OPPOSITE   211

Detail of a contaminated Victimless Leather jacket, from an installation at the Mori Art Museum in Tokyo in 2010.

PROTOTYPE

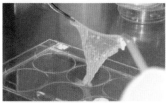

ABOVE   214, 215

From the top: setup for Victimless Leather at the University of Liverpool in 2008; a layer of pig cartilage cells grown by TC&A in in 2001.

These artists have grown a scaled-down 'leather' jacket in vitro using a variety of cell types that are fed with nutrients via a peristaltic pump. A biodegradable polymer provides scaffolding shaped like a tiny coat that grows as living cells slowly envelop and fill it. Exhibited for the first time in 2004 in Perth, Australia, the jacket has since been displayed more than ten times in different configurations and settings, from science museums to art shows with a range of political, biological, and design themes.

Victimless Leather was originally part of a series of works developed under the banner of the Technologically Mediated Victimless Utopia (2000–8). This project explored the use of tissue engineering for the creation of in-vitro meat and leather while questioning the tendency of Western technology to obscure its victims. The artists see their role as that of agitators or provocateurs who set up contentious situations and objects, and welcome critique.

The work aroused much attention in 2008 when exhibited within Design and The Elastic Mind at the Museum of Modern Art (MoMA) in New York. This was the first showing that included what the artists describe as an unplanned 'public death' without the transparent 'killing ritual' that usually closes the exhibition of other living artworks by the Tissue Culture and Art Project, such as 'Semi-Living Worry Dolls' and the 'Pig Wings Project.' These acts were staged and the audience was aware of the artists' intentions. In the context of a design show, however, the unplanned death was construed by many as a type of failure—an ostensible ceasing of function. But the broader discussion that the work generated about responsibilities, ethics, and the use of living materials for human-centric ends was, and continues to be, an artistic success.

LIVING WATCH

Could a living timepiece become the symbol
of an era of biological innovation?

*Bovine chondrocyte cells, alginate scaffolding, DMEM/FBS growth
medium.*

Oliver Medvedik (American)—Bioworks Institute, Brooklyn, USA / Genspace, Brooklyn, USA

IN PRODUCTION

This prototype, slowly growing in a community lab, is intended to be a teaching tool to help illustrate the possibilities of tissue engineering. The idea of forming the object as a watch was originally inspired by the artwork of Swiss surrealist H.R. Giger, the set designer and painter who is best known for his work on the film *Alien* (1979). A watch is a convenient, simple, and familiar form that is imbued with deeper meaning because of its relation to time. The history of design also reserves an important place for timepieces as symbols of the standardization and mechanization that were integral to the Industrial Revolution. Should an industrial-biological revolution come to pass—which some argue has already begun—the **Living Watch** may become ubiquitous.

The construction method depends on primary cells, such as chondrocytes, which deposit collagen to form cartilage. These are allowed to grow around biodegradable scaffolding, constructed from polymers that are more typically used by surgeons. As the fibrous material develops, the support structure gradually dissolves, leaving behind a living object of the desired shape. Oscillatory behavior is well known in nerve cells, but in fact many cells follow regular rhythms in ways that can be predicted and detected, so it may ultimately be possible to harness this natural time-keeping ability in the form of a biological clock or pacemaker. This may be the first of many living objects that become commonplace.

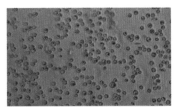

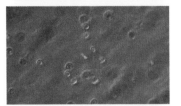

ABOVE 216, 217, 218

From the top: bovine chondrocytes isolated from calf wrist-joint cartilage; embedded in alginate matrix; and embedded in alginate and growing in DMEM media on tissue culture plates.

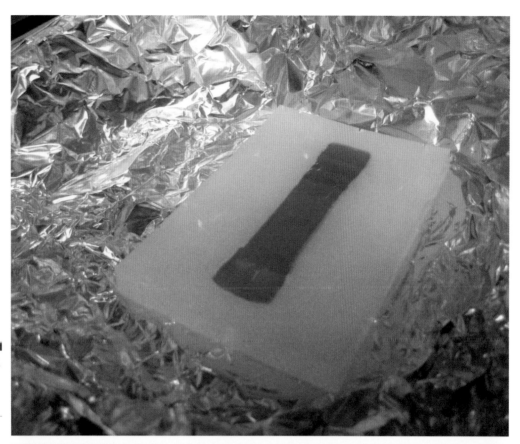

RIGHT / BELOW 219, 220

Bovine chondrocytes in alginate matrix cast in the form of a watchband. This experimental object may foreshadow new types of industrial production to come in an age of biology.

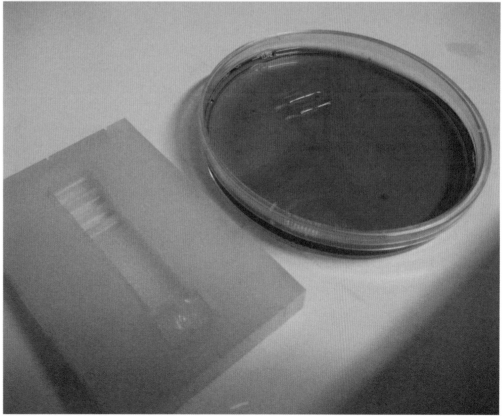

CARNIVOROUS DOMESTIC ROBOTS

The cycle of life on graphic display in your own home.

Rapidform SLA, MDF, perspex, electronic media, motor.

James Auger (British) / Jimmy Loizeau (British)—Material Beliefs, Goldsmiths College, London, UK

PROTOTYPE

This series of three devices provokes questions about what a robot is and what it could be in the context of the home. These prototypes are for utility, drama, and entertainment, serving a role similar to that of an exotic carnivorous pet, such as a snake, piranha, or lizard, where owners provide living prey and become voyeurs in a synthesized glimpse of the violence of the food chain. The predatorial nature of these autonomous entities that rely on living animals raises questions of life and death and our role as mediator, nudging the user out of the moral comfort zone regarding the mechanized taking of life.

Carnivorous Domestic Entertainment Robots pitches otherwise inanimate household objects in competition with life in the home—equivalent to the spectacles more usually witnessed through reality television and edited, dramatized depictions of war. As consumers of these programs, like those who keep vivariums, users may be repulsed, entertained, or both. The question of our complicity as voyeurs is foremost in this provocative scenario scripted by the designers.

Table has a mechanized iris built into its top surface that is linked to an infrared motion sensor. Crumbs and food debris left on it attract mice, which gain access to the top via a hole and tunnel built into one oversized table leg. The rodent's motion activates the iris and triggers a trap. The animal falls into a microbial fuel cell and is slowly digested, generating the energy to power the iris and sensor.

Lamp takes advantage of the natural attraction of flies and moths to light. Its shade is perforated with shapes based on the form of the pitcher plant, offering insects access but no escape. Eventually they expire and fall into the microbial fuel cell underneath, where electricity is produced for a series of LED lights that switch on automatically when the house lights are turned off.

Clock uses flypaper on a roller mechanism to trap insects. As the paper passes over a blade, captured insects are scraped into a microbial fuel cell. This powers the turning of the rollers as well as a small LCD clock.

ABOVE 221

Attracting and capturing insects on flypaper, the device digests each one within a microbial fuel cell and uses the energy to power an LED **Clock**.

OPPOSITE 222

Modeled on a pitcher plant, the **Lamp** attracts insects into a space where they become trapped.

LEFT / BELOW / RIGHT   223, 224, 225, 226

Attracted by food crumbs, a mouse enters the **Table** via a leg. A sensor picks up the rodent's motion and triggers a trap, which captures, kills, and feeds the animal into a microbial fuel cell.

LEFT / ABOVE / RIGHT   227, 228, 229, 230

The flypaper in the **Clock** rotates, pushing any captured insects toward a blade, which then scrapes them off and into the fuel cell below.

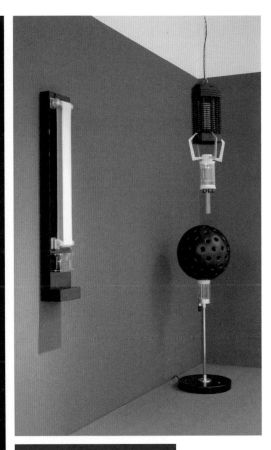

LEFT / ABOVE / BELOW   231, 232, 233, 234, 235

The **Lamp** attracts and traps flying insects, which
inevitably die and are funneled down into the fuel
cell below, the energy of which then powers an
eerie, LED glow, not unlike bioluminescence.

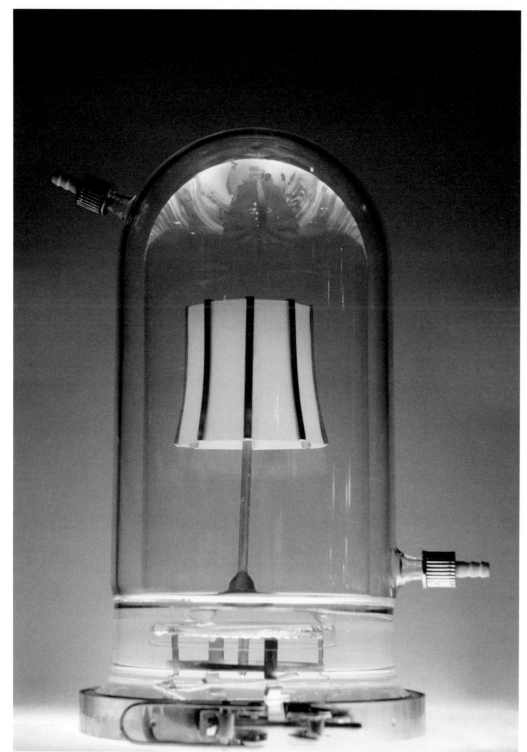

ABOVE   236

Empty of the nutrient medium, the titanium ribs of the lampshade are visible, in between which are base sheets of biopolymer on which the modified cells are grown and maintained. Under the foot of the lamp a small propeller, which circulates the liquid nutrients in the vessel.

ABOVE   237

The lamp complete with the nutrient medium.

HALFLIFE LAMP

Integrating bioluminescence into living cells via genetic
modification to create a simple lighting device.

*Glass, cobalt chrome, genetically modified Chinese hamster ovarian cells,
luciferin.*

Joris Laarman (Dutch)—Joris Laarman Lab, Amsterdam, the Netherlands / University of Twente, the
Netherlands / University of Wageningen, the Netherlands

COMPLETED

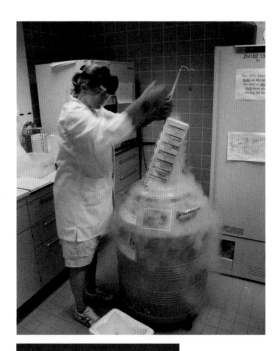

ABOVE   238

Samples of Chinese hamster ovary cells
modified with a firefly's genes for luciferase
and luciferin production, both of which are
necessary for triggering a light reaction.

This work is an exploration of how to create
a biological object that can be functional and
attractive in a form that is easily and immediately
understood. This device creates light through
bioluminescence by incorporating genetically
modified cells. The suspended cells originated from
the CHO cell line, which was first harnessed from
a Chinese hamster's ovaries in the late 1950s.
The line is widely used in research and has become
the mammalian equivalent of *Escherichia coli*—the
workhorse and favorite test subject of biotechnology
today—especially when long-term, stable gene
expression and high-yield proteins are required.

The cells in **Halflife Lamp** were genetically
enhanced by the introduction of a firefly's luciferase
gene. This causes them to produce the enzyme
luciferase, which generates bioluminescence in
the presence of the substrate luciferin. A glass
vessel is filled with a nutrient medium that feeds
the population of genetically modified CHO cells.
These cells grow on the lampshade, on a sheet
of biopolymer. The device anticipates future
collaboration and experimentation in rethinking
objects' functions in relation to biological processes.

In an illustration of the fragility of tissues
used for experimentation, the debut of this design
in New York City was spoiled by the death of its cells.

SYMBIOSIS

Living letters that grow, change color, and eventually die.
Could this herald a future of living, dynamic graphic design?

Bacteria (Escherichia coli), paper, growth media, petri dishes.

Jelte van Abbema (Dutch)—Lab van Abbema, Eindhoven, the Netherlands / Department of Microbiology,
University of Wageningen, the Netherlands

PROTOTYPE

This experimental project responds to the vast
resource consumption and pollution generated
by printed media. Going beyond the adoption of
alternatives such as soy ink or natural pigments to
alleviate the impact of media waste, **Symbiosis** takes
a radical approach, utilizing bacteria to grow letters
in petri dishes. In these experiments, the cultures
—living on growth media configured with nutrients
to guide their development—multiplied, changing
form and color over time, before ultimately dying.

In the larger, poster box format, he appropriated
a piece of public space that usually features an
advertisement and transformed it into a giant petri
dish, the temperature and moisture levels of which
could be adjusted to achieve an optimal outcome.

To control growth so that it would generate
legible type, he experimented with techniques adopted
from the history of print—from screen-printing to
moveable type using authentic wood-cut lettering—
and this resulted in familiar character shapes and
proportions. In essence he created what might be
called the first living typeface, which constantly
shifts in response to changes in the environment.

The designer studied in the Department of
Microbiology at the University of Wageningen to
learn how to go about this work safely and effectively.

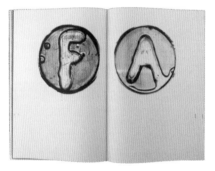 

ABOVE   239

Images of bacteria spread and coaxed into
growing in the form of familiar letters within
petri dishes.

OPPOSITE   240

A poster box repurposed as a growth medium
for biologically rendered letters. The characters
develop in form and color, eventually dying and
decomposing as the nutrients are depleted.

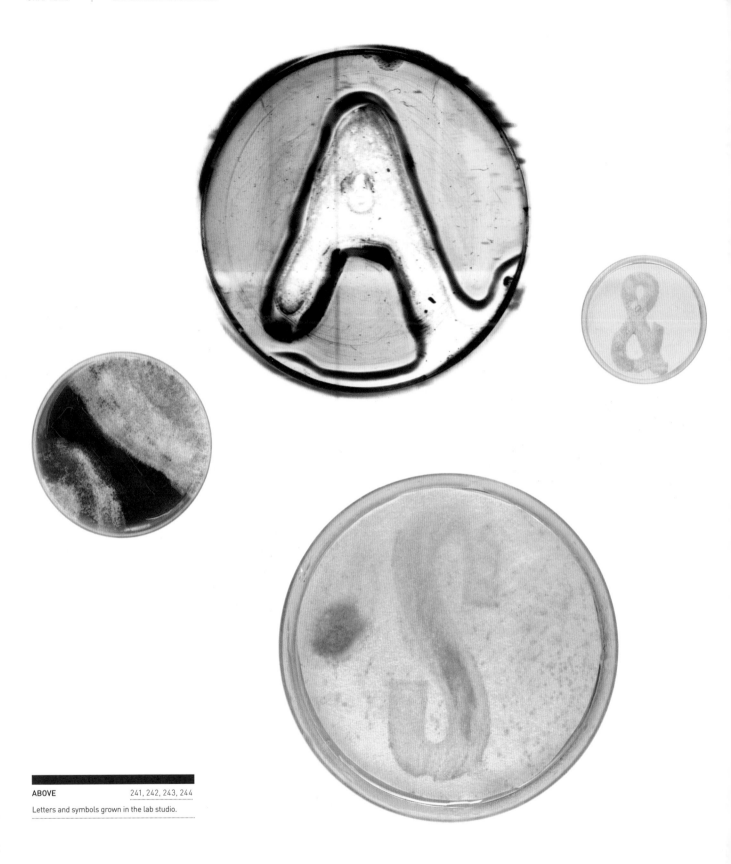

ABOVE   241, 242, 243, 244

Letters and symbols grown in the lab studio.

ABOVE   245, 246, 247, 248

The artist combined traditional printing, movable
type, and screen-printing techniques in his
exploration of using biology to generate form.

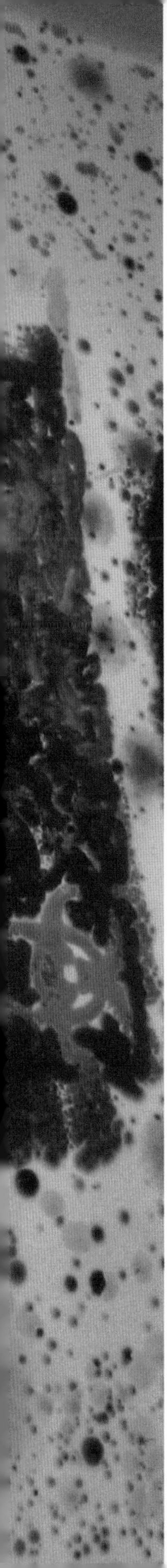

CONTAGION ADVERTISEMENT

Harmless microorganisms help to promote a medical disaster movie.

Nutrient agar gel, fungus (Penicillium sp.), bacteria (Serratia marcescens).

Glen D'Souza (Canadian) / Mike Takasaki (Canadian) / Patrick Hickey (British)—Lowe Roche, Toronto, Canada / CURB Media, London, UK

COMPLETED

To provocatively publicize Steven Soderburgh's 2011 film *Contagion*, this endeavor involved devising a new take on the movie billboard, employing several types of microorganisms and colorants to create dynamic graphics. While the movie presents a dystopian vision of social structures fraying at the threat of a global pandemic, these living advertisements posed no threat to the public.

The team, comprising a creative agency and a sustainable media company, dreamed up a sign that would both grow and decay, creatively linking its message to the film's foreboding themes. To execute their concept, they inoculated two giant petri dishes with a mix of multicolored bacterial and fungal strains. The freshly prepared 'bacteria message boards' were installed in an abandoned storefront window in Toronto's downtown where the kaleidoscope of microorganisms worked their magic. Over the course of the next six days, they grew to resemble the logo and lettering seen on the film's other promotional materials—creating a sight that was alarming to some. Judging by pedestrian reactions, which film crews captured on camera, **Contagion Advertisement** frequently prompted disgust. In this instance, a creative take on promotion neatly combined both medium and message.

OPPOSITE   249

A message board populated with a range of bacterial and fungal species creates an ever-changing and multicolored sinister message.

ABOVE / RIGHT   250, 251, 252, 253, 254

Promotional boards were installed and left in an
abandoned storefront in Toronto. They grew and
changed dramatically over several days, echoing
the film's plot about an out-of-control epidemic.

ABOVE   255

The advertisements provoked varied reactions among passersby, from fear to fascination.

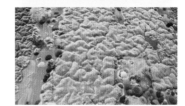

ABOVE   256, 257

From the top: detail of the bacterial and fungal samples before the signs were inoculated; and the cultures by the end of the promotion, by which time the signs had begun to decay.

BACTERIOPTICA

A living chandelier that allows the owner to experiment with the lighting effects offered by different bacteria.

Glass petri dishes, bacteria samples, aluminum rods, fiber optics.

Petia Morozov—MADLAB: Morozov Alcala Design Laboratory, Montclair, USA

IN PRODUCTION

Here the architects have created a custom chandelier that simultaneously reflects the uniqueness of the people who dine below it and the surrounding microbial environment. It is effectively an organism—a household pet as much as the family dog—that lives and breathes alongside the human inhabitants, plants, and other living entities in the home. It is quite literally alive; growing, multiplying and illuminating the lives of both its own family and those of its human cohabitants.

Bacterioptica is adaptive by design, in both its form and its mechanics. Instructions help the owners to experiment with different bacterial samples—from themselves, the yard or dinner guests, for example—and to add, subtract and change components. Thus the chandelier's nature is never static. The modular design can accommodate more than 100 samples. Different sizes of petri dish, hundreds of metal rods, and 4,500 m (15,000 ft) of fiber-optic cable all work together in a complex and organic assembly of bacteria, materials, and light.

ABOVE / RIGHT   258, 259

Samples of bacteria are cultured in petri dishes, which are installed at the illuminated nodes of the modular chandelier. Depending on the type and coloration of each of the samples, the lighting effect can be subtly altered, reflecting the microbial diversity of the surroundings.

BIOLUMINESCENT TOYS

The potential uses of bioluminescence in everyday life range from the utterly serious to the whimsical.

Marine bioluminescent proteins, plastic, glucose.

Bruce Bryan (American) / Terry Willard (American)—Biolume Inc., Wendell, USA / Prolume Ltd, Arizona, USA

PROTOTYPE

These products recreate a natural chemical process that produces light for a variety of functions in nature, from reproductive signaling to thwarting predators. Bioluminescence (the production and emission of light by living organisms) has been observed since antiquity. Numerous sea creatures, including species of squid, mollusk, and jellyfish, exhibit this glow. In the first century AD, Pliny the Elder wrote of the Romans' fondness for bioluminescent piddock, a shellfish they would consume while bathing in the sea at night, their mouths and fingers aglow. The phenomenon also appears in life on land—in fireflies, bacteria, worms and several types of fungi.

The process requires two key components: luciferin, a molecular substrate, and luciferase, an enzyme that speeds up the reaction between luciferin and oxygen, which results in the release of light. It occurs at relatively low temperatures and harnesses more than 90 percent of the reaction's chemical energy to produce illumination—a good deal more than the 10 percent efficiency of an incandescent light bulb, which releases most of its energy as heat.

In **Bioluminescent Toys**, such as water guns and lollipops, the reaction is mechanically choreographed but the requirements are the same as those in living organisms. The objects are synthesized from DNA samples that the team's scientists collected from sea expeditions around the world to discover which animal made the smallest and brightest 'nano-lights.' They turned up *Gaussia princeps*, a tiny copepod living in the ocean 640 m

(2,100 ft) down off the coast of California that features a particularly bright burst of illumination.

Since the process takes place outside of an organism, it is encouraged by introducing metallic ions, such as calcium. There is potential to integrate these natural reactions into many consumer products (such as chewing gum and specialty cocktails) or into medical applications (perhaps replacing radioactive elements in diagnostics, and illuminating internal organs for brief periods during surgery).

ABOVE   260, 261

Prototypes of toy water guns with luminescent ingredient cartridges included in the packaging.

ABOVE 262

Compounds in saliva trigger the luminescent reaction, which lasts for several minutes and replicates the natural glow found within tiny copepod crustacea that live deep in the ocean.

RIGHT 263

Once activated, the bioluminescent water in the toy gun generates intense visible light and it will illuminate any surfaces that it is fired at.

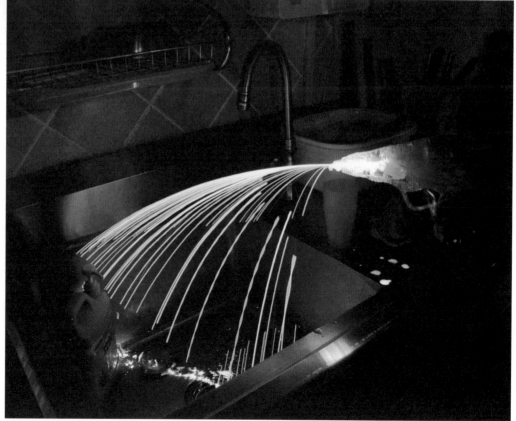

GREEN MAP

Changes in the tension between urban and natural spaces in the UK are represented in this three-part design project.

Mixed media wall installation, artificial turf, plywood panels, concrete, various plant species.

Conny Freyer (German) / Sebastien Noel (French) / Eva Rucki (German)—Troika, London, UK

COMPLETED

These designers developed three immersive installations—Green City, Open City and Living City—for the Shanghai 2010 World Expo. In the walkways leading to and away from the nearby 'Seed Cathedral' by Heatherwick Studio, the narrative focuses on the relationship between nature and cities in the UK—in the past, present, and in the future.

Two of the walkways reflect on the country's long tradition of incorporating nature into urban spaces. The third tries to envision the future, suggesting ways in which nature might be a catalyst for innovation within urban environments.

Green City demonstrates the sometimes surprising amount of green space in the urban environment. It is a series of 'inverted' maps of the four UK capitals—London, Cardiff, Belfast, and Edinburgh—which record every piece of urban greenery but leave out the architecture and infrastructure. Parks, gardens, and avenues of trees are represented by artificial turf that is recessed into the concrete canopy of the walkway.

Open City aims to show how permeable the cities of the UK are to the weather. In these urban spaces, generally widespread and low-profile, with few developments that provide shelter from the elements, dwellers experience wind, fog, and rain directly. The second walkway depicts a city in the sky that is open and transparent. It includes some 300 representations of traditional UK buildings, recreated in clear resin and suspended from the canopy. Finally, groups of small lights hang from the ceiling and cast colorful animated raindrops across the floor.

Living City offers a wide swathe of plants set into the canopy of the third walkway, highlighting species that are likely to be particularly useful in cities of the future. With the guidance of scientists, the team identified some 200 plants that could have a positive impact on urban life, of which 30 species were selected for display. These were chosen for their ability to purify air, remove soil contaminants, offer a food supply, insulate buildings, or provide sources of biofuel and plastics.

Over the course of the project, the designers encountered inspiring research projects in biotechnology and biomimetics. To represent them, eight imaginary plants were made as models and included in the planting scheme. These speculative plants raise questions about the future of recycling biofuel production and biosecurity.

OPPOSITE   264

The Green City installation representing urban greenery—part of the Shanghai 2010 World Expo.

ABOVE / BELOW   265, 266, 267

Patches of artificial turf represent the number and placement of green spaces in four UK capitals while omitting their built environments.

ABOVE   268, 269

The designers investigated the different kinds of plant that might be beneficial to cities both today and into the future—to purify air, remove soil contaminants, provide food, or insulate buildings.

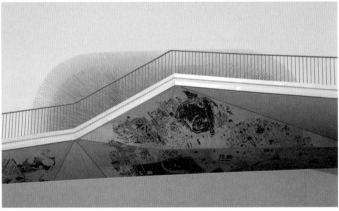

伦敦
London

ABOVE   270

The maps gave an often surprising picture of the
quantity of green space in urban environments.

ABOVE   271

In this fictional narrative, birds hosting modified gut bacteria are released into the environment, ready to defecate soap and help clean our cities.

RIGHT   272

Pigeons would eat a yogurt containing bacteria that would harmlessly alter their metabolism.

PIGEON D'OR

From 'flying rats' to urban sanitation workers—can synthetic biology transform how we think of pigeons?

Modified bacteria (Escherichia coli), pigeons, wood, vinyl.

Tuur Van Balen (Belgian), London, UK; supported by the Flemish Ministry of Culture

CONCEPT

The ubiquitous pigeon has long been viewed as vermin—spreading disease, scavenging through trash, and defecating in populous urban spaces. Yet they are a product of selective breeding for purposes as diverse as racing for our entertainment and, historically, delivering wartime post. Synthetic biology may offer this animal a new chapter within the urban fabric.

Pigeon d'Or recognizes how these birds represent a potentially useful interface for urban biotechnologies. If their metabolism could be modified, they might be able to add a new function to their repertoire. The idea is to 'design' and culture a harmless bacteria (much like the microorganisms in yogurt) that could be fed to pigeons to alter the birds' digestive processes such that a detergent is created from their feces.

Two devices have been prototyped in this fictional narrative. One allows birds to be absorbed into the architecture of the home, from where they can be fed and cared for. The other encourages the birds to perch above the windscreen of a parked car, with the benefit that the glass will receive a dose of detergent.

By manipulating animals for human-centric goals, this project explores the ethical, political, practical, and aesthetic consequences of future synthetic biology for design.

This project was developed in collaboration with James Chappell and the Centre for Synthetic Biology at Imperial College, London.

RIGHT 273

Enlisting pigeons to clean the city with soapy excrement could make the animal useful to mankind once more.

LIFE SUPPORT

Close relationships between humans and animals have a long history, but how might that symbiosis evolve in a biotechnological future?

Leather, foam, acrylic, aluminum, rubber, solid maple, powder-coated steel, stuffed rabbit, peristaltic pumps, vinyl tubes, needles, hay.

Revital Cohen (British, born Israel)—Design Interactions, Royal College of Art, London, UK

CONCEPT

Humans have domesticated animals for thousands of years, using them for food, companionship, security, and assistance for physical disabilities, such as blindness. **Life Support** proposes a scenario in which domestic animals function as 'external organs' in a surprising extension of the service animal tradition.

People often love their pets, but could they love their respirators? The **Life Support Respiratory Dog** is a pedigree greyhound raised for track racing. Around five years of age, when most racing dogs are retired (and thousands euthanized each year), the dog would be acquired for training as a respiratory assistant. Someone suffering from lung disease would then adopt the animal as a replacement for mechanical ventilation. The dog would be fitted with a harness that would use its chest movements to pump air through a trachea tube and into its owner's lungs. This extended symbiotic relationship between patient and pet would then transform man's best friend into man's best augmented-breathing apparatus.

The **Life Support Dialysis Sheep** is a transgenic lamb capable of filtering its owner's blood. Scientists would extract the regions responsible for producing blood and immune responses from the patient's DNA, substituting this for the equivalent genetic material in a sheep. The resulting recombinant DNA would then be inserted into a sheep egg, which would in turn be implanted into a ewe. When born, the genetically modified lamb it would be given to the patient, who would care for it during the day and use it as a substitute for a dialysis machine at night. Prior to sleep, the sheep's kidneys would be connected to the patient's vein and peristaltic pumps would push the patient's blood into the sheep's kidneys, which would clean it before it was pumped back into the patient.

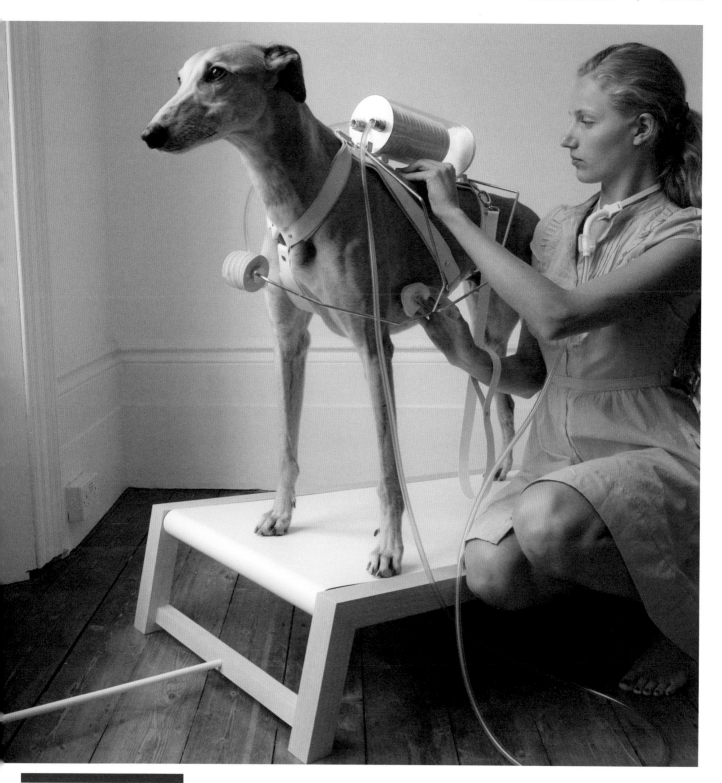

ABOVE 274

In this fictional scenario, the dog is fitted with a
harness that is able to transfer the strength of
its chest movements to pump air into its owner's
lungs, like a living replacement diaphragm.

ABOVE   <u>275</u>

Bred for speed, a greyhound becomes a
service animal following its brief racing career.

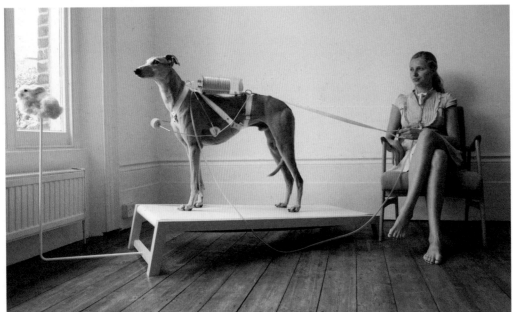

LEFT   <u>276</u>

The dog exercises regularly on a treadmill in
order to deliver oxygen to its debilitated owner.

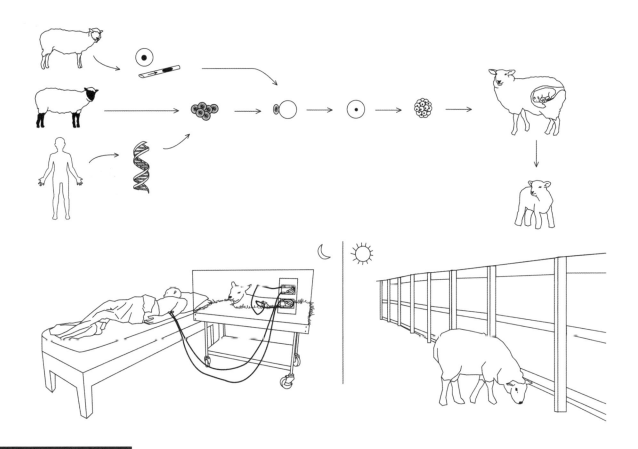

ABOVE   277

In a similar symbiotic relationship, a sheep's DNA
is augmented with that of the patient, preparing a
transgenic offspring that can filter human blood.

RIGHT   278

During the night—in the role of a living dialysis
machine—the sheep's kidneys filter the human
blood before it retureturning it to the patient.

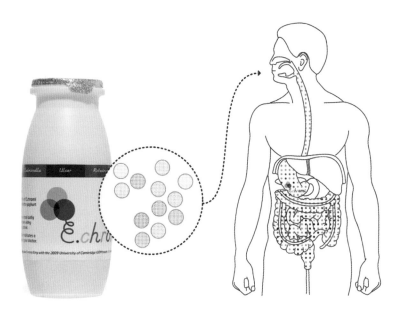

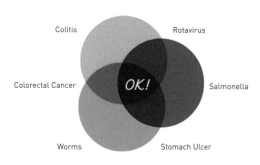

In this speculative work, bacteria modified to work as biosensors are ingested in a yogurt-like culture. The harmless microorganisms take up residence in the intestines. If a chemical marker for one of various diseases is present, the individual's feces are dyed a particular color by the bacteria, signaling the need for treatment.

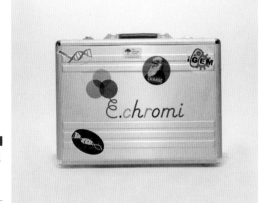

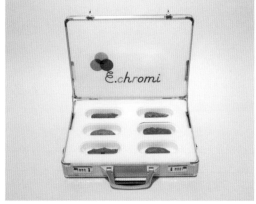

To help illustrate the concept of gastrointestinal biosensors, the designers created color-coded sample feces, naming the collection a 'scatalog.'

E.CHROMI

Synthetic biology is apt to bring still unrecognized benefits
and burdens, from biosensors to bioterrorism.

*Genetically engineered bacteria (Escherichia coli), paraffin wax, aluminum,
polyethylene foam, acrylic case.*

Alexandra Daisy Ginsberg (British) / James King (British) / 2009 Cambridge iGEM team (Mike Davies,
Shuna Gould, Siming Ma, Vivian Mullin, Megan Stanley, Alan Walbridge, Crispian Wilson)—University of
Cambridge, UK

CONCEPT

A group of science undergraduates genetically
engineered bacteria that produce a range of colored
pigments. To achieve this, they created BioBricks—
custom sequences of DNA—and inserted them
into *Escherichia coli*. Each part of these BioBricks
houses genes selected from existing organisms,
and each instructs the bacteria to produce a
color (red, yellow, green, blue, brown, or violet)
under certain circumstances. The 'programed'
microorganisms act as biosensors, turning a
particular color in the presence of a specific
toxin, for example. This work earned the team
the Grand Prize in the iGEM competition in 2009.

The design team worked with the scientists
to explore the potential of the system while it was
being developed in the lab. Together they drew a
timeline illustrating ways in which such a foundational
technology might develop over the next century. These
scenarios include widespread use of food colorants,
contentious patenting issues, promising personalized
medicine, frightening terrorism, and alien types of
weather. Not necessarily desirable, these visions
explore the different agendas that could shape the
use of **E.chromi** and, in turn, our everyday lives. The
collaboration anticipates an approach to innovation
wherein both the genetic and the human scales are
responsibly considered and potential consequences—
positive and negative—are imaginatively explored

One of the speculative outcomes of this work
is displayed in a colorful 'scatalog' and briefcase—
props that describe a future where bacteria work as

an internal medical diagnostic system. A patient
would ingest a a drink containing a dose of the
engineered microorganism, which would blossom
in the gut and color the individual's feces according
to the balance of chemicals present there. The
result would be an immediate, visible indication
of the health of the patient's gastrointestinal tract,
with different colors diagnosing, for example,
worms, colorectal cancer, or a stomach ulcer.

THE SYNTHETIC KINGDOM

New species created by man represent a combination of beauty and terror.

Various media, including graphics, resin, glass.

Alexandra Daisy Ginsberg (British)—Design Interactions, Royal College of Art, London, UK

CONCEPT

Over the millennia the tree of life has grown and evolved slowly, with significant changes taking perhaps a hundred thousand years. More recently, humankind has interfered with natural evolution, the most obvious examples being how we have caused the extinction of huge numbers of species. Now, however, we have the opportunity to create new 'species' through synthetic biology.

The Synthetic Kingdom looks at the consequences of developing and using—or misusing—new life forms for our own ends. While currently we are dependent on petrochemicals and precious metals in manufacturing, soon we are likely to be able to choose desirable features from different organisms, find and duplicate the relevant parts of their DNA, and then synthesize and insert them into a different 'biological chassis,' such as bacterial DNA. As this field of activity expands, a new branch may sprout from the tree of life: that of synthetica—a fourth kingdom of living organisms.

The possibilities of this new biotechnology are almost as endless as the human imagination, such as developing bacteria that deliver drugs to a specified location in the body, or goats that produce spider silk for use in repairing damaged ligament tissue. Typical of new innovations, however, synthetic biology has a darker side, as evidenced by the ongoing debates over the likes of genetically modified food and animal cloning.

Concerns about the future of this field of research are exacerbated by the complex makeup of living organisms, about which we still understand only a small fraction. Biology's agenda—that of reproduction and survival—is entirely divorced from standards that we wish to uphold, such as laws and borders. How we monitor and control our manipulation of evolution is crucial to our future. In this project, several items are presented that create narratives about potential future breakthroughs as well as unintended consequences.

OPPOSITE   281

A fourth kingdom, 'synthetica', is added to the contemporary tree of life on earth. As the name implies, these species are artificially engineered, heralding a new era of evolutionary development.

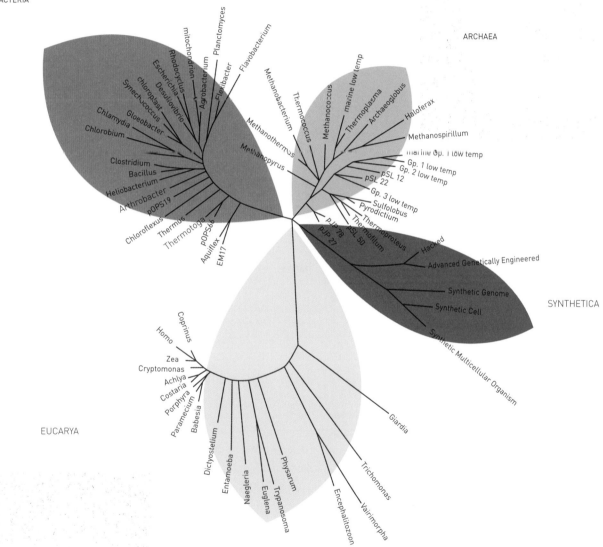

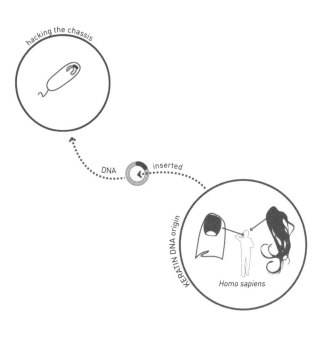
hacking the chassis

DNA · inserted

KERATIN DNA origin

Homo sapiens

ABOVE / RIGHT 282, 283

Bacteria can conceivably be modified to secrete keratin, the protein found in hair and fingernails, which can be used to generate biodegradable products that replace petroleum-derived plastics.

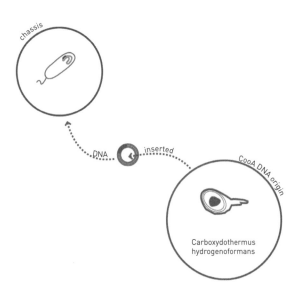
chassis

DNA · inserted

CooA DNA origin

Carboxydothermus
hydrogenoformans

LEFT / ABOVE 284, 285

Left: the genetic codes to trigger color expression are inserted into the 'chassis' that is a bacterial host. Above: a mock-up of what a carbon monoxide sensor might look like, embedded with genetically modified microorganisms.

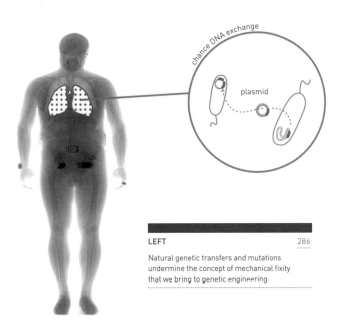

chance DNA exchange

plasmid

LEFT 286

Natural genetic transfers and mutations undermine the concept of mechanical fixity that we bring to genetic engineering

RIGHT 287

In this fictional narrative biosensing microbes wreak havoc on the lungs of a smoker, crystallizing them into fatal but eerily beautiful sculpture.

BIOLOGICAL ATELIER

Growing objects in the lab from our own cells or those of animals fortells a new age for personalized and renewable fashion.

Mixed media including digitally embroidered scaffolds, silicone, enamel, crystals, leather, silk.

Amy Congdon (British)—Textile Futures Programme, Central Saint Martins College of Art and Design, London, UK

CONCEPT

Imagine a world where haute couture relies on the greatest commodity of all: ourselves. This speculative work is set in the year 2082, where new fashions are no longer 'made' but rather grown, and living cells replace fabric and thread as raw materials. Future embroidery and textile design relies on the application of scientific mechanisms that mimic the natural form and function of living beings. Although realized solely through conceptual prototyping, much of this alternate reality is inspired by current scientific research, suggesting that advances in biotechnology and synthetic biology could pave the way for renewable, organic systems in the textile and fashion industries.

The designer's view of the future aligns with developments in other fields. Digital embroidery has been used in the production of medical implants, and its capacity to imitate biological processes could figure greatly in advancements in textile design. Rapid cell modeling, otherwise known as bio-inkjet printing, is currently being explored as a way to 'print' replacement organs, but it could also have practical applications as a means of efficiently reproducing living cells in great numbers. These biomedical approaches could be used to create textiles that are entirely composed and synthesized from living cells.

In exploring the role that current biotechnological research could play in years to come, **Biological Atelier** proposes questions that have, as yet, gone unanswered by the fashion industry. What, for instance, would the world look like if we could grow an ethical, victimless ivory or a cross-species fur? What

sorts of hybridized raw materials can be engineered for use in practical applications such as textile design? How can an industry driven by newness, beauty, and limitless possibilities adjust to a world of dwindling resources? Linking this to current research and focusing on the renewable and organic results in a timely vision for a biotechnologically engineered high fashion that might be realized one day soon.

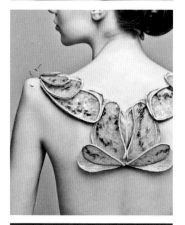

ABOVE / OPPOSITE   288, 289, 290, 291

Accessories from a future where fur- and ivory-like materials can be grown from living cells.

ABOVE   293

Parasitic prosthesis—parasites engineered
to assist the body's temperature regulation are
expressed on the skin's surface through hairing.

LEFT   292

Voluntary mutation—microorganisms engineered
to live in the body to regulate atmospheric toxicity
levels are expressed on the surface of the skin.

DESIGN FICTIONS

The rise of synthetic biology brings ethical questions about the appropriation of life and the alteration of self to the fore.

DIY stem cell biology, home-cultured parasitic organisms, genetic products.

Natsai-Audrey Chieza (Zimbabwean)—Textile Futures Programme, Central Saint Martins College of Art and Design, London, UK

CONCEPT

BELOW   294

Voluntary mutation—fashionable skins grown at home using customizable genes express a variety of prints, patterns, and structures on the body.

ABOVE   295

Bio-collectible—a decorative bacterium lobe pendant cultured and customized by the owner.

This project takes the position that applications of the life sciences will converge in the 21st century to characterize different means of production. This development would generate massive changes and be largely influenced by designers, who might also need to become material scientists, engineers, or synthetic biologists to achieve their goals. **Design Fictions: Posthumanity in the Age of Synthetics**, presents a range of fictional artifacts that tell the story of three future scenarios to spark discussion about ethics in science and its exploitation of life. It also anticipates the role of the designer in 2075, working in a studio-cum-laboratory.

    Voluntary Mutations looks at the aesthetic potential of a subculture in a situation where open-source do-it-yourself stem cell biology becomes as commonplace as computing. **Parasitic Prosthesis** suggests that the post-human body will be synthesized genetically from 'homegrown' parasitic organisms, which will make possible adapting quickly to changed or new environments. **Bio-collectibles** raises questions about the ethics of the worrying market for genetic materials that could see our bodies being viewed as 'farms.' This is represented by a precious genetic first aid cabinet.

    Research for this project was facilitated through collaboration between the designer and John Ward, Professor of Molecular Microbiology at University College London's Institute for Structural and Molecular Biology, and PhD student Lottie Davis, in order to select and safely grow microorganisms.

ABOVE 296

Bio-collectible—adornments grown from bacteria and still living prompt a variety of questions.

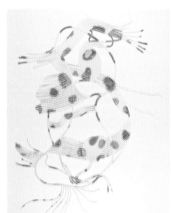

ABOVE 297

Voluntary mutation—a bio-tattoo that is digitally printed onto the skin's surface using stem cell technology achieves a high-resolution pattern.

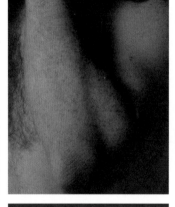

ABOVE 298

Parasitic prosthesis—parasites engineered to grow on the skin release a resist pigment to shield the body from high levels of radiation.

ABOVE 299

Voluntary mutation—body modification via DIY synthetic biology gives rise to new physical traits.

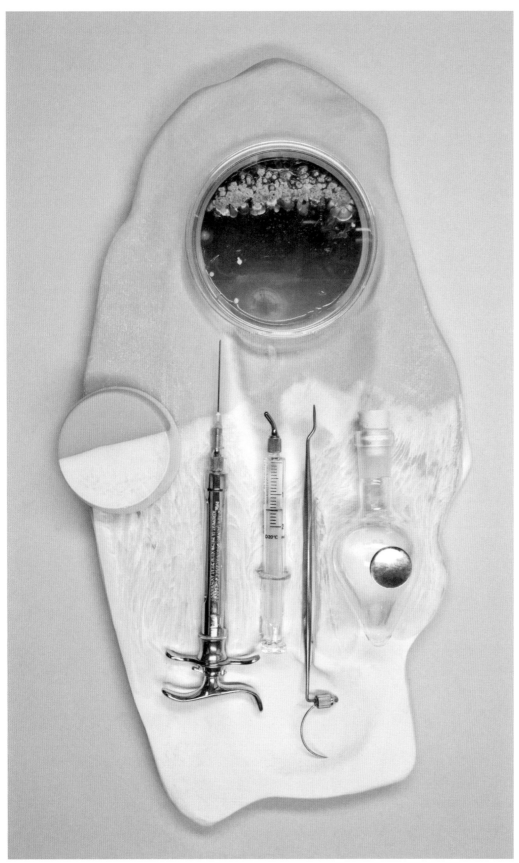

ABOVE   300, 301

Fashionable skins articulated with the help of customized genes are able to express a variety of different colors, patterns, and textures.

LEFT   302

A home kit containing the minimum required tools and ingredients for self-body modification.

PLANT FICTION

Can plants help to redress the balance of nature in the shadow of our increasingly demanding cities?

High-quality digital photographic prints, wooden frames, silver foil.

Conny Freyer (German) / Sebastien Noel (French) / Eva Rucki (German)—Troika, London, UK

COMPLETED

These designers explored the role of nature in the West from the perspective that the city has developed as a social concept that is essentially at odds with its surrounding environment. The seemingly inexorable march toward ever more sophisticated technology and increased cultural refinement demands our control and subjection of nature. This pursuit drives modern natural science to deliver a continuous flow of new innovations that offer improvements to our well-being. However, such progress, puts pressure the environment in the form of, for example, pollution, resource depletion, and loss of biodiversity.

Plant Fiction applies layers of fact, fiction, myth, history, and radical thinking to our relationship with nature, culture, and the city. Five scenarios are presented, each formed around a fictitious plant species that is placed in a London of the near future, each of which is intended to ameliorate a familiar man-made situation. Here, the team envisaged plants that would self-decompose to generate biofuels, or that would excrete unique pigments for use in security devices, creepers that would sense viruses, and shrubs that would reclaim gold from electronic circuits found in landfill sites. This depiction reveals our tendency to enter into short-sighted, self-serving relationships with nature.

OPPOSITE   303

The Weeping Thief plant displays fine silver hairs, to be harvested in the biological brave new world.

RIGHT 304

The Selfeater plant breaks down its own cellulose
in order to facilitate the fermentation of ethanol.

LEFT 305

The Pandemic plant is engineered to change color in the presence of airborne pathogens. Planted on roofs across a community, it allows diseases to be mapped and monitored remotely.

PROSPECT RESORT

In time it may be possible for individuals afflicted with particular conditions to help search for their own cures.

Numerous props, including Prospector's kit, photographs.

Sascha Pohflepp (German)—Design Interactions, Royal College of Art, London, UK

CONCEPT

'Bioprospecting' is the search for plant or animal life for use in research and for the development of novel pharmaceuticals. The activity flourished in colonial times because crops, herbs, and spices were commercially viable in home markets. Now the collection and gene sequencing of organisms that exhibit potentially useful traits is on the rise, and the practice is the subject of both legal disputes and numerous ethical questions.

This conceptual work leverages the increased accessibility and affordability of biological research, supported by the increasingly participatory Internet culture. Bioprospecting for the non-professional is becoming increasingly viable, and it echoes a thriving new branch of the locavore movement that focuses on finding and resurrecting underappreciated grains, corns, vegetables, and other plants that have fallen out of use in commercial production.

A fictional destination in South America, **Prospect Resort** combines a hotel, a top-notch laboratory, and a hospital. After a discovery is made of a species that shows genetic promise, widespread attention is generated that leads to a flood of hopefuls. The site offers them a base from which they can explore the Amazon Rainforest.

With the increasing popularity of amateur science in mind, the narrative presents a potential form of modern-day colonialism, not so different from corporate investment in oil drilling or diamond mining in developing countries. The resort's offering is a response to a trend whereby individuals' involvement in the generation of new information—particularly when it concerns illness or death—could soon be commonplace. Although this project is speculative, there is a distinct possibility for individuals to participate in genetic research for their own medical benefit in the near future, possibly even with the encouragement of poorly funded public health systems.

RIGHT   306

Gathering DNA samples in the wild is a regular practice within pharmaceutical research today but may soon be the pursuit of citizen scientists.

ABOVE   307

A prospector kit, with plant samples collected
from a previously ignored part of the world.

ABOVE   308, 309, 310, 311

In this speculative scenario, prospectors collect
genetic samples that might be repurposed in
industry or medicine for the benefit of mankind.

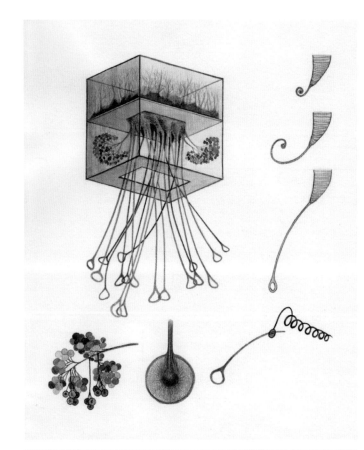

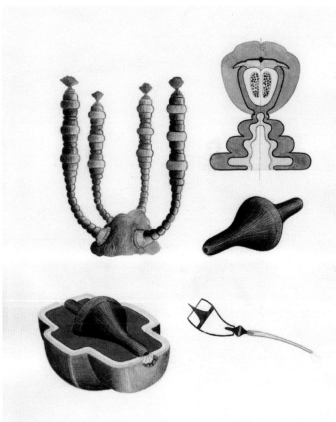

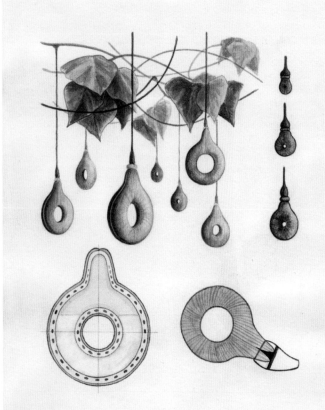

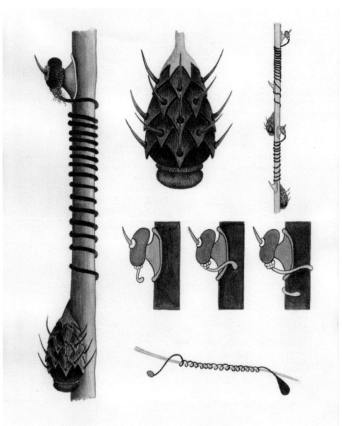

GROWTH ASSEMBLY

Can we source more of the 'things' we need from plant 'factories' rather than resorting to mechanized production processes?

Watercolor illustrations on paper.

Alexandra Daisy Ginsberg (British) / Sascha Pohflepp (German)—Design Interactions, Royal College of Art, London, UK

CONCEPT

Here, the designers envision a future characterized by dramatically high energy costs plus widespread adoption and advance of synthetic biology to fulfill our everyday needs. The illustrations here are reminiscent of the drawings of German biologist Earnst Haeckel of the 19th century, but they depict new plant species that have been manipulated to grow components for assembly. Coded into the DNA of plants, objects develop from literal biological 'factories.' Having reached the appropriate stage, they are harvested like a nut from its shell, ready to be combined with other elements to make a useful device.

Growth Assembly envisages shops being replaced by factory farms, where items are both grown and sold (similar to Freeman Dyson's description of the future in *The Sun, the Genome, and the Internet* (1999)), and the postal service focusing on delivering seeds for domestic manufacture rather than on the distribution of end products. New, slower biological processes usurp high-speed, mechanized production lines. Complex items require longer to grow, making them costly, whereas small, simple ones are cheaper. Relying on biology to produce consumer goods rejects the conventional idea of industrial standards, thus promoting softness and diversity in place of heavy machine-based production and uniformity.

As an example, a herbicide sprayer is built up from a range of parts, each one sourced from a different plant and specified according to the function that it is required to perform.

OPPOSITE   312, 313, 314, 315

'Natural' counterparts of components of everyday products are grown inside genetically modified plants, within vessels such as pea pods or cornhusks.

GOOGOL PUDDLES

Imagining a future where micoorganisms take over
the role of data storage in place of computers.

Graphics, video, drawings.

Mike Robitz (American)—Columbia University Graduate School of Architecture, Planning and
Preservation, New York, USA

CONCEPT

This is a speculative design fiction, developed in the Architecture Bio-Synthesis course at Columbia University, that envisions a natural world contaminated with cells that function as computer processors and digital storage. In this dystopia, advances in synthetic biology allow scientists to program microscopic life to perform logic operations in the way that microchips do, and the base pairs of DNA are translated into the 1s and 0s of binary code.

The startling result is that processes that formerly occurred in sterilized, cooled warehouses of computer servers are released into the natural environment. The concept recalls the fictional 'wet net' envisioned by Neal Stephenson in the 1995 novel *The Diamond Age*, which consists of nanocomputers working and multiplying inside the human body.

Googol, after the ubiquitous search engine, is the name given to these computing cells, the size of which allows for tremendous density of information in a tiny space. Given that common bacteria such as *Escherichia coli* are so small that three million of them could huddle on the head of a pin, and that the DNA within each cell is even smaller, at low concentration a half-gallon puddle of Googol has the capacity to store the amount of digital information that the entire world can produce in a year. Information stored in this way has the potential to be preserved indefinitely since the robustness and fecundity of microbial life is so immense.

The advent of a cellular microprocessor and DNA hard drives transfers the immediacy of computation into the natural environment, altering our perceptions and expectations of it. The data centers in this future are our oceans, streams, . rivers, and puddles—all populated with organisms of our creation. In **Googol Puddles**, cities have to reorganize themselves around this new reality, zoning areas based on bandwidths and memory limitations rather the traditional categorizations of residential, industrial, and commercial. Whole bodies of water, like a Facebook River Estuary, are home to the data storage of a single company.

As computational infrastructure and nature are combined in such an intimate way, corporations in turn vie to preserve or alter nature in order to ensure their competitive success. In this scenario, the public has perhaps its last opportunity to assert itself and take a firm position on the issue of preserving the natural environment.

ABOVE   316

In this fictional narrative, digital information is stored within the DNA of living cells throughout the natural environment, prompting questions about public ownership, security, and control.

ABOVE   317

Data encryption inside cells would capitalize on the extremely small and variable format of DNA.

RIGHT   318

The alteration and control of natural resources using the developing tools of synthetic biology will create issues for public debate in the future.

BLOOD LAMP

Wouldn't you think twice if every time you wanted to switch on a light you had to bleed a little?

Glass bulb, luminol, blood.

Mike Thompson (British)—Mike Thompson Studio, Eindhoven, the Netherlands

CONCEPT

ABOVE / RIGHT 320, 321

The top of the lamp is broken, thereby creating a jagged edge with which to break the skin and to allow the entry of blood into the liquid medium.

OPPOSITE 319

Bioluminescence triggered by the addition of human blood helps to emphasize the value of the energy required to provide us with light—something that we routinely take for granted.

With this project the designer asks some crucial questions to raise awareness about the true cost of energy. Would you turn a light on so readily if you understood the impact it has on the environment? And would you still do it if there were a direct (not simply moneteray) impact on you? Most of us use energy-hungry devices without a thought. In fact, the average American citizen consumes more than 3,000 kwh of energy each year, which is sufficient to light several rooms continuously during that same period.

Blood Lamp makes the point that energy isn't free. The user is required to break off the top of a glass bulb containing luminol. Used in forensic science, this chemical glows bright blue when allowed to react with the iron in blood. They then add a packet of powder that activates the luminol. Finally, they must cut themselves, squeezing droplets of blood into the solution to trigger the light reaction. The lamp can be used only once and the individual has to make a personal sacrifice, so inevitably they consider more carefully their need for light and are prompted to recognize its value.

LATRO

The idea of 'stealing' energy from plants could lead to a means of powering small battery-driven devices.

Glass, algae, electronics.

Mike Thompson (British)—Mike Thompson Studio, Eindhoven, the Netherlands

CONCEPT

As fossil fuel supplies become scarcer, natural sources of energy, such as algae, are increasing in importance. While these can be used in the production of biofuel, much of the energy they absorb from sunlight is lost. By inserting nanosized gold electrodes into the photosynthesizing chloroplasts of these plants, scientists have been able to draw small amounts of electric current. With further advances in nanotechnology, algae are therefore becoming increasingly attractive energy sources.

Latro (Latin for 'thief') is a speculative design for a 'living and breathing' hanging lamp containing algae, which need no more than sunlight, carbon dioxide, and water. Breathing into the device via the handle provides carbon dioxide, while a separate opening allows water to be added and oxygen to be expelled. In sunlight, the plants then have all they need to sustain themselves. Removal of electrons from them is restricted by a sensor that monitors light intensity, thereby preventing malnourishment of the algae. The gathered electrical energy is stored in a battery, ready for use at night.

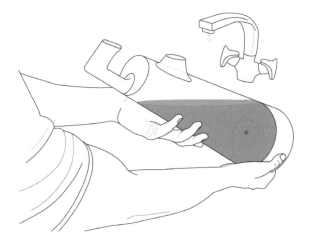

ABOVE 322

Like a house pet, the algae in the lamp must be fed and maintained if they are to function reliably.

ABOVE / RIGHT 323, 324

Exhaling into the vessel provides a supply of carbon dioxide for photosynthesis. In return the algae generate energy to light the lamp.

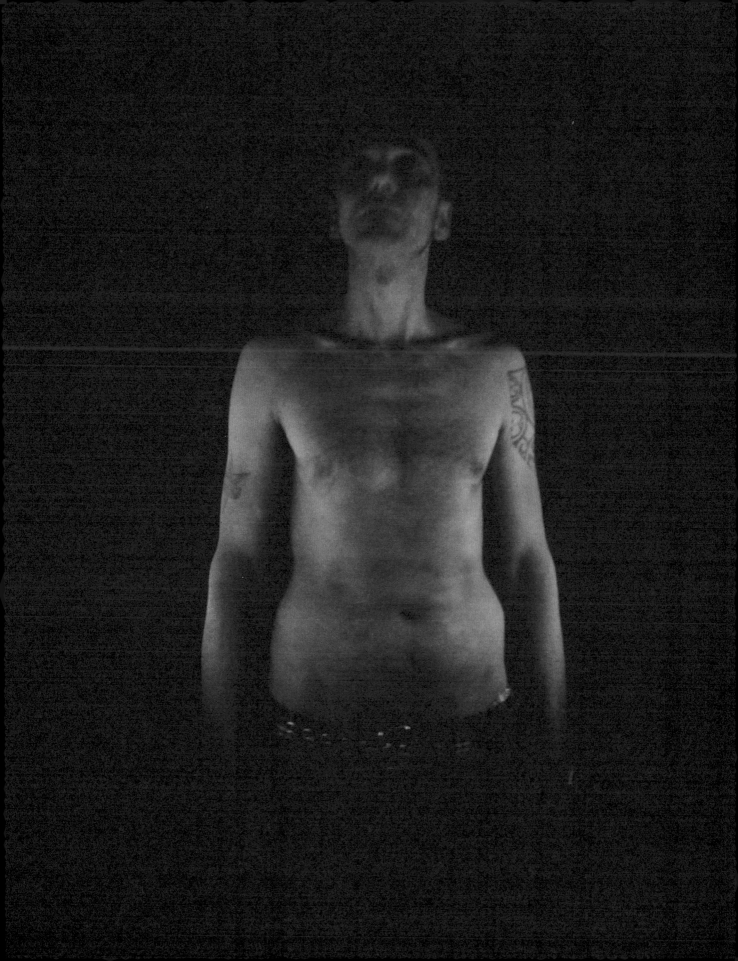

4.
DYNAMIC BEAUTY

Artwork Crawling off the Auction Block

OPPOSITE 325
See 'Exploring the Invisible', page 240.

Here we profile recent works that intersect with biology and harness life in often unexpected ways. Expressing an idea of beauty for its own sake or in search of meaning is different from design in the sense that it need not be directed toward any user or perform a clear function. Nonetheless, these projects reveal opportunities for the field of design while creating original aesthetic experiences and laying the foundation for a new conception of beauty.

In many of these endeavors, biology is both the subject and the medium, reflecting the unmet need to thoroughly examine and decode the cultural meaning of accelerating scientific progress. Different approaches are adopted, from genetic manipulation in the laboratory (such as 'Natural History of the Enigma') to directing the activities of insects and plants to obtain specific formal or symbolic outcomes (for example, 'The Seed of Narcissus'). A thread common to several is a response to the relative apathy or ignorance most people harbor regarding the world of microorganisms and our dependence on it for survival (such as 'Co-existence'). As research advances, greater knowledge of the natural world filters to the public relatively slowly, although some developments readily capture the imagination.

One undertaking that inspired broad understanding and thorough coverage in the press was the Human Genome Project. Launched in 1990 and completed in 2003, it determined the sequence of the base pairs that make up our genetic code, and it mapped the approximately 20,000 genes of the human genome. These achievements have rapidly and significantly influenced art and design, from the popularization of genomorphic forms in architecture to experiments in creating transgenic species as bioart. The concept of DNA as an architectural plan has also firmly embedded itself—despite the limits of the metaphor—in our consciousness through the lexicon: a distinctive approach to management or innovation is said to be 'in a firm's DNA', while 'your genetic makeup' might, with or without basis, be assigned responsibility for unique traits or behaviors.

In contrast, the Human Microbiome Project is not widely understood or discussed. This five-year program was launched in 2008 and employs new techniques to identify genetic material from microorganisms that thrive in environments such as the body but are difficult to culture in the laboratory. The goal is to characterize all of the bacteria, viruses, and so on to which people are host and that may affect our health, with potential applications in biomedical science. Early findings suggest that humans are closely entwined with all of these guest organisms symbiotically. While some projects, such as 'Co-existence', have begun to respond by focusing on these relationships, the full potential of this research as aesthetic inspiration is a long way from full realization. The delicate balance of these intimate associations on which our lives depend is likely to alter our sense of self and our conception of the environments in and around us that teem with invisible life.

Another indication of the future direction of artistic engagement with life appeared in 2010, with the creation of the first synthetic life form—a cell that had been generated entirely from synthesized DNA—by a team led by Craig Venter. The biologist said: 'This is the first self-replicating species we've had on the planet whose parent is a computer.' Although this effort consumed 10 years of time and millions of dollars, it may be a harbinger of an entirely new and virtually limitless medium for creative output. Among those who eagerly anticipate wielding these tools of creation and manipulating life is pioneer Eduardo Kac, who said: 'One of my goals is to completely and thoroughly design a new life form, to conceive every aspect of it.' As they plunge into such uncharted territory of form giving, unconstrained by design objectives such as utility, artists instigate still more collaboration and cross-pollination.

ABOVE 326

The genetically modified 'Edunia' plant exhibited at the Weisman Art Museum, Minneapolis.

ABOVE 328

The flower of the 'Edunia' plant with the artist's DNA expressed in the red veins of the petals.

RIGHT 327

The artist watering his own genetic offspring.

NATURAL HISTORY OF THE ENIGMA

Gene manipulation offers an entirely new and expansive medium to artists.

Petunia DNA, artist's DNA, soil, water.

Eduardo Kac (American, born Brazil)—Studio Eduardo Kac, Chicago, USA

COMPLETED

ABOVE   329, 330

From the top: the transgenic plant exhibited at the Factoría art gallery, Santiago de Compostela and the Weisman Art Museum, Minneapolis.

Transgenic art is a nascent discipline in which portions of genetic code are added to and expressed by a host organism. **Natural History of the Enigma** involves a range of items that include a new life form—a genetically engineered flower that is a hybrid of the artist and a petunia. The result, 'Edunia', was developed through the application of molecular biology and so is not found in nature. The alien, human gene that the plant contains was isolated and sequenced from a sample of blood. It produces an immunoglobulin, a protein that functions as an antibody and is used by the immune system to identify and neutralize foreign antigens (antibody generators that trigger an immune response). The gene produces a protein that makes the veins of the flower's petals red, creating a living image of human blood within a flower. The creation of this novel organism, which entailed using a virus promoter to insert the gene precisely, was overseen by Professor Olszewski in the Department of Plant Biology at the University of Minnesota.

In anticipation that Edunia would be distributed and planted outside of galleries and museums, the artist created limited edition seed packs. Embedded magnets keep them closed while visitors are invited to open and examine them like books. The project includes several watercolors, photographs, and lithographs. All of the blooms featured are genetically identical clones, yet they look quite different, supporting the view that all life, no matter how similar genetically, is fundamentally unique.

This work suggests a broad scope of artistic opportunities offered by newly accessible techniques for synthesizing and working with genes. A couple of decades ago such endeavours would have required thousands of dollars in funding, but today only about one-tenth of the financial outlay is necessary.

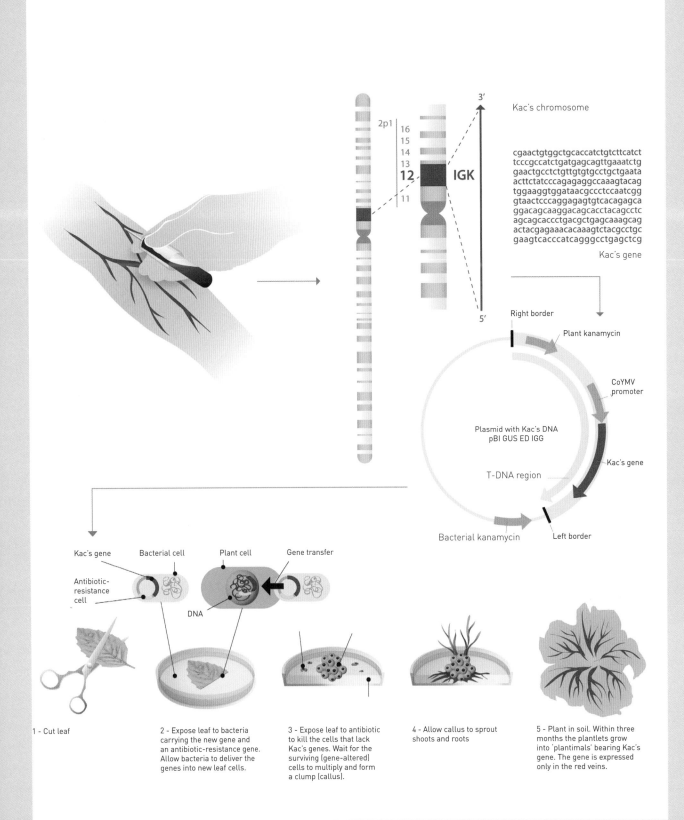

2p1

16
15
14
13
12
11

3'

IGK

Kac's chromosome

cgaactgtggctgcaccatctgtcttcatct
tcccgccatctgatgagcagttgaaatctg
gaactgcctctgttgtgtgcctgctgaata
acttctatcccagagaggccaaagtacag
tggaaggtggataacgccctccaatcgg
gtaactcccaggagagtgtcacagagca
ggacagcaaggacagcacctacagcctc
agcagcaccctgacgctgagcaaagcag
actacgagaaacacaaagtctacgcctgc
gaagtcacccatcagggcctgagctcg

Kac's gene

5'

Right border

Plant kanamycin

CoYMV
promoter

Plasmid with Kac's DNA
pBI GUS ED IGG

Kac's gene

T-DNA region

Bacterial kanamycin

Left border

Kac's gene   Bacterial cell   Plant cell   Gene transfer

Antibiotic-
resistance
cell

DNA

1 - Cut leaf

2 - Expose leaf to bacteria
carrying the new gene and
an antibiotic-resistance gene.
Allow bacteria to deliver the
genes into new leaf cells.

3 - Expose leaf to antibiotic
to kill the cells that lack
Kac's genes. Wait for the
surviving (gene-altered)
cells to multiply and form
a clump (callus).

4 - Allow callus to sprout
shoots and roots

5 - Plant in soil. Within three
months the plantlets grow
into 'plantimals' bearing Kac's
gene. The gene is expressed
only in the red veins.

Edunia Seed Pack Studies I–VI on display in the
Factoría art gallery, Santiago de Compostela.

  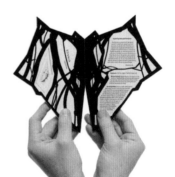 

OPPOSITE   331

Diagram showing how the artist's DNA becomes
part of the plant and is expressed in its flowers.

ABOVE   333

Handmade paper objects with 'Edunia' seeds and
magnets formed part of the installations.

EGG AND SLUG

Inspired by the slug's balletic mating ritual, these artworks reflect the bounty of nature within the confines of custom-made vessels.

Cast acrylic, aluminum, stainless steel, hand-blown glass, full-spectrum lighting with planting.

Paula Hayes (American)—Studio Paula Hayes, New York, USA

COMPLETED

For the installation **Nocturne of the Limax maximus** at the Museum of Modern Art (MoMA) in New York, the artist created two terrarium sculptures, cast from iridescent acrylic and blown glass. One oviform and freestanding on a pedestal, the other fusiform and mounted on a wall, **Egg** and **Slug** were home to miniature forests of lush plant life in the museum's lobby for six months. The pieces were intended to highlight the organic nature of their surroundings—an area chaotically populated and continually changing.

Their forms reflected two characteristic shapes of *Limax maximus*: one a single horizontal slug that suggests slippery, globular movement; and the other the act of fertilization, in which a pair of the mollusks wrap around each other in an elegant spiral, suspended in the air on a rope of mucus. When their sex organs meet, they too entwine to exchange sperm, creating a translucent, flowerlike globe that leaves both partners fertilized. (Slugs are hermaphrodite, meaning that they have both male and female reproductive systems and they each produce eggs and sperm.)

ABOVE   334

Limax maximus ('great slug') exhibits a marvelous mating behavior, which inspired part of this work.

OPPOSITE   335

Installation at MoMA in New York, where the form mimics a pair of *Limax maximus* during mating.

ABOVE 336

Terrarium sculptures in the lobby of MoMA in New York, echoing the forms of a slug in movement (left) and its hermaphroditic mating ritual in suspension from a tree branch (right).

ABOVE 337

The flow of visitors at the museum reflects the temporal and organic nature of the terrariums.

ABOVE RIGHT / RIGHT   338, 339

Close-ups of one of the terrarium plantings, for
which a variety of plant species were selected.

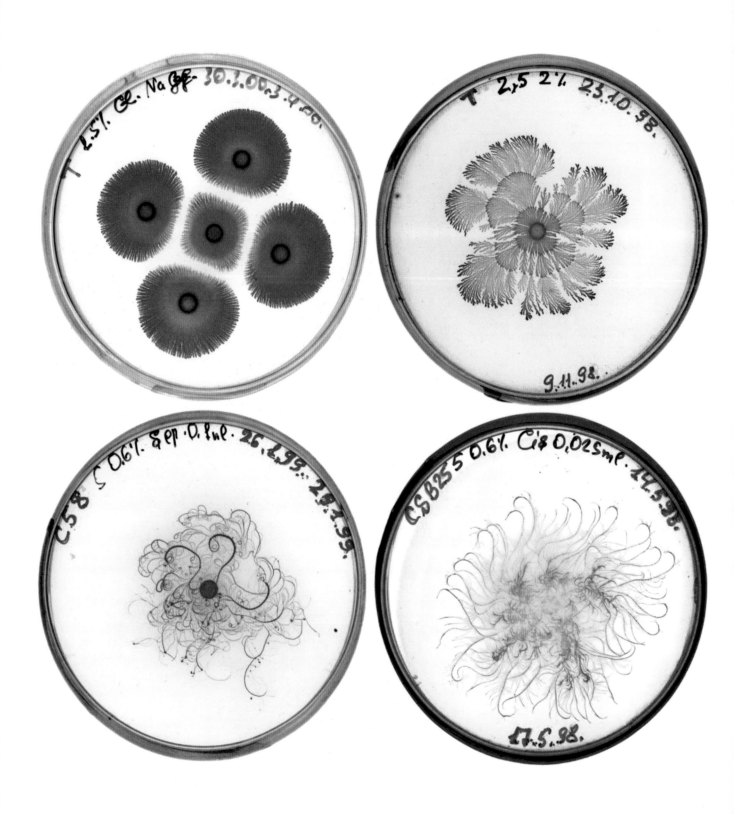

OBJECTIVITY

The surprising ability of tiny organisms to communicate and make decisions is exploited here to form biological sculpture.

Bacteria (Paenibacillus vortex), agar, nutrients, petri dishes.

Nurit Bar-Shai (American, born in Israel)—School of Physics and Astronomy, Tel Aviv University, Israel / Genspace, New York City, USA / MakerBot Industries, Brooklyn, USA

IN PRODUCTION

This work explores the intersection of art, science, and technology in a series of images that capture bacteria displaying social behaviors with rich communication patterns. In visualizing biological systems of self-organization, it is possible to detect surprising complexity and to achieve dramatically varied results with only slight alterations in the initial environment. The project includes a series of three-dimensional agar structures containing nutrients. These pieces examine the decision making of living, performative objects that 'grow images' as a sculptural form.

Objectivity was inspired by the research of Professor Eshel Ben Jacob who studies microbial behavior at Tel Aviv University. Specifically, it builds on his discovery of, and research on, *Paenibacillus vortex*, a bacterium that forms colonies with complex and dynamic characteristics. These microorganisms possess advanced social motility, employing cell-to-cell signaling to prompt activities such as attraction and repulsion under different environmental conditions. When grown on soft surfaces, these 'superorganisms' (many individuals effectively acting as one) exhibit collective motility by forming foraging 'arms' that are sent out in search of food. This 'swarming intelligence' allows the population of bacteria to disperse and then reunite when they detect scattered patches of nutrients.

Once the bacteria have grown into patterns, prompted by the dispersal of nutrients, they are made visible with dye that also halts their growth.

OPPOSITE 340

Paenibacillus vortex exhibits sophisticated social behavior, both scattering and forming foraging swarms to obtain food. The artist uses these bacteria to grow sculptures in three dimensions.

THE SEED OF NARCISSUS

Combining industrial design and natural sculpture.

Beeswax, glass, silver, stainless steel.

Tomáš Libertiny (Slovak)—Studio Tomáš Libertiny, Rotterdam, the Netherlands

COMPLETED

Here, two works harness the industriousness of bees, guiding them to form the shape of specific objects.

Exhibited at the Venice Biennale in 2011, **The Seed of Narcissus** also exploits a juxtaposition of contrasts: industrial and natural processes of form making. The glass bulb was made in a high-speed, high-temperature, machine-driven environment to achieve its specific shape. A silver coating on the inside makes it highly reflective (recalling the myth of Narcissus who fell in love with his own reflection). The outer wax structure was the result of the natural and relatively slow process of honeycomb building.

The materials exhibit strong textural differences too, with the soft, jagged form of the bees' architecture set against the hard, smooth surface of the glass. Uniting the two materials, however, is their extraordinary fragility, an attribute that the artist favors for its ability to create a sense of distance between the work and the viewer. The work was inspired in part by the concept of *Ahimsa*, an important tenet of Hinduism, Jainism, and Buddhism that means 'the avoidance of violence' and implores kindness toward all living things. As a work too delicate to touch, it draws attention to the vulnerability of both biological and material existence.

A separate but technically related work, **The Honeycomb Vase 'Made by Bees'** is the result of the efforts of forty thousand bees, confined by a wooden box and encouraged to cover a vase-shaped scaffold in honeycomb, layer by layer, in the course of a week. Completely natural, this slow process of manufacture is low energy and low temperature, and it deliberately uses a species that is important in agriculture and threatened by changes to the environment. The end product neatly integrates its process and function: as the bees form the vase they spread pollen and aid in the reproduction of flowering plants, the very things that the vessel is intended to display.

ABOVE   341

A concept sketch of a wax-covered glass vessel.

ABOVE   342

The Seed of Narcissus installation at the Venice
Biennale, honeycomb formed around silver glass.

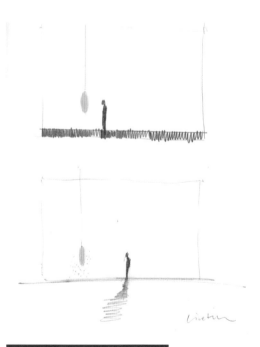

ABOVE   344

Installation sketches show a viewer for scale.

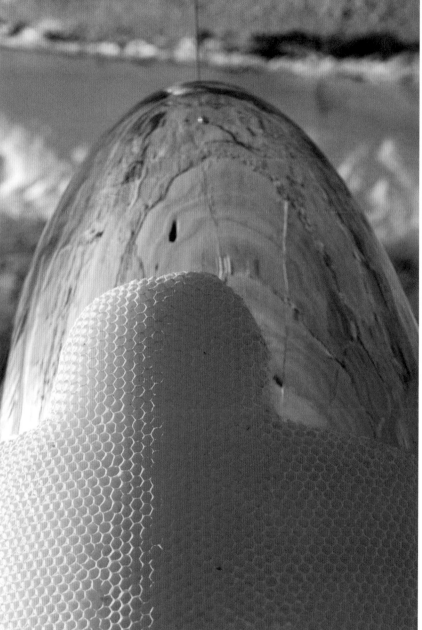

ABOVE   343

Detail of the naturally formed wax honeycomb
alongside the highly reflective silver glass.

ABOVE   345

The Honeycomb Vase, resembling the Greek
krater vase form without handles. The wax
honeycomb is created as a result of the slow and
deliberate work of tens of thousands of bees.

The Honeycomb Vase 'Made by Bees' was recently added to the design collection of the Museum of Modern Art, New York.

ABOVE 347

The vase with some of the bees that created it.

ABOVE / BELOW   348, 349

Suspended intravenous bags containing algae,
to which viewers are invited to add material that
could either promote or hinder their growth.

ABOVE / RIGHT   350, 351

Syringes containing chemicals for injection by
visitors into the algae-filled intravenous bags.

ALGAEBRA

The consequences of human intervention on a small scale offer insights into our potential impact on our environment.

Water samples, algae, intravenous bags, helpful and harmful chemicals.

Jelte van Abbema (Dutch)—Lab Van Abbema, Eindhoven, the Netherlands

COMPLETED

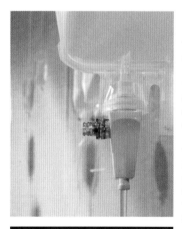

ABOVE   352

The algae were harvested from various locations in the east of the Netherlands.

Unlike more conventional design materials, living organisms are sensitive to changes in their environment and will often provide unique cues to the consequences of human actions.

Created specially for the exhibition Artificial Green in Roombeek, the Netherlands, **Algaebra** is a garden of suspended intravenous bags containing small concentrations of algae that are made dependent on human care for their survival. The initial month-long installation displayed water samples that had been collected throughout the eastern region of Enschede. Water sources ranged from public taps to muddy ditches so that each offered a unique algae ecosystem. Visitors were encouraged to participate by injecting the bags with either helpful or harmful chemicals. Over time, this influence encouraged the algae in many bags to flourish while the viability of others was compromised. Their survival or demise was evident from their color, which ranged from murky brown to vivid green.

This project explores the simultaneous potential for growth and inevitability of deterioration. The interaction of visitors with the algae enabled the piece to change and evolve in unpredictable ways.

GENETIC HEIRLOOM SERIES

Where inherited conditions are viewed as keepsakes, such as gold jewelry.

Hand-blown glass, gold-plated brass, nylon, vinyl tubing, leather, powder-coated aluminum, colloidal gold, colloidal silver, corian, pear wood.

Revital Cohen (British, born Israel)—Design Interactions, Royal College of Art, London, UK; supported by a Wellcome Trust Arts Award

CONCEPT

Here the designer imagines how family behavior might change as a result of the increased availability of genetic information and the growing perception that our identity is closely tied to our particular sequence of genes. This view of the self challenges our conception of responsibility, risk, and autonomy and could also alter our relationships within the family.

The project explores these potential changes through objects designed to be passed down through generations as inheritance, reflecting the passing on of genetic conditions. Increasing use of precious metals in medicine, especially for cancer treatment, draws a parallel between material heirlooms (such as silver candlesticks) and genetic ancestry (such as an inherited disease). The three items in **Genetic Heirloom Series** address different issues that might arise as more genetic information becomes available, such as the emotional impact of disease vulnerability on children.

How we might struggle with knowledge that implies a genetic determinism is the basis of the **Guilt Adjuster**, a device that allows a child to inflict pain on themselves so as to alleviate the guilt they feel for their good fortune in not inheriting the disease from which their parents or siblings suffer. In addition to addressing survivor's guilt, it provides discomfort as an entryway for the child back into the family narrative of enduring disease. To take their body through a journey of pain and healing, the child connects their wrist to the needle, turning one tap to inject colloidal gold poison, another for the antidote.

The **Interventionist** responds to epigenetics —an area of genetic research focused on how environmental factors can effect gene expression. It attempts to control the surroundings by releasing sound, scent, and antibacterial sprays with the hope of suppressing a deadly, inherited genetic disorder.

The **Disclosure Case**, which makes reference to one of the key ethical issues raised by genetic profiling, allows potential inheritors of a trait to decide for themselves if they want to know their fate. Traditional heirlooms of precious metals, an echo of recent treatments for cancer that have relied on gold and silver, are kept alongside audio messages from relatives that disclose inherited genetic traits. Inspired by Pandora's box, the device is left for the next generation to open.

ABOVE 353

The **Guilt Adjuster** allows the individual to self-inflict pain via an intravenously delivered poison.

ABOVE / RIGHT   354, 355

A healthy person whose sibling has inherited
a debilitating or fatal genetic disorder has the
opportunity to alleviate their survivor's guilt.

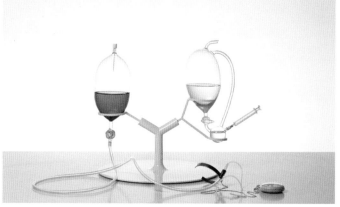

ABOVE   356

One bulb of liquid contains a poison while the
other offers the antidote, allowing the user to
experience the ordeal of pain and healing.

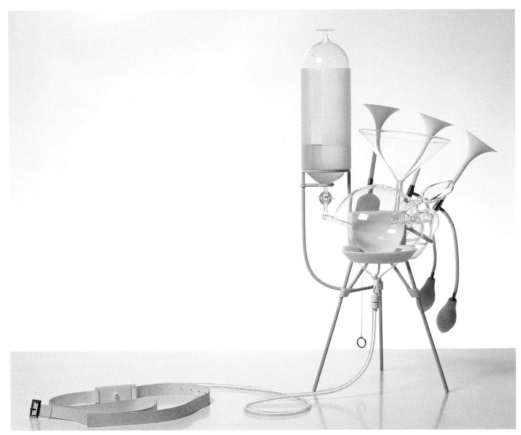

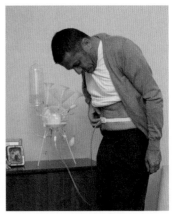

ABOVE 357, 358

The **Interventionist** responds to epigenetics—an area of research focused on how environmental factors can effect gene expression. The device attempts to control environmental factors by releasing sounds, scents, and antibacterial sprays to suppress a inherited genetic disorder.

ABOVE 359, 360

The device includes equipment for administering nanogold-enriched chemotherapy. The main drip leads to a bespoke needle, to be inserted into the navel, highlighting the maternal connection that is characteristic of many inherited disorders.

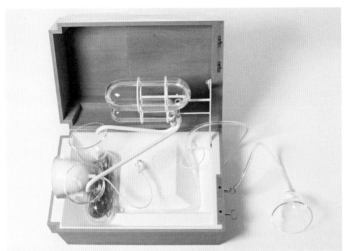

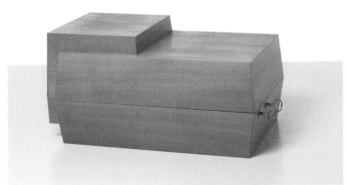

ABOVE / RIGHT   361, 362, 363, 364

The **Disclosure Case** is intended for a child who has a hereditary form of cancer. Within the box is an audio description of the inheritance as well as the family's gold, which begins dissolving into chloride for the first stage of their treatment.

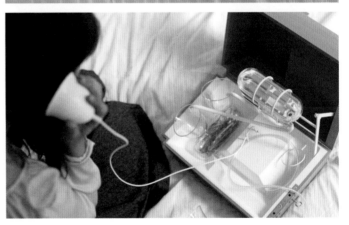

TOP / LEFT / ABOVE 365, 366, 367

A leech is allowed to feed on an individual's arm, collecting blood that is mixed with altered yeasts and stock to create a blood mousse. The end-product contains mood-altering chemicals.

COOK ME—BLACK BILE

Food tailored to the diner's emotions changes the old adage
'You are what you eat' into 'You feel what you eat.'

Leeches, altered yeasts, resin, glass, leather, video (cooking performance).

Tuur Van Balen (Belgian)—London; produced for the exhibition Alter Nature: The Unnatural Animal
(January 29–May 1, 2011), Z33, Hasselt, Belgium

CONCEPT

This work presents a new form of cooking that creates a combined gastronomic-emotional experience for a specific person at a specific time to counteract melancholy. First, a leech is allowed to feed on the individual via their forearm. The sacrificed animal (containing the human blood) is mixed with yeasts and stock, where fermentation reads and responds to chemicals in the blood, such as serotonin, which has mood-altering effects. The resulting combination is incorporated into food and laden with chemicals that will make the eater feel more or less sad. The mixture is prepared in a blood mousse topped with caraway seeds and accompanied by oyster mushrooms, redcurrant sauce, and blood sorrel.

The recipe in **Cook Me—Black Bile** is inspired by Hippocrates' theory of the four humors, which sees the body as made from four essential substances: yellow bile, blood, phlegm, and black bile. The idea is that each is linked to a specific temperament (black bile with sadness) and any surfeit or deficiencies cause physical and physiological alterations. This project, straddling ancient beliefs and future unknowns, unifies the kitchen, the home laboratory, and the pharmacy.

ABOVE 368

This speculative cooking ritual uses synthetic
biology to transform the kitchen into a lab and
pharmacy. A leech collects the diner's blood.

CO-EXISTENCE

The symbiotic relationship between humans and the trillions of microorganisms we host inspires a thought-provoking portrait.

Perspex, lighting, 9000 petri dishes, photographs of various bacteria.

Julia Lohmann (German); commissioned by the Wellcome Trust

COMPLETED

This project was inspired by the universe of unseen organisms that inhabit our bodies. The artist, with the help of microbiologist Michael Wilson, produced a pair of dramatic pixelated images of two reclining nude women. Each 'pixel' was represented by a petri dish containing a photograph of a culture of bacteria—all species that are commonly found in or on the human body. The positioning of each dish within the artwork corresponded to the part of the body in which its inhabitants are usually found. The choice of the female form reflects centuries of art history, as well as the fact that women generally support a greater variety of microorganisms than men.

Underlying **Co-existence** is the recent widespread realization that the human body is essentially a hybrid of human and bacterial cells. We are made up of trillions of cells, of which around 10 percent are human and the rest are of other origin—mostly bacteria that inhabit the gut. We host all this company for our own benefit: critical functions such as digestion and maintaining the immune system rely on symbiotic relationships with other organisms. In other words, we are complex ecosystems in miniature—a blend of human and non-human life working together.

OPPOSITE   369

Petri dishes containing bacteria and other tiny microorganisms that reside on and within our body. These microscopic guests, many of which have adapted to live with us symbiotically, outnumber our own cells by at least ten to one.

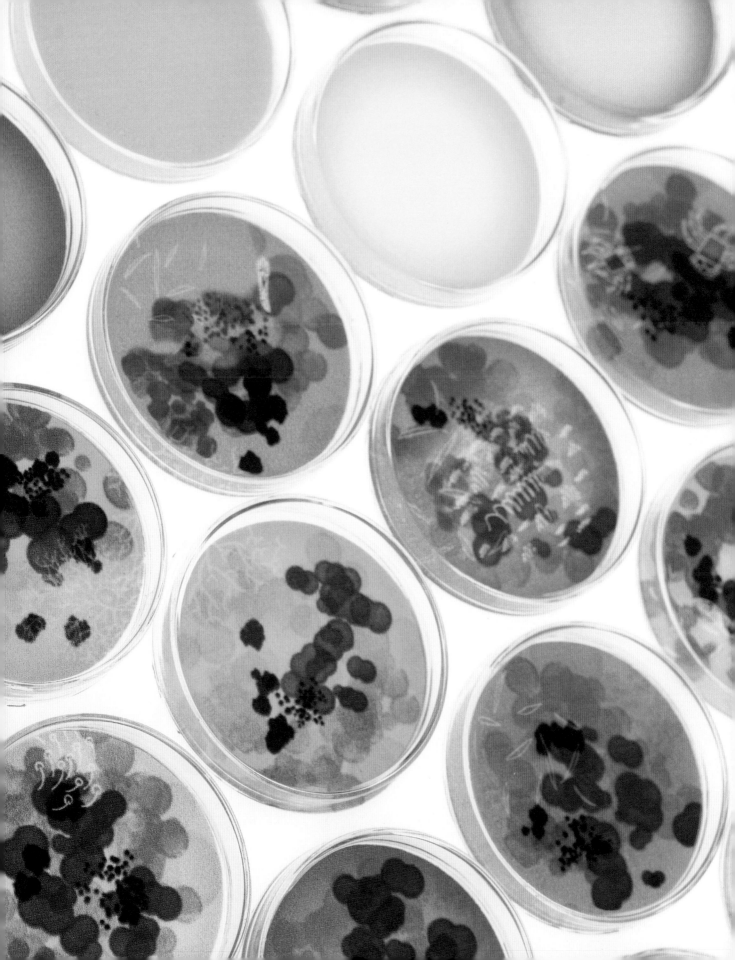

ABOVE   371

Some nine thousand petri dishes, each housing samples of microorganisms from the human body, were dyed and used to represent individual pixels in an image of a reclining nude figure.

LEFT   370

The placement of each dish relates to the origin of those microorganisms on on or in the body.

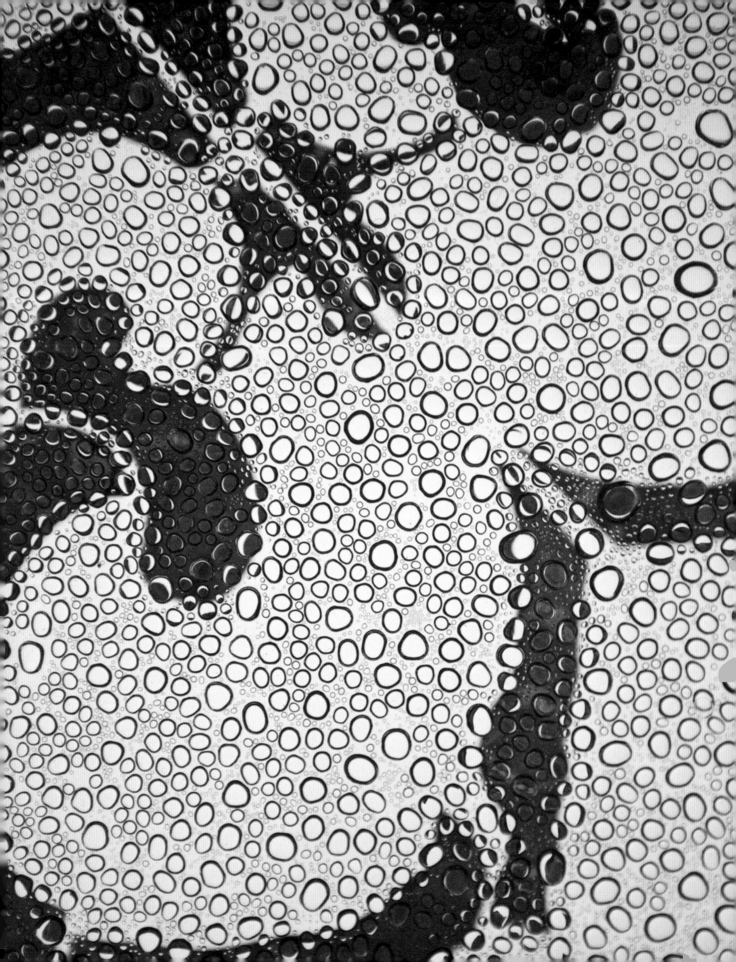

GROWTH PATTERN

A traditional, geometric tile design made from plant matter is allowed to change in unpredictable ways.

Light box, petri dishes, agar, nutrients, hormones, die-cut tobacco leaves.

Allison Kudla (American)—Center for Digital Arts and Experimental Media, University of Washington, USA

COMPLETED

ABOVE   373

Tobacco leaves were cultured in tiling squares with a hormone medium to promote their growth.

Here the artist takes a living system and gives it the form of a manufactured pattern, which is then allowed to develop and change shape naturally. Tobacco leaves are die-cut into a bilaterally symmetrical pattern and suspended in tiling square petri dishes containing the nutrients and hormones necessary to promote new leaf growth. The plant cells, like spores, are totipotent, which means that they are able to multiply and eventually differentiate into all of the different cell types of the whole organism.

In **Growth Pattern** the newly growing leaves undergo morphological changes and thereby extend the form of the traditionally inspired botanical motif over time. Alternatively, although the tiles are sealed ecosystems, accidental pre-contamination can result in the decay of plant tissue or infestation by a parasite, again allowing the design to change in unpredictable ways.

OPPOSITE   372

Detail of the leaf fragment in a sealed petri dish.

ABOVE 374

Tiling squares together on exhibition at the
LABoral Centro de Arte y Creación Industrial in
Gijón, Spain.

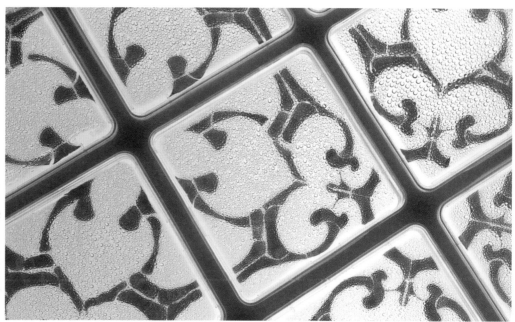

ABOVE 375

The tiles are self-contained ecosystems that usually exhibit only slight variation, but if a parasite enters the vessel during preparation it can alter the intended pattern of leaf growth.

ABOVE / RIGHT 376, 377

The tobacco leaves are cut into specific shapes and prepared beneath a sterile hood to minimize the likelihood of contamination of the dishes.

CONTAMINANT

As carriers of invisible microorganisms, we construct a colorful embroidery of life in the built environment.

Steel, glass, acrylic, tailored agar and BG11 medium, bacteria (including Aspergillus fumigatus, Aspergillus terreus, Penicillium digitatum).

Steve Pike (British)—Unit 20, The Bartlett School of Architecture, University College London, UK

COMPLETED

Microorganisms are present in every earthly environment, from the cleanest hospital room to the murkiest corner of the gutter. Their study reveals otherwise invisible patterns of human activity.

Contaminant is a screen-like architectural installation that displays the growth and colonization of microfungi and dust that were unwittingly introduced by patrons of London's Holborn Station during the course of the sampling phase of the project. As people travel through and occupy various locales, they pick up microorganisms and particulate matter, unintentionally transporting them from one place to the next. A nexus of human travel, the London Underground is also a highway for these microfungi, enabling them to move and mingle throughout the city.

The work visualizes these living traces of place by capturing and fostering the station's ambient particulates within a gelatinous growth medium, much like a petri dish. The result is a visual 'architecture of contamination' formed by the introduction of each speck of life. The diversity of fungi and the variation in the pattern of their colonization of the growth medium illustrate not only human motion through the city but also our relationship with constructed environments. Imbued with themes of colonization, domain, control, and scale, the sculpture can be seen as a metaphor for human colonial behavior and the limits of architecture in the programmatic control of living matter.

The artist collaborated on preliminary laboratory-based experiments with two scientists from University College London: microbiologist Conrad Mullineaux and mycologist Richard Strange. This research helped in the development of techniques of ambient particle capture, tailoring the composition of the growth medium, use of colony facilitators and inhibitors, and a refinement of the design of various monitor vessels.

OPPOSITE   378

Monitor cells were deployed in several locations where they could absorb ambient particles, fungi, and microorganisms specific to each site. The resulting variation in colonial growth hints at the diversity of lifeforms in the built environment.

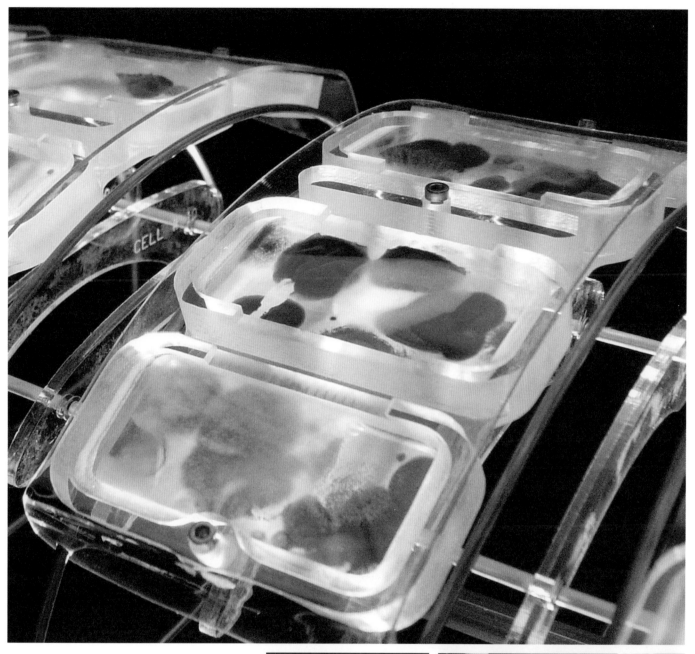

OPPOSITE / ABOVE / RIGHT   379, 380, 381

The growth media within the monitor cells
was tailored to support the specific groups of
microorganisms that were targeted for capture.

SPECIMENS OF UNNATURAL HISTORY

Is it time to redefine the nature of nature?

Artificial grass and mosses, taxidermied animals, animatronics, injection-molded plastic model kits.

Liam Young (Australian)—Tomorrow's Thoughts Today, London, UK

IN PRODUCTION

This project questions our long-held idealistic and preservationist views of the natural world. It imagines a near future in which the slow pace of evolution, relentlessly duplicating and multiplying with gradual mutation, gives way to ever-greater human intervention. **Specimens of Unnatural History** presents a world characterized by robotics, biotechnology, and computing that creates hybrid beings that resist conventional categorization.

Represented by a combination of still life, taxidermy robots, and engineered hybrid creatures, this contemporary work is both an echo of a Victorian-era conception of nature and a meditation on where the interbreeding of biology and technology may lead. The augmented creatures are depicted as guards that are deployed to protect an idealized landscape—Darwin's Galapagos Islands—from invasive, man-made species. Half-animal, half-machine, the living devices call into question whether a managed wilderness is natural.

ABOVE 382

These ground-based herding animals—'Judas Rodents'—drive their invasive cousins into tight packs so that they can be targeted more easily.

ABOVE 383, 384, 385

From the top: the 'Poison Mist Machine' works in much the same way as a crop duster, releasing targeted clouds of poisons and pesticides to kill invasive rodent populations; while the 'Robotic Seed Clouds', made from layers of lightweight fabric, disperse seeds while drifting on the wind.

ABOVE 386, 387

From the top: a collection of stuffed and mounted specimens; and the Galapagos Islands invasive species collection at the Nevada Museum of Art.

RIGHT 388

A nomadic silk factory herd roams across the landscape, tethered to a companion swarm of moths and spinning glistening webs for harvest.

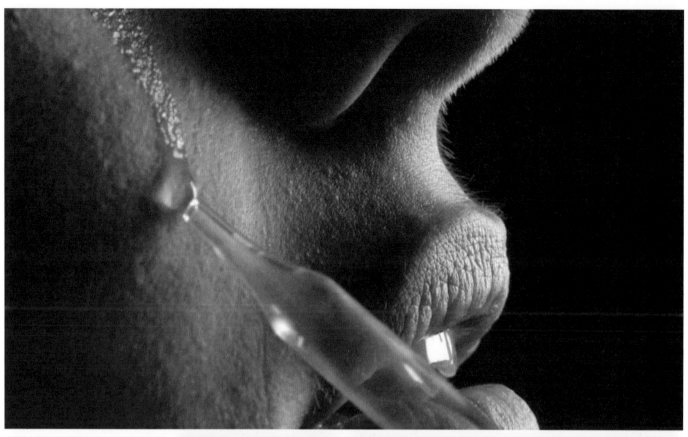

ABOVE / BELOW / RIGHT 389, 390, 391, 392

Various devices for personal health surveillance, each shaped to help the user gather samples from skin, tears, hair, and saliva—environments where innumerable microorganisms thrive.

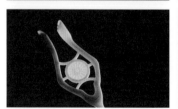

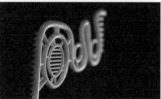

LEFT / ABOVE 397, 398

Embedded with microscopic sensors, these tools can be used to probe either body parts or inanimate objects. The presence of pathogens is signaled by the fluorescing of the objects when they are exposed to a certain wavelength of light.

ABOVE / RIGHT 393, 394, 395, 396

Of the innumerable numbers and species of microorganisms found on our bodies, some are pathogenic but most are harmless and symbiotic.

PATHOGEN HUNTER

How might new tools for detecting dangerous microorganisms alter our current social conventions?

Video, leaflets, probing tools.

Susana Soares (Portuguese) / Mikael Metthey (French)—Design Interactions, Royal College of Art, London, UK / AptaMEMS-ID, Diagnostic and Therapeutic Technologies Department, Newcastle University, UK

CONCEPT

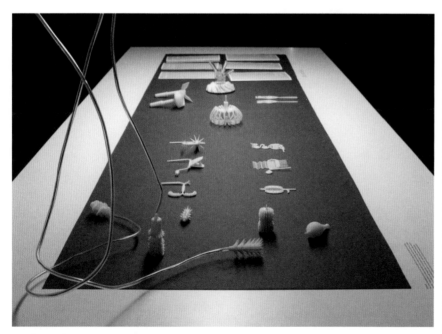

ABOVE   399

These tools are used to discover, capture, and observe infectious microscopic organisms that live on our skin, lurk between our teeth, hide under our nails, and populate everyday objects.

Microorganisms are crucial to our existence, but bacteria and viruses are the cause of some the most devastating epidemics experienced by mankind. This work explores how disease monitoring in the near future might change our health etiquette. It speculates how surveillance personnel would be trained with specific devices to vigilantly predict and manage infectious outbreaks. No matter how clean we are or how healthy we feel, we are continual hosts to trillions of microorganisms on and in our bodies. **Pathogen Hunter** asks: will we change our behavior in order to prevent the spread of pathogens to others and what will be the consequences for our social conventions?

The proposed tools for the discovery and observation of infectious organisms would be embedded with nano-enabled sensor systems that would allow microorganisms to be analyzed and indexed. They are designed to accommodate different sampling contexts and environments, from human skin to door handles. Pathogen balloons would be used to capture volatile organisms that live suspended in the air. The artist developed them in collaboration with a multidisciplinary team of scientists at Newcastle University, who expect the technology to be available within 5–10 years.

GROWING PAINS

What additional meaning is imbued in a memorial object so intimate that it is grown in the giver's body?

Glass, plastic, resin.

Mike Thompson (British)—Mike Thompson Studio, Eindhoven, the Netherlands

CONCEPT

Thanks to advances in the biological sciences, the capabilities of the human body are continually being extended. This endeavor envisions a new frontier in design in which the body is used to cultivate products. It takes on the role of fabricating new material, with both nurturing and monitoring progress becoming part of the everyday routine, and the host necessarily conducting a relationship with the object that they are creating under their own skin. The artifact becomes personalized in this process, accumulating an index of its interactions and experiences as part of its final form.

Growing Pains generally refers to the discomfort often experienced by children during development. It is also applied metaphorically to the changes that we undergo in later life, whether physical or emotional. A new source of such pain might result from generating objects within our bodies through tissue engineering. These could both represent and be involved in some of our most important life experiences. For example, in preparation for their ultimate decay, someone might wish to create a memorial object that could be passed on to their loved ones on their demise—a more literal representation of the self than traditional keepsakes.

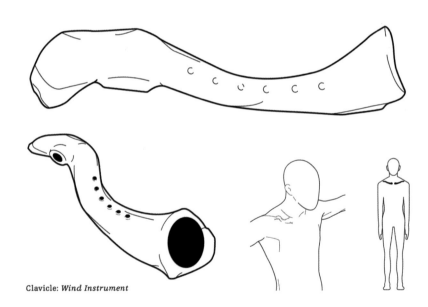

Clavicle: *Wind Instrument*

ABOVE   400

A 'Clavicle Wind Instrument', a bone formation grown beneath the skin over a long period, is intended as a memorial object to be passed to loved ones after one's death. Grown and shaped within the body, it is personalized, carrying traces of its interactions and experiences in its form.

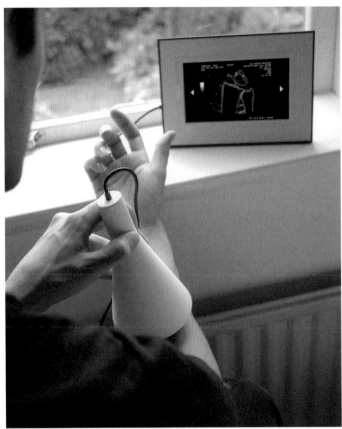

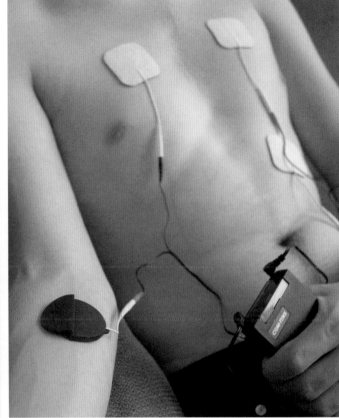

ABOVE / BELOW   401, 402

An image-capture device, similar in function to an ultrasound machine, allows the host to regularly check on the development of the body object.

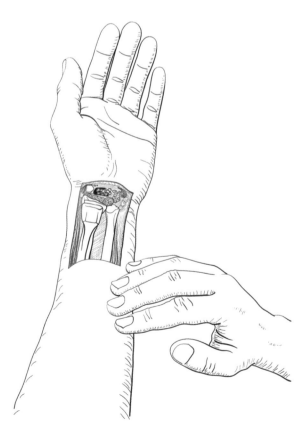

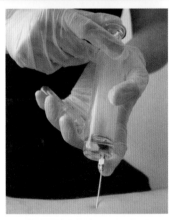

TOP / ABOVE   403, 404

Electrode pads are placed on the body to send a small electric current through the tissue, toning the muscles and stimulating growth of the body object. To prepare for object growth, cells are removed from the body and differentiated in the lab. Once the required bone cells have been isolated they can be injected into the growth site.

THE VISION SPLENDID

A sculpture of living human cells highlights the anonymity
of donors in the face of biotechnological progress.

*Portable bioreactor, hand-blown glass, living human tissue, nutrient media,
PGA polymer, polyurethane.*

Alicia King (Australian)—Hobart Art School, University of Tasmania, Australia / SymbioticA, University of
Western Australia

COMPLETED

This artist investigates biotechnological and biomedical practices and our relationship with the body through the growth and sculpting of human tissue. Living cells are presented in a glass bioreactor, a portable, low-tech, low-cost artificial body. They are grown over glass and polymer shapes to determine their final form. The tissue is a combination of the artist's own and connective tissue cells of an anonymous 13-year-old African-American girl that were isolated from a skin sample on January 31, 1969. The latter were purchased through the American Type Culture Collection. This online catalog of more than four thousand human, animal, and plant cell lines lists cell type, cell characteristics, donor age, and donor ethnicity, among other attributes.

Estranged from the donors' bodies in **The Vision Splendid**, the cells are re-embodied in the form of a contemporary living reliquary, echoing those first religious artifacts that toured between towns like traveling sideshow miracles. Unlike traditional relics, however, this use of tissue outside the body eliminates all traces of the individual from whom they came. In response, the artwork takes the form of fangs, referencing the use of human material in biomedicine that has been so thoroughly commoditized as to appear almost cannibalistic.

ABOVE 405

The portable bioreactor supports the growth of a human tissue sample isolated more than 40 years ago and bought from an online catalog.

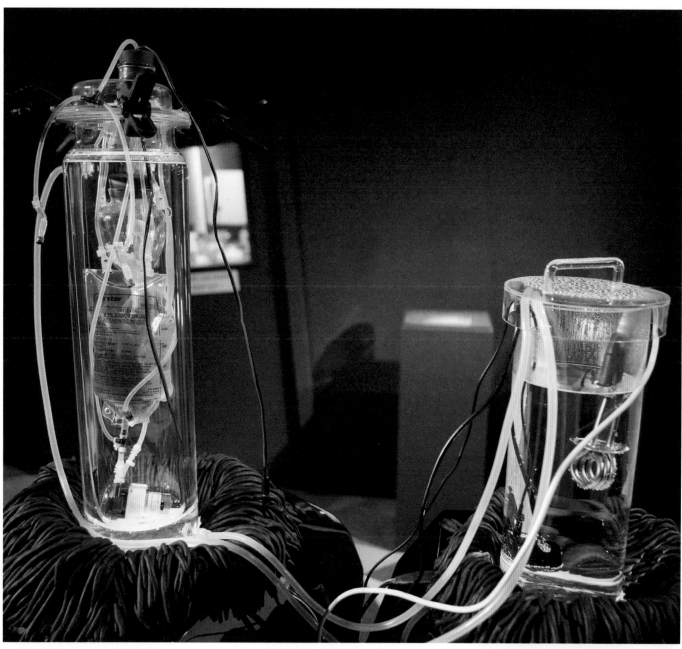

ABOVE   406

Mimicking the human circulatory system, the
intravenous bag contains nutrients that support
the maintenance and growth of the tissue.

RIGHT   407

The tissue slowly forms around a biodegradable
polymer framework in the shape of a set of fangs.

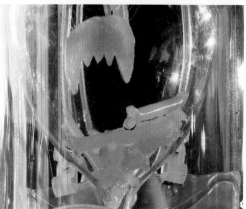

ABOVE   409

Robotic components deliver or withhold nutrients in accordance with instructions generated in a computer-monitored laboratory experiment.

ABOVE   408

An indoor pond containing Azolla ferns and young rice shoots. The system forces mechanization onto, and attempts the control of, an otherwise natural symbiotic process that has been exploited by rice farmers for more than a millennium.

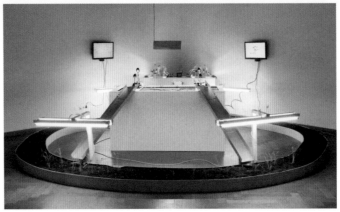

LEFT   410

The system works to mediate the relationship between species in a controlled environment.

AUTOINDUCER_PH-1

Complex control of a traditional rice-cultivation method mirrors the overmechanization of Western farming techniques.

Bacteria (Anabaena cyanobacteria), ferns (Azolla sp.), rice, various audio, computational and robotic components.

Andy Gracie (British)—University of Huddersfield, UK

COMPLETED

ABOVE   411, 412, 413

Observations within a laboratory environment determine the nature of the relationship between two plant species, and this, in turn, controls the behavior of the mechanized fertilization system.

In Southeast Asia, rice yields are maximized by growing aquatic ferns in large numbers in the paddy fields. These provide natural, organic fertilizer. This technique has been practiced for more than 1,000 years and relies on a symbiotic relationship between the ferns and the cyanobacteria that live on their roots and fix atmospheric nitrogen, the ingredient that plants typically absorb from soil. In the installation, this process is repeated but in an elaborate, industrial laboratory style, thus mirroring the contemporary mechanization of Western agricultural practices used to alter natural ecologies so as to increase crop yields.

Employing an arrangement of ponds, electronics, and laboratory and hydroponic equipment, **Autoinducer_Ph-1** oversees and alters the relationship between fern and bacterium, and relies on a software-based system to digitize and mechanize the process. Complex signaling systems and sensors interact to either facilitate or hamper the symbiotic fertilization, based on a virtual modeling of bacterial growth that mimics actual growth in culture chambers. Outcomes from this intricate relationship determine the actions of the robotic rice-farming system. If the software interprets the interaction as symbiotic, it instructs the arms to deliver the fern to the young rice shoots; if parasitic, the arms withhold the nitrogen-rich delivery. In creating an integrated biological, electro-robotic, and computing process, this work generates technologically mediated relationships between species.

EXPLORING THE INVISIBLE

Bioluminescence illuminates the everyday.

Glass, bacteria (Photobacterium phosphoreum), petri dishes, discarded glassware, china cups, camera equipment, film.

Anne Brodie (British)—School of Biomedical Science, University of Surrey, UK / Artakt, Central Saint Martins College of Arts and Design, London, UK; funded by the Wellcome Trust, UK

COMPLETED

This project was conceived and executed by the artist in collaboration with microbiologist Simon Park and curator Caterina Albano in an effort to explore the light-producing properties of bioluminescent bacteria outside the usual confines of scientific practice. Among the outcomes of **Exploring the Invisible**, which spanned several months, was a one-night exhibit of glass objects and a two-day participatory photo booth project.

The brief installation in the Herb Garrett in London questioned the role of certain items in our daily lives. A range of old glassware and vases that had been filled with nutrient agar inoculated with *Photobacterium phosphoreum* were put on display. The bacteria live for around 36 hours, glowing for a brief period during that time and highlighting the impermanence of use of the items. Unsuited for experiments, the microorganisms, along with with the recently orphaned objects, magnify the precariousness of fashion and habits.

The bioluminescent photograph booth was on show at the British Science Festival in London. Packed with hundreds of glowing petri dishes, it engaged children and adults by day, but in the evening it was used to photograph the natural biological light's reflection on nine volunteers. The images, which were first displayed within the booth in the Old Operating Theatre, restaged the long exposure of the camera lens in the improbable and, at times, disquieting bioluminescence, which gradually faded as the bacteria died.

ABOVE / OPPOSITE   414, 415

Nine volunteers posed in a photo booth while being illuminated by hundreds of petri dishes glowing with naturally bioluminescent bacteria.

ABOVE   416

A collection of used glassware and vases that
was purchased at yard sales and charity shops,
filled with bioluminescent bacteria and a nutrient
medium, and put on display for one evening.

ABOVE / BELOW   417, 418

The portraits taken with reflected biological
light were first displayed in the Old Operating
Theatre in London, which is where surgical
demonstrations were given in the 19th century.

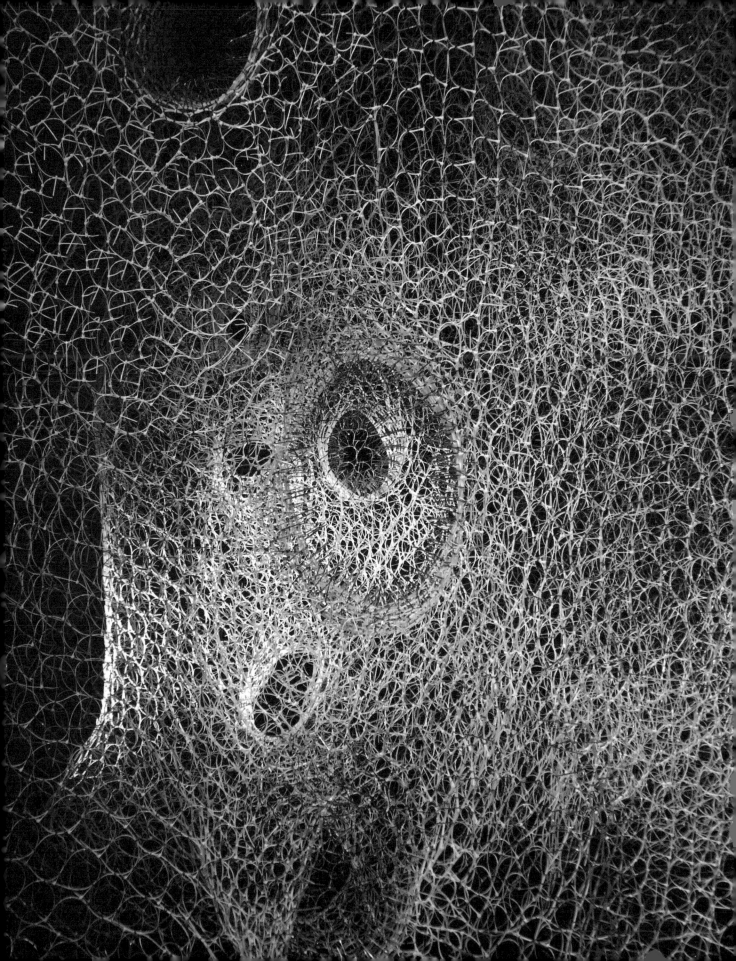

Delft, The Netherlands

OPPOSITE   419

'Branching Morphogenesis' (2009) by
Sabin+Jones LabStudio (page 249). A 'datascape'
of magnified, interacting lung endothelial cells
constructed from over 75,000 cable zip ties.

PROFILING PROGRAMS AND COLLABORATIONS

The many types of biodesign chronicled here, including new ecologically enhanced design, speculative narratives, and experimental works of art, have emerged in recent years, thanks in large part to cooperation between designers, artists and scientists. These exchanges take many forms, from lab projects in a university setting to curated designer–scientist pairings to investigate the potential of new research for product applications. Such collaborations generate benefits to all participants and echo the close ties that science and design once enjoyed in the 17th century, when founding members of the Royal Society in London, such as Robert Hooke, were both practicing architects and leading scientists. For researchers in the sciences today, gains include new tools to visualize and better understand underlying patterns in vast quantities of data, access to rapid prototyping technology to test the efficacy of experimental equipment, and guidance in workspace design (improving both the layout and the material usage in the lab). Working with designers can also come as a welcome respite from the pressures of the contemporary lab, where there is little time for undirected 'thinkering'—brainstorming in three dimensions—a pastime that designers gravitate toward. On the other side, enormous benefits are accumulating for designers and architects, from the availability of new computational algorithms that replicate natural growth patterns, to access to the lux operon, which can be isolated and reinserted into organisms to generate bioluminescence.

There are numerous ways to choreograph this beneficial sharing, which is also referred to as consilience, or reaching across disciplines to collaborate so as to achieve mutual goals. The most common type now is guided by academic institutions, but that is changing, as knowledge is shared ever more quickly and outside of university or corporate laboratories. Social media are amplifying this trend, allowing the like-mindedly curious to find one another and initiate worthy projects. This accelerated cross-pollination is an essential ingredient in fueling innovations that might address the climate crisis or reverse biodiversity loss. It is also a boon to artists who seek to create new aesthetic experiences through engagement with the life sciences and in the effort to translate an evolving conception of beauty into form. By the same token, the collaborations will continue

to produce difficult and often uncomfortable, but ultimately healthy, questions about the implications of new technologies and their effect on human behaviors.

As designers, scientists, and the art community work together more frequently and creatively, challenges will certainly arise along with opportunities and innovations. A study published in 2011 by researchers at the University of Cambridge examined such collaborations and found that obstacles, such as misaligned expectations about how to share intellectual property rights, a lack of common vocabulary, and conflicting working styles and standards, often arise. Clearly, participants in a team are destined for tension and difficulty in achieving their goals if they disagree over the ownership of their creations, don't know how to communicate effectively about their subject matter, and assume vastly different timeframes and standards of rigor for product development, review, and testing. The language issue is particularly problematic, as many participants profiled in this book have noted, largely because each discipline develops nuanced meaning behind many words that can seem impenetrable even to well-intentioned collaborators.

It should be clear that no single solution, breakthrough in technology, or miraculous legislation would be sufficient to 'solve' these issues or universally incentivize innovations that improve lives and spawn wondrous, thought-provoking art while undoing climate change and wasteful design practices. However, the obvious dedication and intelligence of participants in several programs profiled here

LEFT 420

The iGEM (International Genetically Engineered Machine) Competition is hosted each year at the Massachusetts Institute of Technology and involves participants from more than 130 teams worldwide.

BELOW 421

Genspace is a community laboratory dedicated to promoting citizen science and access to biotechnology. The biosafety level one facility is based in Brooklyn, New York, and offers hands-on courses to members of the public.

ABOVE 422

Artist/designer Tuur Van Balen constructs thought-provoking scenarios, as in his project 'Pigeon d'Or,' (page 159) where the ubiquitous bird is conscripted as an urban cleaning apparatus with the assistance of synthetic biology.

provide cause for optimism. They may not present a definitive model for the future but they do exhibit strategies to create productive partnerships.

One leader in facilitating biodesign in many forms is **Delft University of Technology** in the Netherlands. Research there, particularly in the School of Civil Engineering and Geosciences, explores how the built and natural environments interact, with a growing focus on sustainable approaches to design and the integration of natural processes into functional structures. The Dutch are well situated geographically to develop such techniques: much of their country lies below sea level, so inhabitable land must be claimed and continually protected from the sea, a feat that takes no small amount of observation and planning. The urgency to develop viable approaches that curb the output of greenhouse gases follows the logic that as the climate changes and sea levels rise, the Netherlands is at risk of catastrophic damage.

At Delft, researchers harness biology for applications such as microbially grown raw materials for plastics, developing self-healing materials and maximizing the benefits of plant growth on building façades. The school offers a variety of programs that attract students of biology, engineering, civil engineering, architecture, math, and other areas that, together, lend themselves to collaboration to develop technologies for better ecological performance.

Marc Ottelé is one such researcher who is focused on understanding and quantifying the particular benefits of plant coverage of different elements of architecture, from walls beside a road to building façades and roofs. His research examines the rate of particle absorption by vegetation under different conditions, with an eye toward optimizing the absorption of those microparticles that are potentially most harmful to humans. In the course of his research, he has formed natural collaborations with faculty and students from the architecture school. One future possible application of such research is the identification of architectural forms to support dense and human health-supporting foliage.

Robbert Kleerebezem, a faculty member in the Environmental Biotechnology Group at Delft, has examined material technology that could have broad implications for industrial designers and lead to replacements for petroleum-based plastics. In contrast to a genetic engineering or synthetic biology approach, he practices microbial community engineering—the process of applying extreme environmental pressures (heat, withholding nutrients) to select for microorganisms that have particular properties, such as the tendency to efficiently store large quantities of polymers that might later be harvested to make plastic. Considering some of the significant safety concerns and training requirements of other approaches, this is a relatively low-tech and effective way to produce microbial strains that are highly specialized for industrial uses. Microorganisms tend to be inexpensive, fecund, and extremely adaptable, so guiding their development rather than recreating them is increasingly appealing.

Also at Delft, Henk Jonkers ('BioConcrete,' page 80) has been involved in a number of biodesign projects, including a retrofit solution for existing concrete that needs repair, coating underwater pilings with a biofilm that might replace toxic, synthetic paints, and alternatives to cement-making that might replace the process of burning limestone to produce calcium oxide. He also supports the work of his colleague, Leon van Passen, who is studying means of harnessing microbial cementation to solidify soil in an attempt to support roads and other structures and combat soil liquefication. He has called this application 'BioGrout.'

These brief sketches provide only a glimpse of some of the activities and focuses of the programs at the university, which hosts more than 16,000 students from around the world.

In contrast to the formal university structure, a small team of architecture practitioners and academics, biologists, urban planners, and artists are have created a new type of educational lab-studio in New York City that utilizes materials that are unconventional in design: biological matter, including live tissue, bacteria, trees, and fungi. **The One Lab School for Urban Ecology**, organized in 2009 by architect Maria Aiolova, is based in the collaborative Metropolitan Exchange (MEx) Building in Brooklyn and offers workshops on synthetic biology, biomimetic urban planning, parametric scripting, and the use of organisms to grow structures. This cooperative, a burgeoning bio-Bauhaus of sorts, intends to unify several approaches and goals, leveraging expertise from staff at several organizations focused on education and ecology, including Terreform ONE, Genspace, the MIT Media Lab, Columbia University, and the Yale School of Forestry. Although early in its development, its innovative program fosters collaborations between design and the life sciences, and it promises to incubate the type of unorthodox approaches urgently needed in the age of climate crisis and natural resource scarcity. The program also offers a new entry point for non-specialists to contribute to scientific research and experiment with ecological design strategies, as it creates opportunities for design practice to expand into previously uncharted territory.

In the 'Soft Infrastructure' workshop, students are challenged to invent artificial, built infrastructures that maintain positive properties of natural ecologies, including their resilience and complexity. This approach calls for more porous boundaries between built and natural states, such as subterranean wetlands in urban settings to absorb storm water. Students are also introduced to methods for measuring the performance of such systems with the goal of maximizing their ecological performance.

In the 'Synthetic Biology' workshop, students are introduced to contemporary technology that utilizes DNA code to create specialized genetic 'circuits' that can be inserted into host organisms, such as bacteria, and perform specific functions. Learning exercises range from using restriction enzymes, and gel electrophoresis, through

ABOVE   423

Combining living matter with infrastructure is one approach to achieving new levels of ecological performance, as in 'BioConcrete.' Researchers at Delft University of Technology in the Netherlands are at the forefront of important developments.

ABOVE   424, 425, 426

The interdisciplinary format of One Lab helps to encourages biologically integrated design and urban planning, ranging from mushroom-based materials for use in construction through to living, bioluminescent lighting for public spaces.

separating, cutting and pasting genetic sequences, to proposing new types of living machines as potential design and fabrication tools.

A workshop entitled 'Mycoform to Mycotecture' explores the potential benefits of a convergence between design and mycology, the branch of biology that examines the properties and behavior of fungi. Investigations have revealed the ability of mycelia (the vegetative part of fungi) to filter water, remove toxins from soil, provide a viable food source, and even become a material for industrial and building applications. Students consider how these natural processes can be integrated with architecture and urban design, and what opportunities this material presents to enhance ecological performance.

The 'Fab Tree Hab' (page 58) workshop presents students with a promising and critical typology: the house that can be grown to bypass the negative environmental impacts of conventional construction. The workshop teaches a technique for growing housing using native trees and utilizing ancient botanical practices, such as pleaching, grafting, and propagation. Together, these methods are used to train a living structure into shape around prefabricated, computer numeric controlled (CNC) reusable scaffolding. The resulting structures are dynamically integrated into the surrounding environment and offer a foothold to several species, helping to encourage local biodiversity.

In these and other workshops, the One Lab is becoming an important center for exchange and learning between design and the life sciences (processes crucial in transforming design practices). As architecture and design curricula around the world slowly change to address new pressures to improve ecological performance, they will undoubtedly look to this pioneering program—which has taken an early lead in 21st-century education.

Also in the area of architectural practice, **the Center for Architecture Science and Ecology (CASE)** brings together students, practicing architects, and scientists in a collaboration between Skidmore Owings and Merrill and the Architecture School of Rensselaer Polytechnic Institute in New York City to explore and develop emerging building technologies. A core focus of the research pursued at CASE is to push the boundaries of environmental performance in urban building systems. As the research is co-organized by a global architecture firm, new technologies are tested in actual building projects in cities around the world.

CASE research is well positioned to improve the impact of design: the US building sector accounts for approximately a third of the nation's entire energy consumption and nearly half of all carbon emissions. Though large-scale practices in construction and building engineering may be notoriously slow to change, there is little doubt that dramatic change is what is needed. For this reason, far-reaching technologies like those developed at the center have become all the more attractive. CASE aims to implement change in three priority areas: energy consumption, sustainable resource management,

and quality of access to essential elements, such as clean air and water, daylight, and plant and animal life.

The center also co-hosts and is closely integrated with the masters and doctorate programs in architectural sciences with a concentration in built ecologies at Rensselear. Students in these programs work on a variety of projects, from building-integrated solar façade systems through methods of harnessing agricultural wastes to fashioning desiccant building materials that dry interior air in tropical climates. Research is guided by a team of practitioners and academics, and is funded by the US Department of Energy and the National Science Foundation, among others.

Projects under way at CASE are largely a response to antiquated conventions in architecture and planning that are based in the narrow view of structure

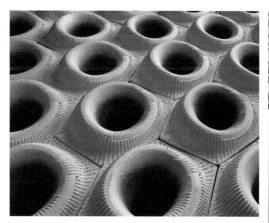

as a self-contained entity. As the built ecologies program suggests, 'the built world can and should operate synergistically within larger ecologies' and, as the built environment represents such a large portion of humanity's ecological footprint, the development and deployment of transformative technologies is an important focus for architecture in the 21st century.

In an effort to look more closely at, and better understand, architectural environments, the University of Oregon's **Biology and the Built Environment (BioBE) Center** was launched in 2010 to investigate built spaces as complex microbial ecosystems influencing and influenced by human life. Microorganisms are constantly introduced into buildings through windows, ventilation systems, and unwitting human and animal carriers. The survival and propagation of these microorganisms depends upon a variety of factors, but their effect on human well-being is undeniable. People living in the developed world spend the vast majority of their lives indoors, unknowingly interacting with trillions of helpful, neutral, and harmful microorganisms. In spite of the significance of these airborne communities, little research until now has focused on them: the built environment microbiome.

BioBE Center Director Jessica Green has said, 'If we are going to continue using energy-intensive design approaches such as mechanical ventilation

Close-up image of mycelia, the vegetative parts of a fungi, which can be hardened into rigid forms and are potentially usable as building components. Students at One Lab examine the properties of such natural alternatives.

LEFT / ABOVE   428, 429, 430

The Center for Architecture Science and Ecology hosts the research and development of new building technologies and materials, from enhanced ceramics and agricultural by-products to building-integrated photovoltaics.

The BioBE center examines the built environment microbiome—trillions of organisms that we interact with every day in our homes, schools, and workplaces. Populations of these bacteria, fungi, and other microorganisms can affect our health and may, in time, be managed by deliberate architectural design decisions.

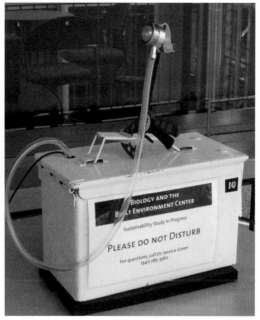

systems, we need to understand how these systems affect the ecology and evolution of microbes indoors, and ultimately our health.' The center's evidence-based investigations are directed toward developing architectural design that will work with the microbial environment to promote human health and environmental sustainability. The core of the research uses next-generation DNA sequencing technology to identify site-specific microbial flora or, if you like, the invisible terroir of architectural spaces. For an investigation of the hospital environment, researchers compared the diversity and composition of microbial communities across two ventilation treatments: a hospital heating, ventilation, and air-conditioning system and window-supplied air from outside. They

At Sabin+Jones LabStudio, participants from several fields, including biomedical science and architecture, work together to research cell surface design, networking behavior, and motility. A focus is sharing digital tools and knowledge across disciplines.

found significant differences in airborne microbial diversity across three sample sites. Mechanical ventilation eliminated many types of microorganism, as its filtration and treatment systems are intended to do, but those that it did not eliminate were much more likely to be harmful and pathogenic.

The current dominant design for hospital ventilation separates the outdoors from the indoors via a sophisticated system of filtering, heating, and air-conditioning. This air system contributes

to the vast energy usage of the healthcare field, the second most energy-intensive industry in the United States. The BioBE Center concluded that increased use of natural air in hospitals might not only promote a healthy microbial diversity and minimize the spread of infectious diseases but also reduce energy consumption. The implications of this research extend far beyond the medical environment. Just as many people consume probiotic yogurt to promote healthy gut flora, we may one day create and inhabit microbially healthy buildings. But in order to progress to this stage of sophisticated environmental control, much more research is required.

The center continues to explore methods of dispersing microorganisms—from ventilation to human occupancy and activity—that significantly influence the built environment microbiome. The researchers also hope to investigate what attributes of the built environment, including building materials, interior temperature, geography, and building use, shape microbial community composition. Applying such information could revolutionize our expectations and experiences of architecture.

In an example of distinctly fluid and mutual exchange, architect Jenny E. Sabin and Professor of Pathology and Laboratory Medicine Peter Lloyd Jones initiated the **Sabin+Jones LabStudio** in 2007 as a hybrid research and design unit based at the University of Pennsylvania. Participants hail from several fields, including mathematics, materials science, cell biology, and architecture. Some of the lab's research has so far focused on ways to leverage the advanced visualization and modeling tools of design to enhance observation and data analysis in biomedical science. Benefits are being generated in both directions—the designers are also discovering, for example, how cell behavior may have implications for optimizing structures for adaptability. To instigate this sharing, LabStudio paired postdoctoral and graduate students from the Institute for Medicine & Engineering with a counterpart from the School of Design, assigning each team a different research brief: cell surface design, cell networking behavior, or cell motility.

Sabin explains: 'The advantage of formulating these scientist–architect pairings was that experiments could be redesigned based on the architect's objective observations, intuition, and requests—and new tools could be developed based on the scientist's specific hypothesis.' One participant, Erica Savig from the School of Design, observed smooth vascular muscle cells under a microscope for months, taking countless photos and importing them into three-dimensional modeling software called Rhino, a tool commonly used in industrial design. This lab work, documenting cell behavioral changes over time and under different environmental conditions, has implications for advancing the treatment of lung diseases. It also introduced architecture students to dynamic biological systems that manage heat, light, energy, and material and nutrient exchanges.

The idea to launch the lab was sparked when Jones attended a conference held by the Nonlinear

Systems Organization, a research group at the Penn School of Design. The event included presentations by architects and engineers involving computational design and parametric scripting. Jones was astonished by the participants' sophisticated modeling and visualization tools, recognizing immediately their potential to enhance his biomedical research. After several discussions about how to form a fruitful multidisciplinary collaboration between Jones and Jenny Sabin, who taught graduate students at the School of Design, plans for the lab were formed and Sabin became the first non-scientist member of the Institute for Medicine and Engineering. Thus far, she and Jones have co-authored publications aimed at illuminating the inner logic of cellular systems, for the benefit of both architecture and biomedical science.

In contrast to internal institutional programs, the **International Genetically Engineered Machine (iGEM) Competition** is a worldwide synthetic biology contest aimed at undergraduate students that is organized and hosted by the Massachusetts Institute of Technology (MIT). Participating student teams are provided with a kit of components from the Registry of Standard Biological Parts at the beginning of each summer, which they are encouraged to contribute to in the course of their project. Working under the direction of advisors from their schools, they combine these standardized parts, called BioBricks (DNA sequences of defined structure and function), in novel ways to create a new practical application that they must present for evaluation. Winning projects often produce cells that exhibit unusual and useful properties, cleverly combining genes along with mechanisms to control their expression, usually in a simple microbial 'chassis' like *Escherichia coli*.

Examples of winning entries include a system to control the spatial and temporal activity of bacterial cultures with the potential application of organizing them in a 'division of labor,' an application to utilize custom bacteria to promote plant growth and combat soil erosion, and a bacterial vaccine for ulcers. More fanciful projects have been proposed, including a scheme to build extremophile bacterial strains that would terraform Mars in several phases, and a design for a new strain of baker's yeast called VitaYeast that would imbue breads with essential vitamins.

The annual iGEM competition has grown rapidly since its inception, from 13 teams in 2005 to 112 teams in 2009 and 160 teams with more than 2,000 participants in 2011. There are now so many participants that the undergraduate competition occurs in stages, with regional jamborees being held in Europe, Asia, and the Americas before the final presentations and judgment at MIT. The competition is also expanding to be more inclusive, allowing high-school students and non-student entrepreneurs to participate. It is simultaneously becoming more common for students of biomedical science, engineering, and design to participate in teams that once comprised only biology students.

The implication of iGEM for design is that microorganisms will become flexible platforms on

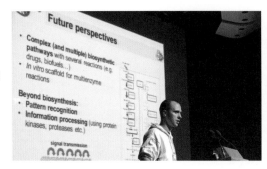

which designers can fashion custom, living machines. Presuming the BioBrick library continues to grow and that techniques for combining and inserting genes continue to be simplified, synthetic biology is on its way to systematization, and will be available through an interface something like Autodesk (computer-aided design software for architects and engineers). This represents two dramatic leaps at once in terms of manipulating matter: in scale, from the micrometer to the nanometer—a jump of three orders of magnitude; and from mechanical to biological. If history is any indication, these changes may enable a second industrial revolution, wherein the products, such as objects and structures, are made up of designed, living organisms. The most important aspect of iGEM foreshadowing these changes is that it is inclusive and open source, creating an inviting safe space for

discovery and speculation, and inspiring others to learn more about the emerging field of synthetic biology.

Also focused on inclusive education and fostering innovation is **Genspace**, a non-profit launched in 2009 that is dedicated to promoting citizen science and access to safe biotechnology. Its activities are focused on the greater New York City area, providing educational outreach, cultural events, classes, and facilities for scientific innovation at the grassroots level. Its lab space is located in the MEx Building, a converted bank in downtown Brooklyn that is currently shared by a collective of organizations focused on education, biotechnology, urban planning, and ecological design. The Genspace lab is a biosafety level one facility, fitted with basic equipment for a variety of experiments with microorganisms, such as common yeast and non-pathogenic bacteria, and safety gear, including gloves, goggles, and ventilation.

Genspace offers classes to the public on the basics of biotechnology, walking students through

ABOVE / LEFT   437, 438, 439

iGEM now includes both high-school and postgraduate participants.

ABOVE / LEFT   440, 441, 442

A Brooklyn-based community lab, Genspace is the first of its kind. Participants include artists, teachers, architects, writers, and entrepreneurs. Community outreach serves to augment science instruction in local public schools and helps build excitement around engagement in lab activities.

ABOVE   443, 444, 445, 446

Students on the Royal College of Arts' Design Interactions course examine the applications and implications of emerging technologies, from the digital to the biological. Research projects take on a range of forms, from creating objects and stories to staging performances.

activities that include isolating and sequencing segments of DNA, and cutting and pasting them using enzymes. It also offers a synthetic biology course that introduces the emerging science of engineering organisms as biological machines. Students perform techniques to alter the functions of microorganisms so that they express colors, emit smells, produce light, and even act as biosensors to detect pollution or pathogens. As well as serving university students and recent graduates, Genspace has become a resource for the business community, with participants from the finance and business sectors, and entrepreneurs who have followed biotech for years and want to understand it in a hands-on way.

Genspace's activities also help to meet the needs of local, underserved communities that have schools with limited science funding. The organization partners with local programs, such as the Urban Barcoding Project, to provide extramural learning opportunities for New York school children at the K-12 level. For older students, it hosts local undergraduates who are competing in synthetic biology competitions, and it has participated in events that include the P.S. 29 Health Fair, Family Science Data at the AAAS International Exhibition, and the Maker Faire.

The founding members of Genspace first met through the do-it-yourself biology (DIY bio) community, a growing network of amateur biologists around the world who meet regularly to collaborate and perform experiments. These groups, like Genspace, find ways to duplicate at home the techniques once used exclusively by government laboratories and large corporations, often in much less expensive ways. DIY bio projects have included coordinating the collection of microbial samples across several cities by swabbing public objects, creating a map showing the distribution of particular microorganisms, and designing a three-dimensionally printed adaptor that can be attached to a Dremel tool to create a centrifuge capable of performing at the standard of professional lab equipment. The ethos common among the loose confederacy of DIY bio groups as well as Genspace is that of the tinkerer or hacker—the pioneer who will take risks and has the confidence to take something apart and try to reassemble it in a more useful or interesting way.

Moving closer to speculative narratives and aesthetic experience, the **Royal College of Art Design Interactions Department** facilitates cross-pollination among disciplines in its broad approach to exploring the social, cultural, and ethical impact of emerging technologies. The program takes the stance that as devices of every kind proliferate and increasingly pervade our lives, there is a growing need for products and systems that are approachable and enjoyable, as well as useful.

Students often develop projects that focus on the expressive and communicative possibilities of digital technology. There is also a growing interest, however, in design that is speculative and critical, aiming to inspire debate about the consequences of different technological futures. A popular topic

is the potential application of biotechnology and nanotechnology, fields that the program's directors Anthony Dunne and Fiona Raby see as moving rapidly from the laboratory to everyday life. Dunne and Raby encourage this development by urging students with science backgrounds to enroll and by offering courses that introduce fields like synthetic biology. Above all, the program stresses the centrality of people, the intended beneficiaries of new interfaces and research breakthroughs, but whose needs sometimes appear to be absent from consideration. Skepticism toward innovation driven by corporate agendas is encouraged. Illustrating a rich duality, the program both fosters a critical point of view of the history of design within industrialized capitalism while simultaneously choreographing collaborations between students and companies such as Intel, Microsoft Research Labs, Philips Design, and Vodafone.

Students in the program are challenged to consider both the implications and the applications of the technologies they research and have been increasingly represented in design exhibitions

ABOVE   447, 448

The Synthetic Aesthetics program, sponsored by the National Science Foundation, brought together teams of scientists and designers to explore the potential of synthetic biology. Projects ranged from an examination of microbial communities and smell to experiments in using bacteria as a medium to cast industrial objects.

around the world, including the Museum of Modern Art in New York. Graduates have also pursued further academic study at the PhD level, joined industry, and launched their own studios, consultancies, and research initiatives.

Among the recent graduates from the Design Interactions Program is artist, designer, and writer Alexandra Daisy Ginsberg. Since 2011 she has worked closely with the University of Edinburgh and Stanford University with funding from the National Science Foundation to coordinate the **Synthetic Aesthetics** program as a design fellow. The program brings together six scientist-designer teams from around the world to explore 'designing, understanding, and building the living world' in the context of recent developments in the sciences, particularly synthetic biology. Each team has developed a research goal based on shared interests and points of connection between issues in participants' respective fields, from biochemistry, molecular biology, and botany to bioart, scent design, architecture, and music. The residents visited one another's working environments over the course of several weeks, and have reported and presented their respective projects through blogs and conferences.

Within one of the teams, architect David Benjamin and postdoctoral researcher Fernan

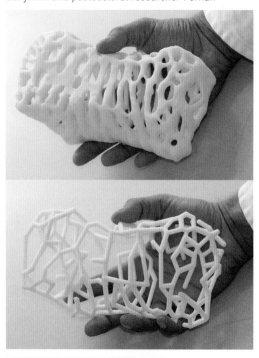

In the Synthetic Aesthetics program, David Benjamin and Fernan Federici sought to apply the optimization behavior of plant cells at the scale of architecture.

Federici have embarked on finding new ways of using biological systems as design tools. In contrast with digital fabrication and computer numerical controlled

milling machines with a fixed and predetermined physical output, they are investigating multiple ways to fabricate synthetic composites by generating novel morphogenetic mechanisms in bacteria and plants.

An outcome of this work has been the creation of prototype software that extracts the complex behavior of xylem cells at the scale of micrometers and applies it to architectural optimization problems at the scale of meters (see 'Bio-processing,' page 83).

In another collaboration curated by Synthetic Aesthetics, designer Will Carey worked with the Lim Lab at the University of California, San Francisco, to develop concepts for customized crop seeds and bacteria-grown consumer goods. The work on plants involves creating a system of sensors to measure the particular conditions of a given plot of land, including rainfall, average temperature, soil pH, and nutrient content. If these conditions are known, it may be possible to customize seeds to thrive in them, effectively mimicking the process of evolution but at a fantastically accelerated rate. The team's idea for growing consumer goods involves the manipulation of bacteria, building on previous, successful genetic alterations that can make microorganisms responsive to light. As the team visualized it, bacteria may be prompted by stimuli (light) to form a hard shell, allowing for a kind of low-temperature kiln firing, creating a form with cellulose, the substance of cell walls, or chitin, the stuff of insect exoskeletons, instead of clay.

The Synthetic Aesthetics program takes the position that, in time, synthetic biology will be critically important to numerous disciplines, from art and industrial design to urban planning, and that cooperation between fields of study is essential to enable inclusive and responsive technology development. The project foreshadows the type of cooperation and cross-disciplinary projects that synthetic biology will invite in the near future as it develops new methods for designing life.

In an illustration of how engagement of science by the arts has yielded effective collaborations, **SymbioticA, Centre of Excellence in Biological Arts at the University of Western Australia**, was established in 2000 by pioneers Oron Catts and Ionat Zurr. Located within the School of Anatomy and Human Biology at the university, it is the first hybrid research-studio laboratory of its kind, enabling artists to participate in wet biology practices in an environment dedicated to the 'learning and critique of the life sciences.'

SymbioticA provides artists with the opportunity to consult experts within a university setting.

SymbioticA also invites artists to engage in both exploration and critique of the life sciences by providing safe wet-lab environments.

In this experimental, interdisciplinary setting, researchers are encouraged to pursue curiosity-based explorations unconstrained by the demands and conventions associated with formal scientific research, such as the focus on publishing and raising funds, but while still complying with regulations.

To date, more than 70 residents have developed projects in the program's labs, actively using the tools and technologies of science, not just commenting on their meaning or form. With the support of the university, the program has grown to include core research projects, residencies, academic courses, exhibitions, workshops, and conferences. In 2006, SymbioticA launched its own postgraduate program, offering a masters in biological art. In 2007 the program received the inaugural Golden Nica in Hybrid Arts at Prix Ars Electronica, and in 2008 the Department of Culture and the Arts of the West Australian Government provided three years' funding that transformed SymbioticA into a Research Centre of Excellence in Biological Arts.

Projects pursued at SymbioticA adopt a range of approaches and objectives, with many responding to rapidly advancing fields of applied research, such as molecular biology, regenerative medicine, synthetic biology, and neuroscience. All of these have an intimate and increasing impact on our everyday lives, but few have yet inspired a thoughtful or thought-provoking cultural response. SymbioticA provides training to help create the vocabulary to formulate such responses, and to introduce scientific concepts that are too often misunderstood outside of small groups of siloed, specialized researchers.

In 2011, the Science Gallery in Dublin hosted the exhibition VISCERAL, curated by Oron Catts and Ionat Zurr and featuring the work of fifteen artists from the first 10 years of research and residencies at SymbioticA. It covered artistic research projects that ranged from working with the elements of the living body (molecules, cells, tissues) through full bodies to ecological systems. All of the works were conceived and developed by artists who spent a significant amount of time in SymbioticA's labs, and went a long way toward introducing the concept of artistic engagement with life to a broad audience.

The Arts Catalyst also supports creativity in this area, commissioning artists' work that experimentally and critically engages with the sciences. Over the last 17 years the London-based interdisciplinary arts organization has publicly presented more than 90 artists' projects in partnership with arts and cultural venues in the UK and around the world. It also organizes symposia and critical debates, artists residencies, and participatory and education projects examining the interrelationships between art, science, and society.

Participating artists work in a range of media, from performance and sculpture to video, music, and living animals or tissues. Often their work is curated into themes, and presented and discussed through events, such as Specimens to Superhumans, which explored how biomedical science, disability, human enhancement, and ethics are represented and critiqued in contemporary art. In another representative program, the exhibition Interspecies brought together works that involve collaboration between artists and animals, touching on questions about the one-sided, manipulative nature of these relationships and how artists have attempted to understand an animal's point of view as a part of their practice. Yet another program, Synthesis: Synthetic Biology in Art and Society, took form as a series of public events and a week-long interdisciplinary exchange lab bringing together scientists, artists, and designers to consider the artistic and wider cultural implications of synthetic biology.

Arts Catalyst encourages artists to take risks and to be provocative and playful with their work so as to produce dynamic conversations about our changing world. Given that the only constant in scientific advancement appears to be its accelerating pace, artists are challenged to synthesize the meaning of new discoveries and to comment on it in their work. Culture may be in continual flux, but the exponential growth in spending on science and research development over time, coupled with the pace of communication and emergence of new media, make it risky for artists to invest time developing a work that might be quickly outdated. Arts Catalyst thus helps to support thought-provoking artwork and programs of the moment to promote public participation and understanding.

The organization partners with a number of groups at University College London, including the departments of Science and Technology Studies, Geography and Chemistry, the Cancer Institute, the Centre for Advanced Biomedical Imaging, the Mullard Space Science Laboratory, and Slade School of Art. Commissioned artists who have taken an intense interest in biology through their works include Andy Gracie, Nicholas Primat, Anne Brodie, and Aaron Williamson.

This surge of cooperation across fields is a promising development and will have consequences for years to come. It provokes difficult questions and poses dangers to be sure, but it is also clearly the path of evolution for biology, design, engineering, and numerous other fields. As living matter becomes a raw material widely adopted and favored above others for its ecological performance or aesthetic value, our very notion of what constitutes life is thrown into flux. What will it mean to be surrounded by hybrid, semi-living objects and structures? What rights and responsibilities will designers have toward such life? And how might such developments alter how we see ourselves? We will also soon be forced to contend with the meaning of widely available cyborg technologies, such as immersive augmented reality overlays on contact lenses and synthetically enhanced internal organs. We are surely at the brink of momentous change in this century of biology and must anticipate that both beauties and horrors will emerge from our pursuits, as they have in every age, thanks to our restless, intrepid curiosity, articulated so well by Mary Shelly in *Frankenstein; or, The Modern Prometheus* in 1818: 'the moon gazed on my midnight labours, while, with unrelaxed and breathless eagerness, I pursued nature to her hiding-places.'

ABOVE   454, 455

The Arts Catalyst has presented more than ninety artists' projects, many of which are provocative and risk-taking, for the sake of promoting public understanding and debate.

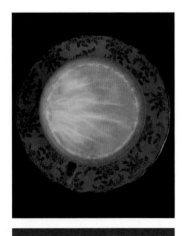

ABOVE   456

Detail of Anne Brodie's work 'Exploring the Invisible' (page 240), showing vases and glassware filled with bioluminescent bacteria and nutrients.

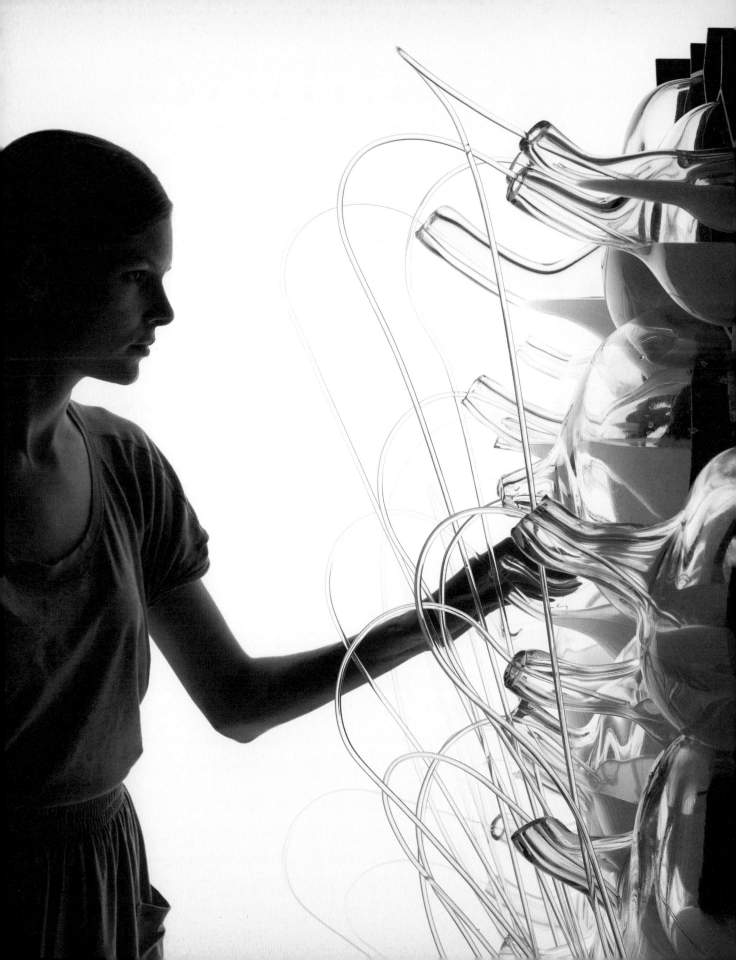

INTERVIEWS

DAVID BENJAMIN

Adjunct Assistant Professor of Architecture at Columbia University

WM: What are the sources of your interest in linking science and architecture?

DB: I've found that collaboration across disciplines is helpful to break out of old patterns of thinking. It turns out that most innovation comes from someone outside the direct field of research. As an undergraduate at Harvard, I majored in social studies, which was an interdisciplinary program. Then I worked at a start-up software company alongside designers, engineers, computer scientists, and 'human factors' experts. By the time I started studying architecture, I already considered it to be a perfect field for interdisciplinary and collaborative projects. My interest in science, and particularly in synthetic biology, is a natural extension of The Living, an architecture firm that I started with my friend and collaborator Soo-in Yang. Our firm explores various ways to bring architecture to life, and recent developments in biology may allow this to become literal.

If the 20th century was the century of physics, then the 21st century is widely seen to be the century of biology. Biology already leads the sciences in terms of budgets, workforce, and innovation. Genetic modification accounts for 2 percent of GDP in the US, and it is growing quickly—for comparison, construction accounts for 4 percent of GDP.

So as an experimental architect interested in new ideas and innovations, I have been studying synthetic biology for several years. Recently I started a collaborative research initiative at Columbia Graduate School of Architecture Planning and Preservation (GSAPP) that involves the intersection of architecture, synthetic biology, and computer science. I have been teaching design workshops at Columbia about these topics, and also, as part of the Synthetic Aesthetics program—an international, National Science Foundation-funded residency that has selected six pairs of scientist–designer collaborators—I am working on applied research with plant biologist Fernan Federici and the Jim Haseloff Lab at the University of Cambridge, UK.

WM: Do you foresee architecture students being required to study biology or synthetic biology in the near future? If so, to what do you attribute this development?

DB: Synthetic biology is a new approach to engineering based on manipulating DNA and establishing a database of standardized biological parts. The biological parts can be assembled in different ways for different applications—similar to how electrical parts, like transistors and capacitors, can be assembled in different ways to create different electrical circuits. This kind of framework is called an abstraction hierarchy, and it is very powerful because it should allow some people to design biological parts while other people design biological devices and systems.

The vision is that some day soon, architects—and other non-specialists—will be able to design new biological devices and systems without needing to understand the detailed molecular behavior of the biological parts.

In addition, biological technologies have been advancing at an incredible speed. It's already possible to buy a desktop DNA printer, which basically allows you to compose a computer file with a sequence of bases—a sequence of the A, C, T, and G of genetic code—and then three-dimensionally print the biological part right in your own studio. This is biological fabrication as an extension of digital fabrication. And these advances are already leading to garage biology, which may trigger an explosion in innovation similar to what happened with garage computing. We may be at a transformative moment similar to the moment in the seventies when Apple Computers started in a garage in Silicon Valley. So I think it's exciting and also probably inevitable for architects to learn about synthetic biology and add these technologies to their palette of design tools.

WM: You recently taught a graduate architecture class in which students proposed ways to harness synthetic biology in designs. Can you describe a few of these student projects?

DB: The students on this course had no prior experience with synthetic biology, but they came up with some amazing applications. One student started with new technology for turning protocells into tiny, self-replicating computers. He designed a hypothetical system for inserting data into cells and then extracting it later. The 0s and 1s of digital code became the A, T, C, and G of DNA code. The division of cells became simple logic gates. The student then imagined how this new bio-computation might lead to rivers and lakes

DAVID BENJAMIN   458

David teaches at Columbia University's GSAPP and is co-founder of The Living, an architecture firm dedicated to creating architecture that is both interactive with and responsive to environmental conditions. His innovative work includes 'Living Light,' a permanent, illuminated pavilion in Seoul that visually reports changes in air quality, and 'Amphibious Architecture,' a floating installation in New York's East River that enabled participants to communicate with fish and learn about water pollution.

that are essentially hard drives—or 'wet drives'—for storing massive amounts of redundant, encrypted data.

Another student started with new genetically engineered yeast and microalgae that convert sugar and sunlight into fuel, without drilling or non-renewable hydrocarbons. By using synthetic biology to redesign the functionality of these cells, the new systems generate around 80 percent less carbon than existing fuels. So the student designed an incredible new fuel cycle, working on vastly different scales at the same time, from DNA with a radius of about a billionth of a meter, to the earth with a circumference of 40 million meters—that's 16 powers of ten in a single design project! The student imagined new desktop devices, new vehicles, new factories and buildings, new agricultural landscapes, and new natural and synthetic ecosystems.

WM: You recently compared the rise of synthetic biology to the development of software and suggested that this made it important for architects to get involved early. Can you explain?
DB: Architects have a tendency to adopt technologies late in their development cycles, after the features and overall frameworks are set and frozen. This can limit design possibilities, and I think we are seeing this now as architects wrestle with modeling and simulation software that was developed by and for other fields. In synthetic biology, the standards, protocols, and applications have not yet been fixed, and I think this is a perfect moment for architects to get involved and contribute to the discussion.

WM: Can you describe your initiative to build a registry of applications for synthetic biology?
DB: While architects may not yet be able to conduct advanced synthetic biology experiments, they are already well trained to imagine potential applications for new technologies—including their impact on buildings, environment, public space, and culture. So in my research and classes at Columbia GSAPP, we have been building a Registry of Synthetic Biology Applications to design and catalog potential projects that use synthetic biology. Drew Endy, one of the leading spokespeople for synthetic biology, suggested this catalog might also be considered a registry of problems or of puzzles.

We imagine that our registry might be a companion to the MIT's incredible Registry of Standard Biological Parts, which already catalogs and characterizes sequences of DNA known to perform specific biological functions. Biology students and professionals already draw on it when they are designing new biological machines. We hope that one day they might also draw on our Registry of Applications. In theory, scientists, designers, and students could review the Registry of Applications for interesting problems to solve, and review the Registry of Parts for relevant building blocks to create the solution.

WM: There is increasing interest in bio-materials that can be grown or manipulated using biological processes. Can this yet be done reliably and functionally, or is it still a long way off?
DB: For new medicines and fuels created with synthetic biology, there are already a handful of new products that are functional and robust. Right now, scaling up for industrial-scale production is a challenge, but many people think we will see these problems solved within the next several years.

So for new building materials created with synthetic biology, I think the limiting factors will be our imagination and our financial investment. If we can imagine incredible new building materials based on known biological functions, and if we can find the money to invest in their development, then we should be able to manufacture and integrate them into our architecture.

WM: What projects will you be focusing on in the near future?
DB: The field is wide open and right now there are amazing opportunities to rethink the design of everything. I have just started working with a large software company to explore the intersection of architecture, synthetic biology, and computation. We are looking to advance the use of software tools in synthetic biology, and we think this might help both experienced synthetic biologists and non-expert designers—architects, artists, material scientists, computer scientists, and all types of students—to improve their capacity to design with biology.

GINGER KRIEG DOSIER

Assistant Professor of Architecture at American University of Sharjah

WM: You generated a lot of interest with your 'BioBrick' project (page 78), which harnesses the natural process of microbial cementation to form bricks from sand. Have you continued to develop this technology?

GKD: Technology development has continued on a number of fronts as we approach readiness for commercialization. With regard to the end product, we have been collaborating with civil engineers and geologists to test and optimize our biocemented materials for structural strength and environmental performance. Our brick is currently exhibiting a compressive strength similar to that of a high-strength brick. We are also developing variations of the process that enable other forms of precast construction units. Simultaneously, we are optimizing the process itself to reduce manufacturing costs while scaling up production.

During this past summer, my partner (Michael Dosier) and I worked with NASA Ames Research Center to explore the viability of this form of biocementation in space application. This work also provided important information relevant to terrestrial production, such as how the cementation performs over a range of environmental temperatures.

WM: What are the biggest obstacles to widespread adoption of the BioBrick as a building material?

GKD: The commercial viability of a fundamental construction material, such as clay masonry and concrete, is intrinsically tied to the economies of scale. Our most significant obstacle currently is the scaling of production. Systems design is intrinsically part of an architect's toolset, so we really view this more as part of the design challenge rather than an obstacle in and of itself. As our biocementation process is distinctly different from the forming of clay or concrete casting, it has required our development of new manufacturing technologies from the ground up. Ironically, and perhaps poetically, the scaled process is beginning to look more like agricultural production than the industrial manufacturing typically associated with construction materials.

WM: What led you to want to incorporate microorganisms and living processes in your work?

GKD: The fundamental materials used in construction have remained relatively unchanged since the invention of steel and concrete technology. During the late 19th century, construction was revolutionized by these materials, enabling architecture to become thinner, lighter, and faster to construct. The Industrial Revolution had little concern for embodied energy or environmental impact. You're essentially taking non-renewable resources, processing them with non-renewable energy sources, and producing unwanted by-products along the way. Although there have been significant gains in reducing the impact of these materials, approaches always felt like patching holes instead of the much needed systematic overhaul. During my education I was inspired by new perspectives on sustainability and materiality, brought to prominence by architects and designers such as Peter Lynch, William McDonough, and Toshiko Mori. Rather than sustainability through reduction, I became interested in material ecologies modeled after natural systems—an approach popularized by Janine Benyus's *Biomimicry*. My first studies with 'materials that are grown' began with researching coral and shell formations. I find it intriguing that a material stronger than concrete can be grown in the low temperatures of seawater. It has been said that the 21st century is the century is of biology, and I believe our technology is one step in this direction for the built environment.

WM: As an architect, how did you go about learning about biology and chemistry?

GKD: The traditional boundaries separating disciplines are constantly receding and reconfiguring. This phenomenon is exhibited both formally by experimental programs, such as MIT's Media Lab, and informally through records of independent inquiry, such as *Make* magazine. One does not need to be a computer scientist to develop software, nor be an engineer to invent new forms of physical computing. My approach to learning biology and chemistry has been similar to these pursuits. I've read through numerous textbooks and journals, audited university courses, and sought consultation with a number of scientists along the way. My curriculum developed organically in parallel with the natural progression of the research. Degrees are benchmarks in one's career but should not become obstacles to academic inquiry. Admittedly, there were technical hurdles in terms of learning proper lab protocols, isolating variables, analyzing and cataloging

GINGER KRIEG DOSIER   459

Ginger Krieg Dosier is an assistant professor of architecture at the American University of Sharjah (AUS) College of Architecture, Art, and Design, United Arab Emirates. Prior to arriving at AUS in 2007, she was a visiting assistant professor at the North Carolina State University College of Design. Over the past eight years she has sought a scientific understanding of the properties of material in relation to architectural performance, engaging in co-research forums and cross-disciplinary collaboration. She received *Metropolis* magazine's 2010 Next Generation design award for her project 'BioBrick.' Dosier studied interior architecture at Auburn University before completing a masters in architecture at Cranbrook. She is interested in exploring the intersection of design practice and the science of materials.

results and producing sound hypotheses. However, it all starts with saying 'What If?' and making the commitment to discover the answer to your question.

WM: Did the iterative process of lab experimentation clash with your training as an architect?
GKD: Iterative process is a common component of contemporary design education, and an integral part of my own pedagogy. Central to iteration is the formulation of a hypothesis, testing that hypothesis, cataloging results, and viewing failure as an evaluative measure to inform improvement. As my own work prioritizes functional performance over formal aesthetic, the continuous cycle of prototyping is an absolute necessity. I think that the distinction between lab experimentation and an iterative design process lies in the nature of the results. In the sciences, a small but accurate result can have a tremendous impact. Individual discoveries act as building blocks that lead to a more comprehensive understanding of how things work, and accelerating the research of others. Alternately, architectural iteration lends itself to a more projective nature: discoveries that have the ability to impact the ways we build, interact with, and live in the world around us. I often find myself straddling both realms. Our collaborators are very interested in certain minutia of the work that exhibits undocumented phenomena, while our colleagues want to know how this material can enable new forms of architecture. While I feel there is tremendous potential in both discussions, our primary focus is to get this material into production and application.

WM: Are you interested in synthetic biology as a design tool? In your opinion, does this field hold significant potential for architecture?
GKD: The field of synthetic biology is rapidly growing and will have a tremendous impact on a range of disciplines. With respect to architecture, I believe there is significant potential for mitigating environmental impact, defining performative criteria, and developing new formal languages. Contemporary design discourse has been addressing relevant topics for over a decade—be it the conceptual frameworks of emergence, morphogenesis, and swarm intelligence; software developments to facilitate coding, scripting, dynamic simulation, and parametric relationships; or the material experiments of Oron Catts.

WM: Do you anticipate the study of biology or synthetic biology becoming integrated in curricula for design and architecture programs?
GKD: Ultimately, yes. Currently I have my students postulate a 'What If?' scenario, and facilitate their interaction with requisite disciplines for answering these questions. I have found in my own experience as an educator and former student that such transdisciplinary work fosters productive collaborations. The move toward sustainability is a good example—it is impacting numerous fields and functions as a platform for multidisciplinary integration. With a rising population and global economic shifts, tremendous problems loom, not least of which is figuring out how to grow food more ecologically. Architecture may provide part of the solution, in the form of vertical farms, for example.

WM: What challenges do you see to this kind of integration?
GKD: One initial challenge will be how to measure learning outcomes in the field of design. Accrediting bodies place intensive criteria on course loads and goals within specific disciplines. However, these are beginning to change. It is critical for curricula to allow personal tailoring to one's education, without compromising fundamental concepts.

WM: What new projects are you working on now or planning to pursue in the near future?
GKD: The 'BioBrick' project has become full time and my current focus is on taking the brick out of the lab and into application. This has become a valuable exercise in the making, from dreams years ago with coral hypothesizing 'what if we could grow construction materials?' into taking a viable prototype from the lab into commercial production. It is quite fulfilling to be a 'principle investigator,' managing the multiple teams and discourse. Three-dimensionally printing with the material has been a concurrent project, and we are continually developing techniques for automation. We keep our minds open to other applications of this technology and how to address the larger question of how to make materials better. 'How can the built environment do more than simply exist?' is always a question in the front of our minds.

SEAN QUINN

Sustainable Design Specialist at HOK

WM: Can you briefly describe your position at HOK and how you were involved in creating the net zero proposal?

SQ: As a sustainable design specialist at HOK, I work directly with both internal and external clients to help guide the application of sustainable strategies, including energy efficiency analysis, renewable energy integration and the building certification process under the US Green Building Council, and other green building rating systems.

I became aware of the Metropolis competition soon after completing feasibility studies for HOK's retrofit design of the office of Housing and Urban Development's headquarters, and after engagement with a Department of Energy program focused on the retrofit of existing commercial buildings. It was a natural extension to lead and manage this effort, and to work with a large and talented team to present a vision and process to achieve net zero in existing building retrofits.

WM: In the 'Process Zero: Retrofit Resolution' project (page 52), it appears that the design goes a step further than just mimicking nature and literally integrates it. Is that a fair assessment?

SQ: The goal as outlined in the competition brief was to generate a zero environmental footprint building, and we decided to push further for a positive environmental footprint building. Relying on the principles of biomimicry, we developed a theme for the project—building as a cell—and designed natural processes alongside the mechanical ones. Every design move was intended to provide both aesthetic and functional benefits, with nature as the guiding force.

The algae bioreactor provides a positive loop cycle for the building as a whole. The feeding vessel in the sub-basement draws carbon dioxide emissions from neighboring Santa Ana Freeway and combines with the algae slurry harvested from the building's wastewater. As the algal fluid flows through the tubular array, the photosynthesis process activates: algae feeds off the carbon, forming lipids for energy production and releasing oxygen, which can be filtered back to the outside environment. In the end, we're harnessing the building's dirty wastewater, dirty outside air, and an onsite supply of algae to generate clean water, clean air and clean energy.

WM: How does this project fit into HOK's approach to ecological performance and innovation?

SQ: HOK has a longstanding relationship with the Biomimicry Group, and our partnership has led to thinking beyond the building scale and modeling nature to developing large-scale, optimized ecosystem solutions. Furthermore, the integrated design process has become embedded within HOK's practice, and we've formalized the use of many of the design analysis tools and techniques that were used in this proposal.

WM: Can you briefly describe how the design team was formed and how it worked?

SQ: The project called for a large, multidisciplinary team in order to address the multiple issues embedded with the retrofit of an existing building of this scale. Anica Landreneau (the sustainable design leader in HOK's DC office) and I recruited members from our office with a broad base of experience. John Jackson, a building façade specialist, invited an old friend and colleague, Brandon Harwick with Vanderweil Engineers, to contribute his expertise to the project. In all, ten designers from HOK DC, one from HOK Tampa and four from Vanderweil contributed to the design of the proposal.

We spent three months developing the proposal for the competition and broke that process into three equal parts: research, integration, and concept development. Very few new and existing buildings have achieved net zero, and certainly none at this scale, so we researched the best emerging technologies to supplement off-the-shelf products. Throwing every idea at this building would have created a confused mess, so we explored which technologies had synergistic benefits and integrated them into the fabric of the building. Those concepts were formalized in the last month, sketches and models were translated to formal renderings, and a refined process to address all federal buildings was developed.

WM: Did the design team consult with a biologist or other life science specialist? If so, can you describe this interaction—was it unusual for HOK?

SQ: We consulted with a biologist, Thomas Nassif, to understand the potential yield of algae in Los Angeles, and an engineering professor, Soolyeon Cho,

SEAN QUINN 460

Sean Quinn was the project manager and lead architect for the HOK/Vanderweil winning net zero building retrofit design for *Metropolis* magazine's 2011 'Get the Feds to Zero' Next Generation Design Competition. *Metropolis* and the General Services Administration challenged designers to develop net zero energy solutions for a 1965 federal office building in downtown Los Angeles. Quinn and HOK DC's sustainable design leader Anica Landreneau assembled a team that included 11 HOK designers and four Vanderweil engineers, each with less than a decade of experience. He is currently working on HOK projects in the district of Columbia, Saudi Arabia, Germany, and Russia.

to understand energy-generation values from algal oil and biomass. This interaction might have been unusual a few years ago but it's more common now and absolutely essential to engage outside expertise to develop environmental solutions. As the energy and environmental impact of buildings has become a forefront issue around climate change, a broader range of consultants is being engaged to develop natural solutions. Their role now and as it expands in the coming years will be invaluable.

WM: Can you explain how algae were chosen to be a feature of the net zero design?
SQ: In an early design meeting, Scott Walzak, a junior designer with HOK, suggested the theme of a building as a cell and presented this fantastic photograph of algae cells. We explored the inherent abilities of algae to purify air and water, and then investigated the means to harness energy from algae. When our research revealed the positive effect of urban environments on algae yield, it became clear that there could be an opportunity to create a carbon sink through a bioreactor. Coupled with the ability to generate energy on site and the means to integrate it as an architectural feature, algae became a unique solution to a complex problem.

WM: Are algae bioreactors currently available as a building technology?
SQ: Industry has explored harvesting of microalgae within power plants in urban areas to use as a power source for nearby buildings. Recently, several universities and colleges have employed the use of biofuels from algae as a campus-wide power source. Our design looks to integrate that power source into the architectural fabric of the building itself.

WM: You've mentioned a desire to create integrated architecture that responds to the environment. Is this what led you to HOK?
SQ: Absolutely. HOK has a strong commitment to sustainability and performance as our design aesthetic. All our design solutions need to address issues of beauty, the urban context, and their impact on the environment. As energy and the environment have become major drivers in all our projects, I've enjoyed active involvement in

assessing impact and integrating sustainable strategies. There is a great team dynamic throughout HOK that allows these goals to be realized.

WM: Can you describe other, new projects you're currently involved in which harness natural processes?
SQ: We have completed designs for the Tribute Garden at Walter Reed Military Medical Center, with a challenge to create a garden experience that provides patients with a space for reflection, healing, and a break from the typical hospital environment. The indoor four-season atrium employs a biomimetic natural ventilation strategy that will assist the project in achieving net zero.

JESSICA GREEN

Director, Biology and the Built Environment Center, University of Oregon

WM: Can you talk about how you became interested in this area of research?

JG: Not long after I started my faculty position in Biology at the University of Oregon (UO), I discovered that it has one of the top architecture programs in the world with an emphasis on sustainable design. This made the biology–architecture marriage ideal. That, and collaborating with the extraordinary minds of architect G.Z. (Charlie) Brown and biologist Brendan Bohannan. Our laboratories are literally a few steps away from one another at UO, which makes working together easy and fun.

WM: Can you briefly describe your findings from your recent research on the built environment microbiome?

JG: In short—architectural design shapes the built environment microbiome, and we are filtering the wrong microbes.

Buildings are complex ecosystems that house trillions of microorganisms interacting with each other, with humans, and with their environment. Elucidating the mechanisms that shape the built environment microbiome—the community of microorganisms that live indoors—is critical for understanding the relationship between building design and human health. We observed that the abundance of potentially pathogenic bacteria was higher indoors than outdoors, and higher in indoor environments with lower airflow rates and lower relative humidity. These building attributes are strongly influenced by architectural design, suggesting that design can be used to manage indoor microbial communities to improve human health and well-being.

WM: Are there any immediate or short-term applications to your research? Could windows render ventilation systems obsolete in certain buildings? If so, what kind of energy savings would this represent?

JG: We are still in the very early stages of studying the built environment microbiome. We are currently trying to understand, using next-generation sequencing technology, how the design and operation of buildings influences the types of microbes that colonize indoor spaces. It is premature to speculate about future decision-making in the architectural world. It is not premature, however, to gather

biological data that is relevant to evidence-based design. If we are going to continue using energy-intensive design approaches, like mechanical ventilation systems, we need to understand how these systems affect the ecology and evolution of microbes indoors, and ultimately our health.

WM: You've mentioned the desirability of creating two sets of blueprints for any building: one that describes structure, the other the microbiome. Can you explain?

JG: I am enamored with the idea of mapping the DNA blueprint of a building. But this is just an analogy I use to visualize a building comprising trillions of microbial genes interacting with each other, with humans, and with the indoor environment. In reality, the genetic make-up of a building could not be mapped onto one static blueprint. Just as light and temperature dynamically varies in a building continuously through time, so does the distribution and diversity of microbes. Perhaps a better analogy is a biology building information model.

WM: Do you feel there are similarities between your work and that of the Human Microbiome Project (HMP)? Why or why not?

JG: Yes, I do feel there are similarities. One goal of the HMP is to understand the causes and consequences of human-associated microbial community assembly. We want to understand the causes and consequences of building-associated microbial community assembly.

WM: As the director of BioBE, can you describe your interactions with architects? What are some of the challenges you've encountered in collaborating with them or setting goals and selecting methodologies for your research?

JG: Collaborating with architects in the Energy Studies in Buildings Laboratory has been one of the most rewarding experiences in my career. I would describe these interactions as enlightening and productive. The biggest challenge in moving forward our research is that there is not enough time to pursue all of our ideas.

WM: What would you say about your research to teachers and students of architecture or industrial design?

JESSICA GREEN 461

Jessica Green is an engineer and ecologist who specializes in biodiversity theory and microbial systems. As a professor at both the University of Oregon and the Santa Fe Institute, she is the founding director of the innovative new Biology and the Built Environment (BioBE) Center, which bridges biology and architecture. She envisions a future with genomic-driven approaches to architectural design that promote sustainability, human health, and well-being. Green spearheads efforts to model buildings as complex ecosystems that house trillions of diverse microorganisms interacting with each other, with humans, and with their environment. This framework uses next-generation sequencing technology to characterize the 'built environment microbiome' and will offer site-specific design solutions to minimize the spread of infectious diseases and maximize building energy efficiency.

JG: I would encourage teachers and students of architectural design to consider microbial diversity as a building attribute.

WM: When people think about microbes, designers included, they most often think of harmful pathogens. What do you think are effective strategies to alter this perception and help people see how much we rely on microorganisms?
JG: I have been thinking about this a lot, and experimenting with different strategies to convey how crucial microbes are for our well-being. One strategy is to introduce microbiology into venues that are not science-centric. I recently collaborated on an illustrated book with Steve Green entitled *The Tiny Shiny*, which uses images from the movie *The Shining* as a platform to discuss microbes. I am currently collaborating with Anita Doron and Adam Huggins on a film that will likely be titled *Talk Derby to Me*. This will use the full-contact sport roller derby to explore the invisible connections uniting humans, including the microbial connections. If these strategies work, I will turn my attention towards urban microbiology.

WM: Are you planning to research other types of spaces to learn about their microbiome? What are some research projects you'd like to pursue in the future?
JG: For logistical and financial reasons we are currently working in or close to where our center is located in Eugene, Oregon. In the future I would like to turn our attention to slums.

DAN GRUSHKIN

Co-Founder, Genspace

WM: Can you relate how you became interested in do-it-yourself biology?

DG: I guess it started in 2008. I was heading to a design conference in Providence for an article, and after I did the reporting I thought I'd go check out iGEM—an undergraduate student genetic engineering competition that was being held at MIT in Boston at the same time. I'd never seen anything like it in my life. While waiting for the judges to deliberate, hundreds of students in the auditorium broke into a dance party in their seats. For the first time, beyond serious, biology looked fun. And, of course, the ideas and projects they had were spectacular. That's a longer conversation though. Who'd ever heard of a vaccine being designed in three months.

During the same event, a young guy named Mackenzie Cowell gave a talk on what would be required to do your own genetic engineering at home. He was talking about DIY bio. I remember commenting that synthetic biology at home sounded dangerous. I pictured anthrax scares and threats of environmental release. How far I've come. Simply put, I looked at what these undergraduates were doing and I thought, 'I want to do that too.' DIY bio still needed fleshing out, but that's where my investigation began.

WM: What led you and your co-founders to formalize your DIY bio meetings into Genspace?

DG: The original reason for founding Genspace as a non-profit was that we wanted to distinguish what we were doing from an amorphous message board. At the time, DIY bio was a lightning rod for negative attention in the press. Journalists were voicing those same fears I first had. Meanwhile, there was deep uncertainty about how law enforcement would respond to our labs. We wanted to distinguish ourselves from the random messages flying back and forth on DIYbio.org, and we wanted to establish our own standards and practices that put us beyond reproach.

Very quickly, we found the limitations of working in my living room and then the NYC Resistor hackerspace. Biology takes time. You can't just pack it up in a box and get to it when you feel like it. So we needed a dedicated space where we could work on projects over weeks and months.

It was amazing to see that idea catch fire. Yes, there are individual biohackers working alone, but the so-called movers and shakers come from organized communities like ours.

WM: How would you describe your role in the organization?

DG: In any startup community, everyone plays multiple roles. I'm most proud of having helped found the organization, and continue to help focus its mission, improve its structure, and strategize for its future. I spend a lot of time talking to those in security and law enforcement, assuaging security concerns about amateur biology. That means frequent talks with the FBI and Washington policy makers. I also feel that we are setting a model for other groups, so figuring out a structure for how to make a community lab work has been a priority. I also have my own biology projects that I work on at the lab. So I'd say I'm part experimenter, part strategist.

WM: Can you describe the multi-school iGEM team collaboration currently under way at Genspace?

DG: Sure. I should warn you, though, that I wasn't on the team. The iGEM team was a collaboration between the Columbia University architecture school, Cooper Union, and Genspace. The goal was to design *Escherichia coli* that would produce quantum dots. Quantum dots are nano-sized crystals whose size determines their output when excited. They appear to glow different colors depending on their size. These are used in solar panels, lighting, medical imaging. The project won a gold medal at the regional iGEM competition and the team was invited to compete in the international competition.

WM: How does Genspace fit in with its neighboring organizations at the Metropolitan Exchange (MEx) Building in Brooklyn? Are there frequent collaborations?

DG: The MEx building has been a blessing for us. We're surrounded by so many talents and skills—architects, artists, designers, electronics experts. We've been working with Amanda Parkes of Bodega Algae and former member of the MIT Media Lab, and have frequent collaborations with Mitch Joachim of Terreform 1. Best, though, is the open discussion that being in the space breeds.

DAN GRUSHKIN 462

Dan Grushkin is co-founder of Genspace and a journalist who covers the cross-section of science, biotechnology, and culture. His articles have appeared in *The New York Times*, *Businessweek*, *National Geographic Adventure*, *Popular Science*, and *Scientific American*.

WM: Can you talk a little about the type of students the classes attract?

DG: We were surprised by the first classes. We expected twenty-somethings and instead drew people who were in mid and late career. These were people in finance, and entrepreneurs who had been following biotech for years and wanted to understand it in a hands-on way. We had beer brewers and distillers who wanted to further understand the microorganisms they were working with. These were followed by a wave of designers who were looking to biology as the next wave in design. Synthetic biology has a strong appeal to engineers and computer scientists, but they are looking for ways to push the envelope of applications.

WM: Sorry, inevitable question: how does Genspace address the public safety concerns that come along with having a biotech lab open to non-specialists?

DG: I was waiting for this question. There are three broad ways we address safety. One, the lab, though it looks hodge-podge, meets biosafety level 1 standards. That means it meets all the requirements you might find in a professional lab. We pair that with a lab safety course for all incoming members, which teaches them about proper lab procedure. The threat here isn't so much about safety to the lab member but to the success of their project. A contaminated project is a failed project. Two, we're very careful about the organisms we bring into the space. We forbid members to work with anything remotely pathogenic. Three, all projects are passed through a biosafety board that advises us on the possible risks of a project. The board includes a biosafety officer from MIT, distinguished geneticists, even a federal biosafety official.

WM: It seems that Genspace can be an effective incubator for entrepreneurial ventures. Have any startup companies yet been formed based on research performed at the lab?

DG: We've barely been running a year, so not yet. However, a number of really exciting projects are starting to emerge. Some have commercial applications, some are pure fun, and others are art projects. I think it's a matter of time.

WM: Are you and your co-founders interested in expanding Genspace? Are you seeking grants or investors to broaden the scope of your activities?

DG: Yes. We're already looking to grow. Genspace is a non-profit so, yes, we're looking for institutions that see the value in bringing bioscience education and innovation to communities in big, hands-on ways. We sent a team to Egypt to teach Egyptian students about amateur science this summer. Though we're a community organization, I see our outreach and our model going global in the next year.

MARIN SAWA

Designer and Researcher

WM: What led you to become interested in incorporating microorganisms and living processes into your work?
MS: The concept of metabolism at cellular levels, which led to the thinking of our spatial envelopes as 'living' entities, creating a new urban 'metabolism' that connects industrial 'metabolism' with that of the natural world. My initial references included the Metabolism movement in 1960s Japanese architecture and the architectural protocell research led by Rachel Armstrong, where an artificial cell was created and programed with a basic behaviour.

WM: Can you briefly describe the goals of your 'Algaerium' project? At some point, did you have to begin studying biology or collaborate with a biologist?
MS: The project was underlined with a vision of textiles as living surfaces that possess the intelligence of life and connect the built environment with the natural world, in search of a smart and ecological textile design and practice. At a more pragmatic level, it was an attempt to craft algae's biological attributes—such as photosynthesis and bioluminescence—in response to our contemporary 'environmental conscientiousness.' Through installations in urban conditions, the applications of 'Algaerium' aimed to visualize otherwise invisible natural phenomena to raise awareness of our coexistence with microspecies, as well as to directly contribute to our ecosystem.

So the very aim was to weave the life of microalgae as materials in a way that they act as the spine of design aesthetically and functionally. This led to recontextualizing them out of their natural habitats and embedding them as active cells in my design. I tried to re-apply their innate living properties, such as respiration (photosynthesis), reproduction (photosynthetic pigments), and the innate abilities found in some of the algae species, such as phototaxis and bioluminescence.

As I had no experience or knowledge in biology or chemistry, I talked to a few biologists prior to the start of the project. Then I gathered basic support and inspiration when I needed it from Dr Masa Tada at the Research Department of Cell and Developmental Biology at University College London (UCL), whose research looks at the zebrafish embryo, and Dr Tammy Kalber at UCL's Centre for

Advanced Biomedical Imaging, who specializes in metabolism and experimental therapeutics.

It would have been ideal to have found expertise in algae cultivation, but I didn't at that time, and I managed to drive the project using an online catalogue of algae on the website of the Culture Collection of Algae and Protozoa at the Scottish Marine Institute, through which I communicated with Joanne Field, who looks after the algae strains and their cultivation. As the project developed, I familiarized myself with algae cultivation and basic biochemistry experiments. I then realized that what I was doing in a lab could be done simply at home in my kitchen, as long as my work tools and surfaces were sterilized against any contamination by fungi and bacteria.

WM: What were the biggest challenges in completing 'Algaerium'?
MS: Most challenges were centered on conditions of containment, and a degree of containment such that the metabolism of the algae could be sustained in my textile structures. This meant the integration of the necessary wet environment (media water, light, and carbon dioxide) into design aesthetics, while creating a semi-open system allowing carbon dioxide/oxygen chemical exchange, while preventing contamination from both outside and inside.

Because in this case containment meant immobilization and loss of a sustainable supply chain, my algae's biological abilities necessary for the design were often suppressed: with the bioluminescent algae, *Pyrocytsis lunula*, it stopped their biological illumination mechanism. Some microalgae, such as *Tetraselmis* sp. (green algae), used in this project are robust and resilient to changes in their environment, while *Pyrocytsis lunula* is extremely sensitive and fragile. The most painstaking challenge was in making bioluminescence occur unnaturally, because this biological ability is only triggered by a strict set of both biological and environmental conditions. The design process therefore involved (1) reprograming their nocturnal illumination to daytime under the reversed light cycle in a cupboard; (2) designing a system of flow to trigger their automatic response to glow; and (3) making an enclosed space for the bioluminescent 'Algaerium' to provide a regular light–dark cycle to sustain its bio-feature.

MARIN SAWA 463

Marin Sawa is a designer and researcher who specializes in a multidisciplinary design approach that combines textiles, biology, and architecture. She is the creator of 'Algaerium' and focuses on how smart materials can be engineered to be responsive at the same time as being elegant, minimal, versatile, and not flooded by electronics. Sawa earned her BA at the Architectural Association in London, a masters degree in the Textiles Futures program at Central Saint Martins College of Art and Design in London, and is a PhD candidate at the Textile Futures Research Centre at the same institution, in a collaborative program with the Energy Futures Lab, Imperial College, London.

WM: What are your research goals for your new 'Micro Algaerium' project?

MS: Through interdisciplinary collaboration with the Energy Futures Lab at Imperial College, my research explores a metabolic synthesis between algal biotechnology, textiles, and urban pollution, with the particular aim of weaving a textile form of algal culture into sustainable fabrics of our everyday spaces: the research tries to connect textile's micro-matrices as culture 'skin' and urban conditions as culture 'media.' At this point I am hoping to draw a picture of the micro-ecology and evolution of spaces inhabited by algal living textiles by planting a series of installations.

WM: Are you interested in synthetic biology as a design tool?

MS: As far as algal fuels are concerned, I am interested in current inventions of what's called 'hybrid' algae species, which are embedded with bioprocesses such as oil secretion and ethanol release. This kind of biotechnology in synthetic biology can directly prevent and eliminate pollution and waste. On the other hand, in today's world, we realize that the creation of an engineered biological entity must be contained within the lab and not outside the lab because of its unverified synthetic biohazards to our ecosystem. The idea of genetically encoding a biological logic of death in the case of unwanted leakage is great, but I think if we were to get new designs of synthetic biology out of the lab, it would be equally interesting and imperative to design secure containment and disposal systems in our physical world as a natural by-product. In this sense, this design tool actually contradicts my interest in creating an open metabolic relationship between 'living' textiles and the rest of the biosphere.

WM: Do you view your work as linked to a movement toward ecological design?

MS: My concerns are in sync with the fundamental visions of ecological design to lower environmental impacts and create positive connectivity between people and the biosphere. However, the bottom line of my work is design for urban living, and the use of living systems as part of the aesthetics and function of my design is not only because they are ecological but also because they are smart and engaging to our contemporary psyche.

WM: Can you describe if/how your architecture studies have influenced your approach to design?

MS: I feel that my interests have not really changed since specializing in textile design a few years ago. Rather, I have found that textiles and their close associations with both high and low technologies are enabling me to freely materialize lasting interests that came out of the realm of architecture. Those lie in studying materials' intrinsic properties as ways of finding form/structures (as in the works of Frei Otto) and the concept of porosity of the skin in relation to temporal fluctuations between inside and outside environments. These are ways by which I see textiles as material structures responsive to their environments, but much closer to the scale of the body and senses than I previously thought in my architectural studies.

WM: Do you anticipate that the study of biology or synthetic biology becoming integrated into curricula for design and architecture programs? Why or why not?

MS: I think it is quite clear that academia has already played a massive role in fostering interdisciplinary projects between design and science, and recently between design and architecture, and biology and synthetic biology: Suzanne Lee's 'BioCouture' project (page 109), for example, is now being developed in collaboration with Imperial University London. The 'Living Plant Construction' project by PhD students, Gerd de Bruin, Ferdinand Ludwig, and Oliver Story of IGMA, University of Stuttgart, is the fruit of inter/multidisciplinary collaboration. 'Biological Habitat' by Zbigniew Oksiuta, 'Victimless Leather' by SymbioticA (page 133), and architectural protocell research led by Rachel Armstrong at Bartlett School of Architecture, UCL, are all products of collaboration with science experts working in labs. For the integration, it is completely feasible right now to form transdisciplinary platforms across different universities and institutions, depending on their expertise, by setting common goals, such as tackling the energy challenge or food crisis.

EDUARDO KAC

Artist

WM: In what ways do you think the artist's toolkit has expanded since your pioneering works 'Genesis' and 'GFP Bunny' were created at the turn of the millennium?
EK: One important factor is that costs have dropped dramatically. It cost me more than $8,000 to make 'Genesis' gene back in 1999. Today the same gene can be made for a few hundred. Generally speaking, due to these lowering costs, access to standard tools has certainly increased. Beyond that, while it would be a truism to say that new techniques and tools are constantly being invented (such as genome sequencing on a chip and the ongoing drive to synthesize complete genomes), we should also point out that there are intellectual changes that lead to new insights. For example, while the general public still has a genocentric conception of life, science itself is moving more towards a network model. In other words, the gene is no longer ascribed centrality; we are beginning to have a better grasp of how multiple factors interact in a living organism. For example, instead of focusing only on genes, we might consider the complexity of 'genetic pathways.'

WM: Have you observed major changes in the public's view of transgenic art over the last 10 years?
EK: Definitely. In the beginning there was a strong sense of polarization, either in favor or (mostly) against. You would be surprised by the number of individuals who consider themselves liberal and progressive who attacked me for using the 'enemy's tool,' as if Paik was the devil because of Murdoch. In the course of time, as I predicted, it has become clear that in the hands of an artist any tool becomes a medium, and biotech is no exception. Now it's evident that the question is not whether an artist uses molecular biology to make art, but if this or that work is visually engaging and emotionally compelling. I'm extremely pleased to see that specialized audiences and the general public alike are focusing more on the work itself and its cultural implications rather than on the particulars of the technique. In 1999 I was attacked for showing 'Genesis,' and since then it has traveled to forty museums and galleries worldwide. I think this is symptomatic of the change you refer to.

WM: What is your opinion of the rise of do-it-yourself biology groups of non-scientists who perform basic genetic engineering experiments such as altering *Escherichia coli* bacteria to glow in the dark?
EK: It's wonderful to see the medium becoming more accessible. It happened with video, it happened with the computer, it will happen with biotech. What's especially significant is that a whole new culture develops when individuals, rather than corporations, employ new media to freely express their ideas, emotions, and points of view.

WM: Can you describe what inspired 'Cypher,' your work that includes a poem embedded in DNA?
EK: My background is in literature and philosophy. I have a body of work in the realm of digital poetry that goes back to 1982, when I created my first digital poem. In 1983 I created my first holographic poem, and in 1985 I created my first online animated poems using the French Minitel system. This body of work, spanning approximately three decades, is documented in my anthology *Hodibis Potax*, published in 2007. So, poetry has always been an important part of my life and my practice. As mentioned above, in 1999 I presented the transgenic artwork 'Genesis,' in which I encode a biblical passage into DNA and allow local and Internet participants to cause real mutations in the gene (and thus in the biblical passage). In a sense, 'Cypher' can be seen both in relation to 'Genesis' and as part of my preceding poetic trajectory. While in 'Genesis' one is physically immersed in the work and causes mutations in a gene that is already inserted into the bacteria, 'Cypher' is much smaller; it is a portable, nomadic lab. 'Cypher' presents the viewer with the inert DNA in a vial and asks him or her to endow the encoded text with life by carrying out the lab procedure.

WM: Can you explain what you were thinking when you composed the short poem: 'A TAGGED CAT WILL ATTACK GATTACA'?
EK: In reality, the poem cannot be reduced to the linear sequence of these six words. In its actual material and semiological reality, its instantiation, its manifestation, it exists in multiple states that are complementary. The poem is never experienced like this, as it is seen above in the question. The poem encompasses not only the visual composition, with its

EDUARDO KAC 464

Eduardo Kac integrates robotics, biology, and networking to explore the fluidity of subject positions in the post-digital world. His work has been exhibited internationally at venues such as Exit Art and Ronald Feldman Fine Arts, New York; Maison Européenne de la Photographie, Paris, and Lieu Unique, Nantes, France; OK Contemporary Art Center, Linz, Austria; and in biennials such as Yokohama Triennial, Japan, Gwangju Biennale, Korea, and Bienal de São Paulo, Brazil. His work is part of the permanent collection of, among others, the Institut Valencià d'Art Modern, Spain. Kac has received many awards, including the Golden Nica Award. He lectures and publishes worldwide.

specifically chosen typeface, but also its simultaneous existence as a gene and as a code—a code that can be read in alternate directions. Neither of these elements is external to the poem. In other words, the poem is a network of elements that should be considered together. As for my motivations, I would prefer for the work to resonate with individual viewers, rather than suggest a specific interpretive framework.

WM: What do you think of the growing interest among artists and designers in synthetic biology and the annual iGEM competition, as is seen in works like Alexandra Daisy Ginsberg's 'E.Chromi'?
EK: I think it is encouraging. It confirms my vision of a biotech culture of the future, in analogy with what happened with video and computers. However, in light of the fact that these competitions have the ultimate goal of product development, I must say that the experimental and open-ended nature of the DIY scene is closer to my heart.

WM: Do you sense potential problems or opportunities in synthetic biology's engineering approach—moving toward standardization, modularity, and abstraction with 'BioBricks'?
EK: Sure, both. Let's not forget that 'brick' is a metaphor, just like 'code' (as in 'genetic code') was a metaphor, coined by comparison with Morse code. There's a lot that can be done by embracing the 'brick' metaphor—that is, by thinking about and working with genetic components as discrete units. However, this metaphor and physical model can only go so far. Eventually a firm limit will force the architectural analogy to be displaced, and a true network model will emerge and become predominant.

WM: What are common obstacles you've experienced as an artist collaborating with scientists? What have you found to be the best ways to overcome these issues?
EK: I always have a very clear notion of what I want to do, so it's not difficult for me to articulate it to any member of my team, be it a scientist, a production coordinator, or a studio assistant. We then engage in dialogue about the best way to get there, the best way to fulfill my aesthetic vision. In my work I create new life—that is, life that did not occur

in nature in nearly four billion years of evolution. This process is hard, costly, laborious, slow, and offers no guarantee of success. Unfortunately, that's just the way it is. So the most important factors for me are patience and perseverance.

WM: Can you describe types of transgenic art you would like to create in the future and which you think will be made possible by the advance of technology?
EK: One of my goals is to be able to completely and thoroughly design a new life form, to conceive every aspect of it and then synthesize its genome, as well as the fundamental cell in which this synthetic genome will be introduced. This full synthesis is indeed far into the distant future, but the integral creation of life, bottom up, is an exciting horizon for transgenic art.

ORON CATTS

Director of SymbioticA, the Centre of Excellence
in Biological Arts, School of Anatomy and Human
Biology, The University of Western Australia

WM: The 'Victimless Leather' project garnered much attention in the 2009 show Design and the Elastic Mind at the Museum of Modern Art (MoMA) in New York. Were there surprises for you in how people reacted to this work? Also, how do you think this project has influenced designers and artists since the exhibition?

OC: The 'Victimless Leather' project was exhibited for the first time in 2004 as part of a show called The Space Between at the John Curtin Gallery, Perth. The exhibition dealt with the future of textiles and fashion. Since then it has been exhibited more than ten times in very different configurations, contexts, and settings—from science museums through to political arts, design, and biological arts shows. The audience reaction would change, depending on the context and configuration. The 2004 showing seemed to generate the most heated reactions from people, who seemed to be very disturbed by the idea of growing leather in such a way. The way we choose to exhibit the work contributed quite a lot to these feelings as we staged the piece in a very dark room alongside a video piece that showed the cells growing (time-lapse) and still images of labs and monsters. Other reactions took it on face value as an innovative way of producing leather without harming animals, while some reacted with a visceral sense of non-articulated disgust.

It is important to note that 'Victimless Leather' was a rather ironic artistic project and was part of a series of works developed under the banner of 'The Technologically Mediated Victimless Utopia' (2000–8). This explored the use of tissue engineering for the creation of in-vitro meat and leather while questioning the tendency of Western technology to obscure its victims. As with our other projects, we see our role as that of agitators, or provocateurs, who set up contestable situations and objects, therefore we welcomed any type of reaction to the work.

The 2008 MoMA show was interesting as this was the first time that 'Victimless Leather' death took place in public. We have performed 'killing rituals' with some of our other projects, such as the 'Semi-Living Worry Dolls' and the 'Pig Wings Project,' but they were staged and the audience was aware of our intentions. In the MoMA show, the death of the jacket appeared to be accidental, and it generated discussion because it was the first time that one of our works

publicly died in a context of design rather than art exhibition. The discussion that ensued highlighted the difference in the framing and reading of the work as a design object rather than an art project, and the fact that what was considered a failure—the death of the jacket—in the design reading of the work was actually a great artistic success in generating the type of broader discussion about responsibilities, ethics, and the use of living materials for human-centric ends.

Regarding the ways the project influenced designers and artists, we have been working with living tissue as a medium since the mid-1990s, and many of our other projects have been exhibited and discussed since then. When we started, no one else was working with living tissue in such a way, and now there are quite a few artists and designers who are working and speculating about the use of living tissue for different ends. Since 2000 we have trained artists and designers in using different types of biological technologies, including living tissues through SymbioticA, the research center we set up at the University of Western Australia. Since 2003 I have been in close contact with Tony Dunne from the Royal College of Art (RCA), who was using our work as a starting point for the biological design projects he sets to his students at Design Interaction. I also know that our work is often used in an architectural context as examples of precursors for biological architecture. Margaret Atwood referred to our work as inspirational, including aspects in her book, *The Year of the Flood*, and a few of our projects appeared in Michael Crichton's last book, *Next*. Saying that, after showing our work at the Design and the Elastic Mind exhibition, we have noticed that some of the designers and architects that had work in the show have started to work with living tissue and employed similar language. Most notable are Joris Laarmen from the Netherlands, who developed a piece entitled 'Halflife Lamp' (page 141) using genetically modified hamster cells, and architect Mitchell Joachim from the US, who developed a concept for an in-vitro meat habitat that he called 'Victimless Shelter.'

WM: Have architects and industrial designers contacted you with an interest in collaborating to grow objects or structures?

OC: The initial research I conducted in the mid-1990s

ORON CATTS 465

Oron Catts is an artist, researcher, and curator whose work with the Tissue Culture and Art Project (which he founded in 1996 with Ionat Zurr) has been exhibited and presented internationally. In 2000 he co-founded SymbioticA, an artistic research laboratory housed within the School of Anatomy and Human Biology, University of Western Australia. Under Oron's leadership, SymbioticA has gone on to win the Prix Ars Electronica Golden Nica in Hybrid Art (2007) and became a Centre for Excellence in 2008. In 2009 Oron and Ionat were recognized in Thames & Hudson's book *60 Innovators Shaping our Creative Future* in the category 'Beyond Design,' and by *Icon Magazine* (UK) as one of the top 20 designers 'making the future and transforming the way we work.' Oron has been a researcher at the University of Western Australia since 1996 and was a research fellow at the Tissue Engineering and Organ Fabrication Laboratory, Harvard Medical School, Massachusetts General Hospital, Boston (2000–1). In 2007 he was a visiting scholar at the Department of Art and Art History, Stanford University, and is a visiting professor of Design Interaction, Royal College of Arts, London.

dealt with design and biotechnologies and was part of my product design degree. Since then, for various reasons, I have decided to pursue the research as an artist but maintained a dialogue with design. When our work started to become better known, we were also approached by architects. As mentioned above, I have been in close contact with Tony Dunne from the Design Interaction Department at RCA, and since 2010 I have been a visiting professor in that department. I also hold a joint grant with Pia Ednie-Brown from the Spatial Information Architecture Laboratory at the Royal Melbourne Institute of Technology entitled 'Ethics and Aesthetics as Criteria for Innovation.' Designers such as Alexandra Daisy Ginsburg have been residents at SymbioticA, and in recent years I have been invited to give lectures in architecture schools and at design events, such as the Bartlett, Columbia University School of Architecture, Experimenta Design, and State of Design.

WM: What major changes has SymbioticA undergone since its inception in 2000? Can you talk a little about the type of students the program attracts?
OC: SymbioticA has grown quite significantly. We started as a bottom-up initiative—basically a couple of artists and a couple of scientists working on a research project. In 2000 we received funding from the West Australian Lotteries Commission and the University of Western Australia to build a dedicated space (lab/studio) for art and life science collaboration. We started a small residency program in 2000 and shortly after that we offered an academic unit in art and biology for undergraduate students. Through the support of the university, the program has been further developed with core research projects, residencies, academic courses, exhibitions, workshops, and conferences. As we are part of the School of Anatomy and Human Biology, we emulate much of the academic science lab model. This allows our residents and researchers equal access to shared laboratories and resources. The idea is that we are an integral part of the science school with a specialized research area—artistic research into the life sciences. In 2006 we started our postgraduate program, offering a masters in biological art. In 2007 SymbioticA received the inaugural Golden Nica in Hybrid Arts at Prix Ars Electronica, and in 2008 the Department of Culture

and the Arts of the West Australian Government gave us three years' funding that transformed SymbioticA into a Research Centre of Excellence in Biological Arts.

WM: In your view, what are the developments in biotechnology over the last few years that have most expanded artists' means of expression?
OC: Let me start by saying that my interest is in life, and the changing relationship we have with the concept of life. My role as an artist (and to some extent as a critical designer) is to culturally scrutinize that which we still do not have a (cultural) language to engage with. The knowledge about life generated in the past 200 years provides a fertile ground for cultural scrutiny. However, the major transformation of biology from a descriptive discipline into a perspective one is what I am interested in. The last few decades have seen an acceleration in the rate at which what we call biology (or the life sciences) is becoming more engineering than science. Areas of applied research, such as molecular biology, regenerative medicine, synthetic biology, and neuroscience, urgently need to be culturally unpacked; partly also because these fields are becoming more standardized. Non-biologists, such as engineers, artists, designers, and architects, now have a new (wet) palate of possibilities to work and engage with. Some of my thoughts concern one aspect of developments in the applied life sciences—regenerative medicine.

The idea of growing products rather than manufacturing them has been explored and critiqued through the notion of the semi-living by the Tissue Culture and Art Project (TC&A) since 1996. This stems from the developments in biomedical research in the 1990s, in particular tissue engineering and regenerative medicine. The premise was that we can evoke the latent regenerative abilities of the biological body to grow organs and tissues either inside or outside of biological or techno-scientific bodies. TC&A postulated that the same logic can offer the growth of semi-living products for uses other than medical. In a series of hands-on artistic experiments, involving the construction and growth of symbolic to pseudo-utilitarian objects, TC&A has explored the philosophical, ethical, epistemological, and practical aspects of the creation of semi-living 'products.'

For example, 'The Pig Wings Project' (2001) in which TC&A developed CAD-CAM protocols for the Tissue Engineering and Organ Fabrication Laboratory at Harvard Medical School and used degradable scaffolds and differentiated stem cells, was also used as a critique of 'genohype' (hype generated with regard to genetic research). Another series of works developed under the banner of the Technologically Mediated Victimless Utopia (2000–8) explored the use of tissue engineering for the creation of in-vitro meat and leather while questioning the tendency of Western technology to obscure its victims. These works can illustrate and critique the notion of the post-sustainable by presenting tangible and evocative ways in which the regenerative logic of life is transformed into a raw material for human-centric ends.

WM: What is your view of the burgeoning DIY bio movement and the increasing availability of tools to bioengineer life forms?
OC: The DIY bio movement goes hand in hand with the increase in engineering of biology, which standardizes and simplifies many of the tasks associated with the manipulation of life. This very same engineering logic oscillates between openness and control—hyping the possible outcomes of biology as engineering and making it more accessible to non-biologists. The DIY movement can play an important role in democratizing the knowledge of life by allowing more access and openness to knowledge and know-how, and hopefully providing alternatives to mainstream agendas that drive the current direction of research and application. My view is that if we allow engineers access to biology, we should allow others the same privileges, including the DIY movement.

WM: Do you anticipate that the study of biology or synthetic biology might become integrated into curricula for designers and architects in the future?
OC: It already happens to some degree in art, design, and architecture courses around the world. Students are at least being introduced to the prospects of using living materials and biological technologies in this context. As parts of biology are now becoming more like engineering, and, for better or for worse, life is becoming a raw material for human use, it is imperative that interested

artists, designers, and architects have a deep knowledge of biological processes and techniques.

WM: What have you observed to be the biggest challenges when designers or artists try to collaborate with scientists, such as biologists?
OC: The main issue with almost all types of cross-disciplinary collaboration is that of language. The same words and expressions can mean totally different things for different disciplines, let alone the specialized jargon that each discipline maintains. There are also the differing methodologies and the meanings of experimentation in science and art/design.

WM: You've written about the potential of 'semi-living' products and structures that might enhance performance (from an ecological standpoint, for example) but would not be fully living, since they would require human maintenance. Can you briefly describe how you developed this definition and comment on whether or not we're nearing a time when such objects will exist in everyday life?
OC: The idea of the 'semi-living' came from my exploration of growing functional parts of living bodies with technological support. Something as 'simple' as ivy growing over a wall can illustrate the basic principle behind the 'semi-living.' Technology is needed to maintain it (a wall to support it, secateurs to prune it); ivy not only serves an aesthetic function but it acts as an insulator from the environment, produces oxygen, and removes pollutants (such as heavy metals).

There are already examples of more- and less-sophisticated approaches that can be considered semi-living 'machines' or products— from biological filters to drug-producing genetically modified cells in large bioreactors. The field of in-vitro meat, where mammalian muscle cells are grown for meat production, is one of the most obvious areas in which the research of TC&A has been picked up for potential 'real-life' products.

What were some of the outcomes of the recent VISCERAL exhibition you curated with Dr Ionat Zurr at the Science Gallery in Dublin? How did this experience compare with exhibiting at MoMA?
The show was a retrospective show of fifteen artists

from the 10-year history of research and residencies at SymbioticA. As such it covered artistic research projects that ranged from working with the elements of the living body (molecules, cells, tissues) through full bodies to ecological systems. All the works were conceived and developed by artists who spent a significant amount of time in SymbioticA's biological labs. The outcomes where very positive—exposing this type of artistic engagement with life to a wide audience and receiving great reviews. We hope to tour the show to other places in Europe and beyond.

VISCERAL was very different from the Design and the Elastic Mind exhibition at MoMA because it was conceived as an art, rather than design, show. The reading of the work was different because it presented mainly critical artistic meditations on l ife as distinct from attempting to propose solutions or functional outcomes. My own experience of the two shows was also very different: in the MoMA show we were part of a huge assembly of designers and artists, and the work was framed and positioned according to someone's else agenda; while curating VISCERAL (and four other shows in the past) presented the opportunity to create a narrative concerning artistic engagement with life.

MARIA AIOLOVA

Director, One Lab School for Urban Ecology

WM: What are the sources of your interest in the confluence of architecture and the sciences?

MA: My early studies of architecture were at the Technical Universities of Sofia and Vienna, where the engineering and science students were always together in their labs conducting experiments, while we architecture students were trapped in our own silo, often at the edge of the campus. We were encouraged to be individualistic and reject things that came before. I found the scientific approach more constructive—working collaboratively and building upon earlier findings. I've always wanted to bridge the gap between these approaches. As I see it, practicing architecture in the 21st century is not only a creative process but also a focused scientific endeavor. My current research at Terreform ONE addresses this change and works to establish new forms of knowledge and new processes of practice at the interface of design, computer science, structural engineering, and biology.

WM: Can you describe how the idea for ONE Lab developed and how the program started?

MA: ONE Lab was founded as a non-profit independent group concerned with research and education in the synthesis of design and technology. It began as a core of young architects, engineers, biologists, ecologists, robotics experts, industrial designers, urban agriculturists, physicists, and media artists all seeking alternatives to traditional forms of teaching and professional practice. They included Mitchell Joachim, Oliver Medvedik, Ellen Jorgensen, Alex Felson, and Vito Acconci. Through our interactions, we discovered the need for an interdisciplinary pedagogical zone, where students can freely inquire, discuss, conduct experiments, and take actions that have a positive effect on the global community.

WM: In what ways is the approach to instruction in ONE Lab different from other design studios or workshops?

MA: ONE Lab offers a new means of design inquiry where students will actively use the tools and technologies of the life sciences. In a period of a few weeks in the summer, the participants learn the basics of biotechnology, including genetic engineering, tissue culture, and cloning; how to grow materials for design, including trees, plants and mushrooms;

and they are introduced to computational scripting and modeling for controlled growth. Students have access to a bio laboratory, specialized equipment, and expertise. More importantly, we create an extremely charged interdisciplinary knowledge zone to facilitate free interaction and cross-pollination of ideas.

WM: What type of students does the program attract, and what sort of projects have been produced?

MA: ONE Lab participants range from design, science, and art students to young and mid-career professionals from all around the world. They are attracted by the possibilities of experimenting freely and breaking out of the silos of their own academic institutions or professional practices. The students are asked to rethink what is salubrious about the city, in both its forms and its life. Projects developed vary from movable urban farms and structural walls grown from living trees and mycelia, to phytoremediation cells for filtering gray- and blackwater and phosphorescent bacteria-based paint.

One group of students started their own non-profit organization that works with inner-city residents in Chicago, teaching them how to construct movable farms and concentrate sunlight. Another student, Eduardo Mayoral, received this year's Holcium Award 'Next Generation' for his project, 'Bioluminescent Devices for Zero-Electricity Lighting' (page 123), which originated in our lab under the supervision of Oliver Medvedik.

WM: In descriptions of the program and its outcomes, it appears that you prefer the term 'ecological design' as opposed to more prevalent phrases like 'biomimetic,' 'cradle to cradle,' or 'sustainable,' which are often used interchangeably in the press. Can you explain?

MA: First, I disagree with the interchangeable use of 'biomimetic,' 'cradle to cradle,' and 'sustainable.' The term 'sustainable' is reductive; it implies the bare minimum. 'Cradle to cradle,' on the other hand, outlines a highly beneficial strategy. At the moment we lack suitable theories on architecture's ability to respond to the environment. Our goal is to unravel the code of ecological design and simply create good design that is interdependent with the natural world. ONE Lab sets out to do just that.

MARIA AIOLOVA   466

An architect and urban designer based in New York City, Maria Aiolova co-founded Terreform ONE and Planetary ONE with Mitchell Joachim, and she directs the ONE Lab School for Urban Ecology and the One Prize Design and Science Award. Most recently, she was faculty at Pratt Institute, the Graduate School of Architecture and Urban Design, and Parsons the New School for Design. She has been honored with the Viktor J. Papanek Social Design Award and the Zumtobel Group Award for Sustainability and Humanity. She received her masters in architecture and urban design from Harvard University, B.Arch. from Wentworth IT, and Dipl.-Ing. from the Technical University of Vienna, Austria and Sofia, Bulgaria.

WM: Do you foresee architecture students being required to study biology or synthetic biology in the near future? If so, to what do you attribute this development?

MA: I do, but that will take some time. Architecture schools have to comply with National Architectural Accrediting Board requirements, which are slow to change or adopt new trends. The study of biology and synthetic biology, on the other hand, is racing ahead and essential to bridging the gap between designers and the natural world. It also offers a wealth of new possibilities and creative solutions to the current global environmental crisis. Independent schools such as ONE Lab have the ability to create a curriculum inclusive of biotechnology that enables us to address the significant problems of our time and opens us up to the possibilities of self-sustenance, organic growth, and perpetual change.

WM: In what ways do you think the location of the program in the Metropolitan Exchange (MEx) Building influences the content or experience of the workshops for students?

MA: The whole idea of ONE Lab was born in the MEx Building, which comprises an immensely diverse group of companies and individuals, but we have in common our creativity, productivity, and professionalism. We benefit from the inspiring energy and camaraderie of our shared spaces. Terreform ONE was the first architecture practice to build a biology lab, which has evolved into educational infrastructure shared with Genspace, another non-profit dedicated to providing wider access to biotechnology. For ONE Lab students, lab activity in such a setting is invaluable. Additionally, we never have to look far to recruit faculty—more than 50 percent of our recent intake of instructors was from MEx Building organizations.

WM: If there were just one element of the urban form of New York City that you could change instantly and permanently, what would it be, and why?

MA: New York is a city of water. I'd love to see the water and the waterfront of New York City become a truly exciting public space integrated with energy production, water cleansing, and habitat creation. Last summer we ran a competition, Water as the Sixth Borough, focused on New York and its waterways, concentrating on recreational space, public transportation, local industry, and native environment in the city. So if I were king for a day, I would open up all 600 miles of the waterfront to the public, create a soft edge, and implement some of the winning designs.

WM: What projects, outside of One Lab, are you focusing on now or in the near future?

MA: We are working on turning ONE lab into a year-round school and a degree-granting institution. We are considering the options to do this independently or in conjunction with an established academic institution. We are also working on a Brooklyn Navy Yards project called 'Super Dock.' Using the principles of industrial ecology, we propose that the underused dry docks become a vibrant manufacturing and incubator space, which will address community needs, public access, storm runoff, water filtration, and rising currents.

BIOGRAPHIES

CHAPTER 1

Triptyque is a French-Brazilian Architecture firm founded by Grégory Bousquet, Carolina Bueno, Guillaume Sibaud and Olivier Raffaelli, graduates from the Ecole d'Architecture de Paris-La-Seine, France. The firm addresses the problems of emerging cities and develops methods and tools for questioning and/or modifying the evolution of urban spaces and modern construction. Triptyque has been lauded for projects such as 'Harmonia 57' and 'Colombia 325' in Brazil. The firm's work was presented in 2008 in Venice for the Architecture Biennale, within the Optimiste exhibition at the French Pavilion; and in 2010, for the AFEX prize exhibition. The firm was also invited to the Hong Kong/Shenzen's Biennale in 2009, with 'Creatures.' Their work was also seen in the Guggenheim Museum of New York in 2010 within the exhibition Contemplating the Void, and at the London Festival of Architecture 2010 with 'Swarming Futures' and in the Victoria and Albert (V.&A.) Museum's 1:1 exhibition.

url: http://triptyqueblog.blogspot.com
email: com@triptyque.com

Weinstein-Vaadia Architects is a Tel Aviv-based firm that specializes in architectural, interior, and landscape design. Founded in 1993, the practice's portfolio includes a range of public and private projects throughout Israel. Their buildings celebrate the beauty of simplicity and natural elements, such as light, air, vegetation, and movement. The firm strives to be both precise and relaxed, like nature, not by imitation but by an exploration of the interplay between these two positions. Their work ranges from hospitals, such as the Childrens Hospital at the Sieff Medical Center in Tsfat, and wineries, such as the Galil Mountain and Golan Heights Wineries, to educational projects such as the Center for Environmental Education at the Hiriya Recycling Park. The firm is led by Shai Weinstein and Gil Vaadia.

url: http://www.zwwv.com
email: wv@zwwv.com

Giuliano Mauri was an artist and architect who used organic and living materials to construct poetic environmental interventions deemed 'natural architecture.' As some materials disintegrated over time, the young trees and living materials would insert themselves in the gaps, generating a work that was never wholly natural nor wholly man made. Mauri created these dialogues with nature in many works, including 'I Mulini' (windmills caressed by what he poetically termed 'imaginary' winds), the 'Scala del Paradiso,' and the 'Bosco sul Isola' project on the Tromo del Lodigiano, other works include the 'Osservatori Estimativi' realized in Gorlitz, Germany, and Zgorzelec, Poland. In addition to his site-specific works all over Europe, Mauri participated in the 1976 Venice Biennale, the 1992 Milan Triennale, and the 1994 Biennale of Penne. He sadly passed away in 2009. Detailed plans and notes for 'Cattedrale Vegetale' enabled it to be constructed posthumously by his son Robert Mauri under the artistic direction of Paola Tognon.

url: http://www.cattedralevegetale.oltreilcolle.info

Ferdinand Ludwig is an assistant professor at the Institute for Basics of Modern Architecture at the University of Stuttgart and a pioneering architect in the field of living plant constructions. He has designed and realized several projects that combine growth processes of living plants with an engineering approach. In his PhD studies, he developed multiple horticultural construction techniques and analyzed botanical rules of growth to deduce construction parameters for living plant architecture. In 2007 he co-founded the Research Group Baubotanik at the Institute of Architectural Theory at the University of Stuttgart. Since then he has organized workshops and lectured on living plant constructions at the University of Stuttgart and worldwide.

www.ferdinandludwig.de
email: baubotanik@ferdinandludwig.de

Stefano Boeri is an architect and editor-in-chief of *Abitare* magazine. He is Professor of Urban Design at the Politecnico di Milano and has taught at Harvard Graduate School of Design, Massachusetts Institute of Technology (MIT) and the Berlage Institute, among others. He is the founder of multiplicity, an international research network dedicated to the study of contemporary urban transformations. He is also the co-author of *Mutations* (Actar, 2000), *USE* (Skirà, 2002), and *Cronache del Abitare* (Mondadori, 2007). Boeri is a regular contributor to several magazines and newspapers, and he was previously editor-in-chief of the international magazine *Domus*. Together with Richard Burdett, Jacques Herzog, and William MacDonough, he is part of the Architecture Advisory Board in charge of developing the guidelines for the urban transformations to be implemented to coincide with the 2015 Milan Architecture Expo.

url: www.stefanoboeri.net
email: boeristudio@boeristudio.it

HOK is a global architectural firm that specializes in planning and design solutions for sustainable buildings, communities, and organizations. Through its collaborative network of 25 offices worldwide, the firm is committed to developing resources and expertise to help lead the world toward a sustainable future. Founded in 1955, HOK's oeuvre includes architecture, engineering, interiors, planning, sustainable consulting, lighting, graphics, facilities planning and assessment, and construction services. HOK collaborated with Vanderweil and Eleni Reed, GSA on 'Process Zero: Retrofit Resolution,' the algae-powered winning entry for *Metropolis* magazine's Next Generation Competition.

url: http://www.hok.com/
email: HOKContact@hok.com

Höweler + Yoon Architecture LLP/My Studio is a multidisciplinary practice operating in the space between architecture, art, and landscape. Founders Meejin Yoon and Eric Höweler believe in an embodied experience of architecture, seeing media as material and its effects as palpable elements of architectural speculation. Their work has been featured in *Expanded Practice* by Princeton Architectural Press, *Architect Magazine*, *Domus*, *I.D.* magazine and *The New York Times*, among others. J. Meejin Yoon is an architect, designer, and associate professor in the Department of Architecture at MIT. She is the recipient of the United States Artist award, the RISD/Target Athena Award and the Rome Prize Fellowship. Eric Höweler is an architect and assistant professor of architecture at Harvard University's Graduate School of Design. Prior to forming Höweler + Yoon Architecture, he was a senior designer at Diller + Scofidio. He is the author of *Skyscraper: Vertical Now*, published by Rizzoli/Universe Publishers. Höweler + Yoon Architecture LLP is based in Boston, Massachusetts.

url: http://www.hyarchitecture.com/
email: info@mystudio.us

Kate Orff is an architect, writer, and educator focused on sustainable development, biodiversity, and community-based change. She is an assistant professor of architecture and urban design at Columbia University, and founder/co-director of the Urban Landscape Lab where she leads studios and seminars that integrate the earth sciences into the design curriculum. Orff's architectural studio, SCAPE, has won local and national design awards. She was named a *Dwell* magazine 'Design Leader' and she received a 2008 National ASLA award in the communications category. She lectures widely in the United States and abroad on the topic of urban landscape and new paradigms of thinking, collaborating, and designing for the anthropocene era. Her work has been cited in publications such as *The New Yorker*, *The Economist*, *The New York Times*, and *New York* magazine, in addition to architecture and planning publications, such as *Metropolis*, *Dwell*, *Azure*, *Landscape Architecture Magazine*, and *Harvard Design Magazine*. She has been interviewed on National Public Radio, Queens Public TV, and The Brian Lehrer Show. Orff received a BA in political and social thought from the University of Virginia and an MLA from Harvard University.

url: http://urbanlandscapelab.org/
email: kate@scapestudio.com

Mitchell Joachim is a leader in ecological design and urbanism and associate professor of architecture at New York University. He is a co-founder of Terreform ONE and Planetary ONE. In 2011 he was awarded a Senior TED (Technology, Entertainment and Design) Fellowship, the Moshe Safdie Associate Fellowship, and the Martin Society for Sustainability Fellowship at MIT. His project 'Fab Tree Hab' has been exhibited at the Museum of Modern Art (MoMA) in New York and widely published. *Rolling Stone* magazine honored Joachim in 'The 100 People Who Are Changing America.' He was interviewed on *The Colbert Report* and *Popular Science* magazine featured his work as a visionary example of 'The Future of the Environment' in 2010. Joachim earned a PhD at MIT, a masters in architecture and urban design at Harvard University, an M.Arch at Columbia University, and BPS with honors at SUNY at Buffalo.

url: http://www.archinode.com/
email: mj@terreform.org

Magnus Larsson is a Swedish architect, writer, and translator splitting his time between Stockholm and London. He has contributed as a writer to publications that include *Frame*, *The Wire*, *Another Magazine*, *Kultureflash*, and *Bon International*, in addition to publications in Sweden. His architectural proposal 'Dune' won him a 2008 'Next Generation' Holcim Award, as well as recognition from *BLDGBLOG*, *Wired*, and *Slashdot*. He earned a BA from the Oxford School of Architecture and completed his diploma studies at the Architectural Association in London in 2010.

url: http://www.magnuslarsson.com/
email: studio@magnuslarsson.com

IwamotoScott Architecture is committed to pursuing architecture as a form of applied design research, and it engages in projects at multiple scales and in a variety of contexts. Led by Lisa Iwamoto and Craig Scott, the firm focuses on the perceptual performance of architecture and aims to produce an experiential synthesis of formal affect and spatial effect, while balancing specificities of context, economies of construction, particulars of program, and desires of the client. The firm has received numerous awards and honors and has been widely published. Iwamoto has worked as a structural engineer at Bechtel Corporation, as an architectural designer at Schwartz Silver Architects, and Thompson and Rose, and as an architectural intern at Morphosis. Lisa Iwamoto is an architect and educator, and the author of *Digital Fabrications: Architectural and Material Techniques*, published by Princeton Architectural Press. Craig Scott is an architect and an associate professor of architecture at California College of the Arts.

url: http://www.iwamotoscott.com/
email: contact@iwamotoscott.com

Alberto T. Estévez has been a practicing architect, designer, professor, and photographer for more than 20 years. He studies architectural practice and theory, and is the founding director of the Biodigital Architecture program at the International University of Catalonia. His research interests include biomimetics and the potential of applying synthetic biology in architecture. Estévez has published numerous articles in national and international publications, including *Editorial Gustavo Gili*, *El Croquis Editorial*, *Actar*, *Editorial Susaeta*, *Arquitectura Viva*, *Temple*, *Ábside*, and *Arquitectura*. He has participated in or organized 27 exhibitions at venues including the Biennial of Barcelona and the Academy of Fine Arts in Vienna. Estévez has received a degree in architecture from Polytechnic University of Catalonia and studied art history at the University of Barcelona, where he received an Extraordinary Prize of Final Studies in 2008.

url: http://www.albertoestevez.com/
email: estevez@uic.es

Rachel Armstrong is a medically trained interdisciplinary researcher focused on the development of metabolic materials for living buildings. She has collaborated with international artists, such as Helen Chadwick, Orlan and Stelarc, who engaged with the technologies of extreme body modification and the impact of extreme environments on biological systems. These projects exemplify the way in which the environment can directly shape organisms through biotechnological interventions. Armstrong is also an author and teaches at the Bartlett School of Architecture, exploring the connections between biology, medicine, and architecture.

url: http://www.rachelarmstrong.me/
email: rachel.armstrong@ucl.ac.uk

T.R.Hamzah & Yeang Sdn.Bhd. is an international architectural firm best known for designing innovative green buildings and master plans. Founded more than 30 years ago by principals Tengku Robert Hamzah and Ken Yeang, the firm has received accolades for their consideration of ecological impact and a building's use of energy and materials over its life cycle. Much of the firm's early work pioneered a passive low-energy skyscraper design, the 'Bioclimatic Skyscraper.' Key projects include the high-rise National Library Board building in Singapore, the 40-storey Eco-Tower at Elephant & Castle in London, the 24-storey IBM Building in Malaysia, the 15-storey Mesiniaga Building (IBM franchise) in Malaysia, and Wirrina Cove Condominium in Australia. The firm has received more than 20 awards, including the Aga Khan Award for Architecture (1995) and the RAIA (Royal Australian Institute of Architects) International Award (in 1997 and 1999). Its work has been published extensively in the international press.

url: http://www.trhamzahyeang.com
email: trhy@trhamzahyeang.com

CHAPTER 2

Ginger Krieg Dosier is an assistant professor of architecture at the American University of Sharjah (AUS) College of Architecture, Art, and Design, United Arab Emirates. Prior to arriving at AUS in 2007, she was a visiting assistant professor at the North Carolina State University College of Design. Over the past 8 years she has sought a scientific understanding of the properties of material in relation to architectural performance, engaging in co-research forums and cross-disciplinary collaboration. She received Metropolis magazine's 2010 Next Generation design award for her project 'BioBrick.' Dosier studied interior architecture at Auburn University before completing a masters in architecture at Cranbrook. She is interested in exploring the intersection of design practice and the science of materials.

http://vergelabs.com
email: gkrieg@aus.edu

Henk Jonkers is a research scientist at the Microlab within the school of Civil Engineering and Geosciences at Delft University of Technology in the Netherlands. His research examines the impact of microbial communities on natural and man-made materials and ecosystems, with a focus on development and application of bio-inspired sustainable materials in civil engineering. He has published multiple papers on self-healing 'BioConcrete,' a material that has earned wide recognition for its potential to enhance concrete's performance while decreasing its ecological impact. Before joining Delft in 2006, Jonkers worked as a research scientist at the Microsensor Research Group of the Max-Planck-Institute for Marine Microbiology in Bremen, Germany. He earned both his MSc and his PhD from the University of Groningen, the Netherlands, specializing in microbial ecology.

url: http://citg.tudelft.nl
email: H.M.Jonkers@tudelft.nl

David Benjamin and Fernan Federici explore new ways of using biological systems as design

tools. Collaborating through a residency in the Synthetic Aesthetics program, they investigate ways to combine synthetic biology and architecture, particularly the use of living cells as bioprocessors. Benjamin is Principal at the architecture firm The Living and Director of the Living Architecture Lab at Columbia University's Graduate School of Architecture, Planning and Preservation. His recent projects include 'Living City' (a platform for buildings to talk to one another), 'Amphibious Architecture' (a cloud of light above the East River that changes color according to conditions underwater), 'Living Light' (a pavilion in Seoul that displays air quality and collective interest in the environment), and 'Proof' (a series of design studios at Columbia that explore testing as a design methodology and evolutionary computation as an exploration technique). Federici is a postdoctoral researcher at the University of Cambridge working in the area of synthetic biology. Federici is interested in how cellular circuits in plant cells can be designed to self-organize and interact with adjacent plant cells and bacteria in a predictable and robust fashion.

url: http://www.syntheticaesthetics.org/residents/federici-benjamin
email: life@thelivingnewyork.com

Damian Palin is a research engineer at Nanyang Technical University, Singapore, and is guided by the belief that biotechnology will play a key role in the development of sustainable societies. He studied at the National College of Art and Design, Dublin, before co-founding kernel32, a furniture design company that exhibited in designersblock at the London Design Festival in 2004. After studying leadership for sustainable development at Queen's University Belfast, he designed and implemented a number of appropriate technologies for the development of micro-industries in two Ecuadorian townships, as well as several technological solutions for the preservation of food. Palin's 'Radical Means' project was developed in his final year of study on the innovation design engineering course at the Royal College of Art and Imperial College, London.

url: http://www3.ntu.edu.sg/r3c
email: damian.palin@network.rca.ac.uk

Marin Sawa is a designer and researcher specializing in a multidisciplinary design approach that combines textiles, biology, and architecture. She is particularly interested in 'smart' materials intrinsically engineered to be responsive while also elegant, minimal, versatile, and not flooded with electronics. She earned her BA at the Architectural Association in London and spent several years in Tokyo working on various fashion, web, interior, and lighting design projects, as well as numerous projects for the architectural offices of Kengo Kuma and Associates. She earned a masters in the Textiles Futures program at Central Saint Martins, London, from which she graduated with distinction. Sawa is currently a PhD candidate at the same institution in a collaborative program with the Energy Futures Lab, Imperial College, London.

url: http://www.marins.co.uk/
email: atmarin@marins.co.uk

Don Ingber is Founding Director of the Wyss Institute and a leader in the emerging field of

biologically inspired engineering. He oversees a multifaceted effort to identify the mechanisms that living organisms use to self-assemble, and to apply these design principles to develop advanced materials and devices. He also leads the Biomimetic Microsystems platform in which microfabrication techniques from the computer industry are used to build functional circuits with living cells as components. Ingber's most recent innovation is a technology for building tiny, complex, three-dimensional models of human organs. He has made major contributions to cell and tissue engineering, angiogenesis and cancer research, systems biology, and nanobiotechnology. He has authored more than 300 publications and 40 patents and has received numerous distinctions, including the Pritzer Award from the Biomedical Engineering Society and the Lifetime Achievement Award from the Society of In Vitro Biology. He holds the Judah Folkman Professorship of Vascular Biology at Harvard Medical School and Children's Hospital Boston, and he is a professor of bioengineering at the Harvard School of Engineering and Applied Sciences. Ingber also serves on the Board of Directors of the National Space Biomedical Research Institute and was recently elected to the College of Fellows of the American Institute for Medical and Biological Engineering.

url: http://wyss.harvard.edu
email: info@wyss.harvard.edu

The Center for Architecture Science and Ecology (CASE) is a multi-institutional research collaboration co-hosted by Rensselaer Polytechnic Institute and Skidmore, Owings & Merrill. It develops next-generation building systems to address the need for radically new sustainable built environments, pushing the boundaries of environmental performance in urban building systems on a global scale through actual building projects. Co-located on the Rensselaer campus and in lower Manhattan, CASE unites advanced architectural and engineering practices with scientific research through a unique and intensive collaboration between multiple institutions, manufacturers, and professional offices within the building industry. Research and system development conducted at CASE aims to implement changes to building practices with international impact in three priority areas: energy consumption; sustainable resource management; and quality of access to essential resources: fresh air, clean water, natural daylight, and plant and animal life.

url: http://www.case.rpi.edu
email: bermie@rpi.edu

Royal Philips Electronics of the Netherlands is a diversified consumer products and services company that is focused on improving people's lives through innovations. As a market leader in healthcare, lifestyle, and lighting, it seeks to integrate technologies and design into people-centric solutions, based on customer insights and the brand promise of 'sense and simplicity.' Philips is headquartered in the Netherlands and employs approximately 128,000 people in more than 60 countries.

url: http://www.design.philips.com/

Micromidas is a California-based company that has developed an innovative microbial process to convert raw sewage into high-quality disposable

plastics in order to address two fundamental issues: sewage and plastic waste. The company collaborates with wastewater-treatment plants to alleviate the costly problem of bio-solid waste, as well as with plastics producers to help bring to market a cost-competitive, biodegradable plastic. It refers to itself as a provider of microbial biorefinery technology for wastewater treatment. In 2010 the Artemis Project, a consulting practice focused on 21st-century water management, selected the Micromidas as one of the Top 50 Water Innovation Leaders.

url: http://micromidas.com/
email: info@micromidas.com

Cityroofs offers a range of innovative products and systems for soft landscaping, hard landscaping, and sustainable drainage, including living (green) roofs and walls, planting and water roofs, paving systems, street furniture, and photovoltaics. The UK-based organization provides design, manufacturing, supply, and installation services to suit the requirements of the developer and contractor. As part of the international building materials group CRH, and with a unique technical perspective covering all aspects, Cityroofs offers complete elevated landscape solutions on projects of all types and sizes.

url: http://www.cityroofs.com/
email: info@cityroofs.co.uk

Ecovative Design LLC was founded in 2007 by Eben Bayer and Gavin McIntyre and focuses on developing naturally grown replacements for unsustainable synthetic materials. It has developed products such as 'Ecocradle' and 'Greensulate,' which harness fungal mycelia to create a rigid, biodegradable composite for applications like packaging and insulation. The New York-based company has won numerous awards for sustainability and materials innovation. In June 2010, Steelcase, a leader in supporting environmental initiatives, adopted 'Ecocradle' packaging for its ready-to-assemble office furniture. The company's research and development efforts have also recently won grants from the New York State Energy Research and Development Authority and the Environmental Protection Agency to further develop its products.

url: http://www.ecovativedesign.com/
email: sales@ecovativedesign.com

Suzanne Lee collaborates with scientists to unite design with cutting-edge bio- and nanotechnologies. She is a senior research fellow at Central Saint Martins College of Art and Design, London, and Director of the 'BioCouture' project, investigating the use of microorganisms to grow a textile biomaterial. 'Biocouture' garments have been displayed in the Science Museum, London, and the ModeMuseum in Hasselt, Belgium. Lee is the author of Fashioning The Future: Tomorrow's Wardrobe, published by Thames & Hudson, and is also a 2011 TED Fellow. She lectures internationally and has coordinated workshops in conjunction with the chemical engineering and synthetic biology departments at Imperial College London.

url: http://www.biocouture.co.uk/
email: info@biocouture.co.uk

Mathieu Lehanneur opened his eponymous design studio in Paris in 2001. He was awarded the Grand Prix de la Création from the city of Paris for 'Andrea,' an air-filtration system utilizing plants. In 2009 he presented at TED Global about his fascination with the sciences, and how they influence and enhance his work. He has worked with a variety of clients on design projects, including Cartier, Nike, Yohji Yamamoto, Issey Miyake, Veuve Clicquot, Schneider Electric, and the Centre Pompidou. In 2010 he received the 'Intelligence de la main' Prize awarded by the Bettencourt-Schueller Foundation for his series of ceramic jars entitled 'L'Âge du Monde' (The age of the world), which visualize in three dimensions the age distribution of a nation's population.

url: http://www.mathieulehanneur.fr
email: m@mathieulehanneur.com

Carlos Peralta-Mahecha is a researcher interested in exploring the intersection between science and design, and the ways in which designers and scientists collaborate. He is a PhD student at the Centre for Technology Management at the University of Cambridge working on the Design in Science project. He has worked as a lecturer at Central Saint Martins College of Art and Design, London, and on the Faculty of Architecture and Design at the Universidad Javeriana in Bogotá. Peralta was Course Leader and Head of the Product Design Department at the Glasgow School of Art between 2003 and 2007, and in the last two years he has worked in design in higher education in Singapore and Spain. His professional design experience includes work for industry, a design consultancy, and design entrepreneurship. He has developed projects in different areas, ranging from lighting to exhibition stands, and from furniture to product interfaces.

url: http://www.ifm.eng.cam.ac.uk/dmg/projects/dis.html
email: cmp60@cam.ac.uk

Alberto T. Estévez, see page 277

Eduardo Mayoral González is an architect and researcher using life manipulation and biotechnology in architectural contexts. He aims to use hybridization and strategies of crossbreeding living and non-living materials for the purpose of sustainable design and production. González earned his masters in sustainable city and architecture from the IUCC, ETSA University of Seville, a masters in advanced architecture from the IAAC, UPC in Barcelona, and a masters in advanced architectural design from the Graduate School or Architecture, Planning and Preservation (GSAPP), Columbia University in New York. He is currently developing his PhD as a member of the research group Out_Arquías at the ETSA University of Seville and is pursuing a year-long independent study through the Advanced Architectural Research program at GSAPP. González was honored in 2011 with a 'Next Generation' Holcim Award for his proposal to create architecture-integrated, zero-electricity bioluminescent lighting.

url: http://eduardomayoral.wordpress.com
email: emg2161@columbia.edu

MADLAB is an award-winning and internationally published architecture firm noted for its research and innovative design services. Founded in 2003 by Petia Morozov and Jose Alcala, it is committed to environmental sensitivity, intelligent creativity, and client service. MADLAB's disciplinary core comprises architecture, industrial design, and urban design, with professional and research influences from the fields of landscape, ecology, art, cognitive sciences, engineering, and urban theory. Morozov is an architect, educator, and writer whose work has been featured in various publications, including Architectural Design, Yale Constructs, Journal of Architectural Education, Performance Art, and a number of ACSA proceedings. Alcala is an architect and Interim Director at the New Jersey Institute of Technology's School of Industrial Design, where he co-founded a lab dedicated to renewable technologies.

url: www.madlabllc.com
email: info@madlabllc.com

The 2010 Chinese University of Hong Kong iGEM team comprised ten undergraduates, who were majoring in biochemistry, and food and nutritional science, from the School of Life Science. Six advisors helped to guide the team's efforts to create a system for encrypting and storing data in DNA. Their work was awarded a gold medal at the annual competition, which is hosted at MIT. It was the first year that the university participated in the competition.

url: http://2010.igem.org/Team:Hong_Kong-CUHK
email: allenyu@cuhk.edu.hk

CHAPTER 3

Ionat Zurr and Oron Catts are considered to be pioneers in the field of biological arts and are renowned for their Tissue Culture and Art Project. They were central to the establishment of SymbioticA in 2000, and they publish widely and are invited regularly as keynote speakers, to curate exhibitions, and to exhibit internationally. They have recently exhibited as part of the Corpus Extremus (LIFE+) Exhibition at the Exit Art Gallery in New York City, and the Design and Elastic Mind Exhibition at MoMA, New York. Oron is the Director of SymbioticA. Ionat, who received her PhD from the University of Western Australia's Faculty of Architecture, Landscape and Visual Arts, is a researcher and SymbioticA's academic co-ordinator.

url: http://tcaproject.org/
email: contact@tcaproject.org

Oliver Medvedik is the principal investigator at the Bioworks Institute Laboratory for Art and Biology in Brooklyn, New York. He obtained his bachelor's degree in biology from Hunter College and his PhD from Harvard Medical School in the Biomedical and Biological Sciences program of 2006, using single-celled budding yeast as a genetic system to map pathways that underlie the processes of aging in more complex organisms, such as humans. Before co-founding the Bioworks Institute, he worked as a biotechnology consultant for Sirtris Pharmaceuticals, taught numerous undergraduates at Harvard University, and mentored two of Harvard's teams for the annual synthetic biology competition (iGEM) held at MIT.

Medvedik is on the board of directors for the non-profit organization Genspace, a biological research incubator that is dedicated to teaching genetic engineering.

url: www.bioworks.com
email: om@bioworks1.com

James Auger and Jimmy Loizeau have collaborated on design projects since October 2000 and the conception of their award-winning 'Audio Tooth Implant.' They develop speculative and critical products and services in order to instigate a broader analysis of what it means to exist in a technology-rich environment, both today and in the near future. Their work has appeared in a variety of publications, from Wired magazine to The Sun newspaper, as well as in public spaces from Austria to China. Their recent 'Carnivorous Domestic Entertainment Robots' has been exhibited in the Science Gallery at Trinity College, Dublin, featured on BBC1, and nominated for a 2010 Transmediale Award. Auger is a tutor of design interactions at the Royal College of Art, London. Loizeau is a design consultant and tutor of design at Goldsmiths College, London.

url: http://www.auger-loizeau.com
email: info@auger-loizeau.com

Joris Laarman is an experimental designer and co-founder of Joris Laarman Lab, which aims to create objects and installations that add cultural meaning to technological progress and show the beauty of how things could work. He first gained notoriety with his functional rococo radiator 'Heatwave,' first picked up by the conceptual design company Droog and now also produced by Jaga. He has contributed articles and seminars to Domus magazine and has been a guest instructor at several institutions, including the Architectural Association in London, Rietveld Academy in Amsterdam, and the Design Academy in Eindhoven. Laarman is a native of the Netherlands and attended the Design Academy in Eindhoven, where he graduated cum laude in 2003.

url: http://www.jorislaarman.com/
email: info@jorislaarman.com

Jelte van Abbema is a designer and artist who is interested in exploring reality through living media. As a young gardener, he learned about the beauty and peculiarity of nature, qualities that inform how his work has developed over time. Abbema studied in the Man & Communication program at the Design Academy in Eindhoven, graduating cum laude in 2006. His work has been nominated for the René Smeets and Melkweg Design Awards and received the Willie Wortel Award for invention. In 2007 he founded Lab van Abbema to investigate how design, science, and technology can combine to shape a new landscape that reflects the contemporary nature of our world. His ongoing search to make the unfamiliar familiar has resulted in numerous collaborations, and his work has been exhibited and published internationally.

url: http://www.vanabbema.net/
email: jelte@vanabbema.net

Lowe Roche is a creative marketing and advertising design agency located in Toronto, Ontario. Its work ranges from the more traditional advertisements seen on subways, streetcars, and buses to logos, corporate identities and unorthodox promotional campaigns. Founded in 1991 by Chief Creative Officer Geoffrey Roche, the company has received hundreds of major awards, including Canada's Agency of the Decade and Marketing magazine's 2007 Agency of the Year Award. It has been featured in Adweek, The New York Times, and Communication Arts, and on CTV and CBC. Clients include Audi, Purina, Johnson & Johnson, Unilever, Miele, and the Toronto Zoo. Lowe Roche is part of the Lowe global agency, headquartered in London, England.

url: http://www.loweroche.com/
email: inquiries@loweroche.com

Terry Willard is President and CEO of BioLume, a privately held biotechnology company developing a portfolio of proprietary bioluminescent proteins with applications in the food, beverage, cosmetic, and diagnostic imaging markets. From 2001 to 2006 he was Executive Vice President of Xsira Pharmaceuticals, Inc. (formerly Norak Biosciences, Inc), where he was primarily responsible for sales, marketing, licensing, and business development. He has worked as Vice President, Marketing and Business Development, at Medco Research Inc. and SONUS Pharmaceuticals.

url: http://www.biolume.net/
email: twillard@biolume.net

Troika is a London design collective founded by Eva Rucki, Conny Freyer, and Sebastien Noel. Its experimental sculptures and projects employ a cross-disciplinary approach at the intersection of sculpture, architecture, and contemporary installation. The firm's work explores the convergence of scientific thought, observation, and human experience in a rational and rationalized world, aiming to describe how logic and reason live in the presence of the metaphysical and surreal. Troika's work is represented in the permanent collections of the Israel Museum Jerusalem, the British Council, the Art Institute of Chicago, and the V.&A. Museum, London. Recently, the firm was invited to create three art installations for the UK Pavilion at the World Expo Shanghai. The firm's founders have authored Digital by Design (Thames & Hudson, 2008) and Moscow Style (Booth-Clibborn Editions, 2005). In 2009 Troika won the D&AD Yellow Pencil for its digital sculpture 'Cloud in London Heathrow Terminal 5' and its kinetic installation 'Palindrome' for the V.&A. in 2011.

url: http://troika.uk.com/
email: studio@troika.uk.com

Tuur Van Balen uses design to explore the political implications of emerging technologies. He aims to confuse, question, and confront different publics with the possible (and impossible) roles of technologies in our everyday lives. Since 2008 he has been working on bringing design into the world of synthetic biology, and biology into the world of design. This has led to collaborations with the Centre for Synthetic Biology at Imperial College in London, the BIOS group at LSE, and the Haseloff Lab at the University Cambridge. He has exhibited and presented his work in various contexts within the UK and abroad. Van Balen is a visiting tutor at the

Royal College of Art and a freelance designer in service and interaction design.

url: www.tuurvanbalen.com/
e-mail: tuur@tuurvanbalen.com

Revital Cohen develops critical objects and provocative scenarios juxtaposing the natural with the artificial. Since graduating from the Royal College of Art in 2008, she has been exhibiting and lecturing within varied contexts and locations—from scientific and academic conferences to art galleries and design fairs. Her work has been exhibited at MoMA, New York, the Cooper-Hewitt National Design Museum, Ars Electronica, the National Museum of China and London's Design Museum. She has given talks at Tate Britain, Design Indaba, the RSA, the Battle of Ideas, and the Foundation for Art and Creative Technology. Cohen is a winner of the Science Museum's Emerging Artist Commission and has produced work on commission for Z33, the Engineering and Physical Science Research Council, and the Icsid World Design Congress. She often collaborates with scientists, bioethicists, animal breeders, and physicians. She is developing an experimental installation investigating the mechanical translation of organic functions, supported by a Wellcome Trust Art Award.

url: http://www.revitalcohen.com/
email: mail@revitalcohen.com

Alexendra Daisy Ginsberg is an artist, designer, and writer who uses the medium of design to interrogate emerging technologies, science, and the function of design itself. As Design Fellow for the Synthetic Aesthetics program, a project at Stanford University and the University of Edinburgh (funded by the National Science Foundation [NSF] and the Engineering and Physical Sciences Research Council [EPSRC]), she is curating an international program that explores the shared and shifting territory between synthetic biology, art, and design. Her recent projects include 'The Synthetic Kingdom,' a proposal to recognize a new branch of the biological tree of life, 'E.Chromi,' a proposal to utilize synthetic biology to diagnose illnesses, and 'The Well Oiled Machine,' a science fiction short story (co-written with Oron Catts) for *Icon* magazine. After graduating in 2009, Ginsberg was a resident at SymbioticA, the art and science collaborative laboratory at the University of Western Australia. In 2010 she spent time at either end of the synthetic biology/design and art spectrum, teaching both the ArtsScienceBangalore and University of Cambridge iGEM 2010 teams. She has studied architecture and design at Cambridge, Harvard University, and the Royal College of Art. She exhibits, lectures, and publishes internationally.

url: http://www.daisyginsberg.com/
email: hello@daisyginsberg.com

Amy Congdon is a designer whose work revolves around the blurring of roles between science and design. After completing a BA in contemporary textiles at the Norwich School for Art and Design, she attended the pioneering MA textile futures program at Central Saint Martins College of Art and Design in London. She has worked on projects for companies such as Nissan Design Europe and Microsoft, presenting her winning 'Data Hungry Skin' at the 2010 Microsoft Design Expo in Seattle. She has exhibited work at the V.&A. Museum, London, as part of CSM Design Explorations and her project 'Biological Atelier' previewed at the Milan Design Fair. Following graduation, Congdon went on to complete a residency at the Australian art lab SymbioticA, working under the supervision of Oron Catts and Ionat Zurr on digital embroidery to produce scaffolds onto which she seeded skin cells. A continuation of her 'Biological Atelier' work, the project further explored the creation of bespoke biological textiles, considering ideas of ownership, commodification, and the ethical implications of using living materials for design.

url: http://www.amycongdon.com/
email: amy.congdon@ymail.com

Natsai Audrey Chieza is a designer, materiologist, and trend researcher born and raised in Zimbabwe. Having completed her architectural education at the University of Edinburgh, she is now based in London, where she participated in the MA textile futures program at Central Saint Martins. Her 'Design Fictions: Posthumanity in the Age of Synthetics' is a collection of crafted surfaces and objects designed to provoke debate and discussion about the life science industry and the appropriation of life. These research-driven future scenarios raise critical questions over current understanding of the potential cultural and environmental implications of synthetic biology and stem cell research.

url: http://natsaiaudrey.com/
email: natsaiaudrey@ymail.com

Sascha Pohflepp is a designer and artist who is interested in past and future technologies and concepts of art, commerce, and idealism. He explores what these ideas mean to us as historical beings and how they inform which realities come to pass and which are discarded. His work has been shown at the the Art Institute of Chicago, the Wellcome Trust, Ars Electronica Festival, the V.&A. Museum, London, and the Talk To Me exhibition at MoMA, New York. He received a special mention at the 2010 VIDA award for art and artificial life. Pohfelpp has been a researcher-in-residence at the Art Center College of Design, Pasadena, and throughout 2011 he was a resident in the Synthetic Aesthetics program, an NSF/EPSRC-funded research project focusing on synthetic biology. He holds a master of arts in design interactions from the Royal College of Art, London, and a degree from the Berlin University of Arts.

url: http://pohflepp.plugimi.com/
email: sascha@pohflepp.com

Mike Thompson's work explores both old and new technologies in order to generate fresh relationships between function and behavior, questioning common codes of conduct. His work touches upon issues such as sustainability, biotechnology, and psychology. After graduating from the Design Academy in Eindhoven in 2009, he set up his own eponymous studio. His work has been widely publicized in both the design and popular press, including magazines such as *Wired*, *Frame*, and *Icon*. He currently works from Eindhoven, the Netherlands.

url: www.miket.co.uk
email: info@miket.co.uk

CHAPTER 4

Eduardo Kac integrates robotics, biology, and networking to explore the fluidity of subject positions in the post-digital world. His work has been exhibited internationally at venues such as Exit Art and Ronald Feldman Fine Arts, New York; Maison Européenne de la Photographie, Paris, and Le Lieu Unique, Nantes, France; OK Center for Contemporary Art, Linz, Austria; and in biennials such as Yokohama Trienniale, Japan, Gwangju Biennale, South Korea, and Bienal de São Paulo, Brazil. His work is part of the permanent collection of the Institut Valencià d'Art Modern, Spain, among others. Kac has received many awards, including the Golden Nica Award. He lectures and publishes worldwide.

url: http://www.ekac.org
email: ekac@saic.edu

Paula Hayes is a New York-based artist whose work often incorporates living materials, from the composition of landscape to the creation of 'living necklaces.' Solo exhibitions of her work include 'Paula Hayes: Aquatic Garden' at Lever House, New York, and 'Paula Hayes' at the Wexner Art Center in Columbus, Ohio. Her work has also been displayed at MoMA, New York, and the Marianne Boesky Gallery, among others. She has lectured internationally and her work has been featured in various publications, including *The New York Times*, *Los Angeles Times*, *Dwell*, and *Architectural Record*. Hayes attended Skidmore College and earned an MFA in sculpture from Parsons School of Design.

url: http://www.paulahayes.com/
email: info@paulahayes.com

Nurit Bar-Shai is an artist working at the intersection of art, science, and technology. She composes video and live telematic installations in addition to conducting experiments through creative collaborative inquiry. She earned her BFA from the Bezalel Academy of Fine Arts and Design in Jerusalem and her masters from the Interactive Telecommunications Program at Tisch School of the Arts, New York University. Her work has been exhibited at the Brooklyn Museum; the OK Center for Contemporary Art, Linz; the National Art Center,Tokyo; and the SESI Gallery in São Paulo, among others. Bar-Shai received a Prix Ars Electronica 2007 Honorary Mention, the 11th Japan Media Arts Festival Jury Award, an Experimental Television Center Finishing Funds award (funded by New York State Council on the Arts), and ARTIS (Contemporary Israeli Art Fund Grant). She is co-founder and Arts and Culture Program Director of Genspace, a community biology lab in Brooklyn, New York.

url: http://nuritbarshai.com/
email: n@nuritbarshai.com

Tomáš Gabzdil Libertiny's focus is on exploring design strategies in art. He founded his Rotteram-based studio after completing an MFA at the Design Academy in Eindhoven in 2006. His artworks have been acquired by MoMA, Museum Boijmans van Beuningen, and the Cincinnati Art Museum. He studied industrial design at the Technical University in Slovakia and the University of Washington in Seattle, as well as conceptual design at the Academy of Fine Arts and Design in Bratislava.

url: www.tomaslibertiny.com/
email: info@studiolibertiny.com

Julia Lohmann is a London-based designer who is interested in unusual and undervalued natural and man-made materials. Her work is exhibited worldwide and is part of major private and public collections, including MoMA, New York. She teaches at the Royal College of Art in London and in 2008 was selected as one of four 'Designers of the Future' by Design Miami. Her work was selected for the Design Mart exhibition at the Design Museum, London, by then director Alice Rawsthorn. Since then, her work has been shown as part of the Great Brits touring exhibition organized by the British Council, and numerous exhibitions in galleries and museums in the UK and abroad, as well as on *The Culture Show* (BBC, 2007), and in books, international magazines, and newspapers. Lohmann earned a BA in graphic design from the Surrey Institute of Art and Design, University College (now the University for the Creative Arts), and an MA in Design Products at the Royal College of Art in London.

url: julialohmann.co.um
email: julia@julialohmann.co.uk

Allison Kudla is an experimental artist who is interested in using digital media to preserve and discover environments that are in a continual state of flux. In her more recent projects she has been exploring the combination of patterns, fabrication technologies, and plant tissue culture to make living installations. Her piece 'Growth Pattern' was exhibited in Alter Nature: We Can at Z33 in Hasselt and When Process Becomes Paradigm at LABoral Centro de Arte y Creación Industrial in Gijón. She returned to the United States after working as an artist in residence at the Srishti School of Art, Design and Technology in Bangalore, India. Kudla holds a BFA from the School of the Art Institute of Chicago and is also a doctoral candidate at the University of Washington's Center for Digital Arts and Experimental Media. She has recieved an honorable mention in Hybrid Arts at Ars Electronica 2010 and an honorary mention in the Vida Competition for Art and Artificial Life. Her work has been publishd in *Art + Science Now* (Thames & Hudson, 2010).

email: allisonkudla@mac.com
url: http://allisonx.com/

Steve Pike spent a number of years as a designer before studying at the Bartlett School of Architecture, University College London. He received a masters in 2003 and subsequently founded arColony, a forum for experimental architecture. His work has been included in a number of publications and various international exhibitions. He currently divides his time between architectural practice in London and progressing his research.

url: www.arcolony.com
email: steve@arcolony.com

Liam Young is an independent urbanist, futurist, designer, and curator. He was named by *Blueprint* magazine as one of 25 people who would change architecture and design in 2010. He is a founder of the futures think tank Tomorrow's Thoughts Today (TTT), a group whose work explores the consequences of fantastic, perverse, and underrated architectures and urbanisms. His projects deploy fictional near-future scenarios as critical instruments for instigating debate about the social, architectural, and political consequences of emerging biological and technological futures. With TTT he has consulted and conducted workshops on speculation, emerging technologies, and future forecasting for firms including Arup—Drivers for Change, Phillips Technologies, and various arts and science organizations. His projects include the stuffed and mounted biotech creatures of 'Specimens of Unnatural History: A Near Future Bestiary' and 'Where the Grass Is Greener,' a set of picturesque postcards from an ecotopian micronation. Young curates international events and exhibitions, including the multimedia series Thrilling Wonder Stories: Speculative Futures for an Alternate Present with Bldgblog's Geoff Manaugh and the Imaginarium Exhibition in Berlin with *Beyond Architecture* editor Lukas Feireiss.

url: http://www.tomorrowsthoughtstoday.com/
email: l.young@tomorrowsthoughtstoday.com

Susana Soares employs design to explore technological implications for public engagement, developing collaborative frameworks between design and emerging scientific research. She is a senior lecturer at London South Bank University and has held research fellow positions at the Impact! project, at the Royal College of Art and Material Beliefs, and at Goldsmiths University of London. She has lectured internationally and has presented her work at Networkshop at Caltech University; the Creative Engagement/Medi(t)ation of Survival symposium at the National Museum of Modern Art, Kyoto; and Headspace—Scent as Design conference, organized by the New School in New York. Her work has been featured within design and scientific publications and exhibited at MoMA in New York, the Science Gallery in Dublin, and the Southbank Centre and Royal Institution in London. Soares completed her BA in product design at the Escola Superior de Artes e Design, Portugal, and earned an MA in the design interactions program at the Royal College of Art, London. Her work is in the permanent collection of MoMA. Her research focuses on how the understanding of technologically redesigned living systems can generate new frameworks for design practice.

url: http://www.susanasoares.com/
email: susana@susanasoares.com

Alicia King is an Australian interdisciplinary artist exploring biological permutations in humans, animals, and the wider environment, alluding to that which generally lies outside of the everyday category of the 'living.' In recent years she has focused on biological technology at SymbioticA, the Art and Science Collaborative Research Laboratory, University of Western Australia, and the University of Tasmania School of Medicine. King has exhibited throughout Australia and beyond, and is the recipient of numerous grants and residencies throughout Australia, Europe, and Asia, with the generous support of the Australia Council for the Arts, Arts Tasmania, and the Australian Network for Art and Technology. She is the 2010 recipient of the Rosamond McCulloch Studio at the Cité Internationale des

Arts, Paris, and a residency in the Galapagos Archipelago, South America.

url: http://aliciaking.net/
email: alicia@aliciaking.net

Andy Gracie explores information systems contained within living organisms and ecosystems, as well as how they might be accessed and processed through the use of technology. His work has always been linked to scientific practice as both contextual and methodological reference, and as a subject of critique. He also focuses on the science of astrobiology and its concomitant theories on the very origins, constitution, and boundaries of life. Gracie's work is often realized in installation, employing robotics, custom electronics, sound, and video, alongside biological processes. His works have appeared in, among others, the 2011 Translife Biennial in Beijing and the 2011 Synth-Ethic, the Natural History Museum in Vienna.

url: http://www.hostprods.net/
email: info@hostprods.net

Anne Brodie is an artist whose work subverts the usual confines of scientific practice. After earning a degree in biology, she completed an MA at the Royal College of Art in 2003. Working experimentally with glass, film, and photography, she jointly won the international Bombay Sapphire Prize for design and innovation with a short film, *Roker Breakfast*, in 2005. The next year she was awarded the British Antarctic Survey/Arts Council Artists and Writers fellowship to Antarctica, where she lived and worked at isolated scientific bases for nearly three months. Operating at the boundary between science and art, her current work explores questions of ownership and the decision-making processes involved in determining what constitutes 'valid data.' Brodie was awarded a Wellcome Trust arts award for a collaborative project exploring bacterial bioluminescence and its external relationship with the human body. Her work has been shown nationally and internationally, at venues that include the V.&.A. Museum, London, the Royal Institution of Great Britain, the Old Operating Theatre museum in London, and the Maison Européenne de la Photographie, Paris.

url: www.annebrodie.co.uk
email: annebrodie01@hotmail.com

CREDITS & INDEX

CREDITS

INTRODUCTION

1 Fab Tree Hab. Mitchell Joachim, Terreform + Planetary ONE; **2** BioConcrete. Image courtesy Henk Jonkers; **3** Process Zero Retrofit Resolution. Images courtesy HOK / Vanderweil; **4** Tassel House. Image courtesy Henry Townsend; **5** SymbioticA. Image courtesy The Tissue Culture and Art Project; **6** Human Microbiome Project. Image courtesy Darryl Leja; **7** Ernst Haeckel. Image from Kunstformen der Natur; **8** BioBE Center. Image courtesy the Biology and the Built Environment Center; **9** Pantheon. iStockphoto: © Tobias Machhaus; **10** Port Said Lighthouse. Shutterstock: © Antonio Abrignani; **11–13** BioConcrete. Images courtesy Leon van Paassen; **14–16** BioConcrete: Images courtesy Henk Jonkers; **17** Dune. Image courtesy Magnus Larsson; **18** Symbiosis. Image courtesy Jelte van Abbema; **19** E.Chromi. Image courtesy Alexandra Daisy Ginsberg; **20** Synthetic Kingdom. Image courtesy Alexandra Daisy Ginsberg.

CHAPTER 1

21 Baubotanik Tower. Image courtesy the designers; **22** Harmonia 57. Image courtesy Nelson Kon; **23** Harmonia 57. Image courtesy Greg Bousquet; **24** Harmonia 57. Nelson Kon; **25** Harmonia 57. Image courtesy Leonardo Finotti; **26** Harmonia 57. Image courtesy Nelson Kon; **27–31** Gutman Visitor Center. All images courtesy Amir Balaban; **32–35** Root Bridges of Meghalaya. All images courtesy Lambert Shadap; **36–38** Vegetal Cathedral. Photo by Aldo Fedele © Arte Sella; **39–41** Vegetal Cathedral. Photo by Giacomo Bianchi © Arte Sella; **42** Baubotanik Tower. Image courtesy the designers; **43–48** Lake Constance Footbridge. All images courtesy the designers; **49** Bio Milano. Image courtesy Boeri Studio (Stefano Boeri, Giandrea Barreca, Giovanni La Varra); **50** Bio Milano. Photo: Iwan Baan; **51** Bio Milano. Image courtesy Boeri Studio (Stefano Boeri, Giandrea Barreca, Giovanni La Varra); **52–54** Bio Milano. Stefano Boeri Architetti; **55–61** EDITT Tower. Image courtesy © T.R. Hamzah & Yeang Sdn Bhd; **62–65** Filene's Eco Pods. All images courtesy Höweler + Yoon Architecture and Squared Design Lab; **66–71** Process Zero Retrofit Resolution. All images courtesy HOK/Vanderweil; **72–76** Oyster-techture. All images courtesy SCAPE/LANDSCAPE ARCHITECTURE PLLC; **77–81** Fab Tree Hab. All images courtesy Mitchell Joachim, Terreform + Planetary ONE; **82–90** Dune. All images courtesy Magnus Larsson; **91–93** Hydronet SF 2108. All images courtesy IwamotoScott Architecture; **94–97**

Genetic Barcelona Project. All images courtesy Alberto T. Estévez; **98–103** Kindergarten. All images courtesy Alberto T. Estévez; **104** Future Venice. Image courtesy GMJ; **105** Future Venice. Image courtesy Christian Kerrigan (studio@christiankerrigan.com); **106** Future Venice. Image courtesy Rachel Armstrong; **107** Future Venice. Image courtesy Rachel Armstrong.

CHAPTER 2

108 Microbial Home. Image courtesy Philips Design; **109–12** BioBrick. Image courtesy Ginger Dosier; **113** BioBrick. Picture by Altaf Qadri © AP/Press Association Images; **114–16** BioBrick. Image courtesy Melina Miralles, Petroleum Institute, Abu Dhabi; **117–26** Bio Concrete. All images courtesy Henk Jonkers; **127–30** BioProcessing. All images courtesy David Benjamin and Fernan Federici; **131–35** A Radical Means. All images courtesy Damian Palin; **136–40** Algaerium. All images courtesy Marin Sawa; **141–42** Algaerium. Photography by Sue Barr; **143–44** Algaerium. All images courtesy Marin Sawa; **145–47** Lung-on-a-chip. All images courtesy the Wyss Institute for Biologically Inspired Engineering at Harvard University; **148–51** Active Modular Phytoremediation System. All images courtesy CASE, the Center for Architecture Science and Technology at RPI; **152–63** Microbial Home. All images courtesy Philips Design; **164–69** Bio Plastic. All images courtesy Micromidas; **170–73** Aquadyne Living Wall. All images courtesy Cityroofs UK Ltd; **174–78** EcoCradle. All images courtesy Ecovative Design; **179–81** BioCouture. © BioCouture 2011; **182–85** Local River. Image courtesy Mathieu Lehanneur; **186** Moss Table. Picture by Toby Summerskill; **187–92** Moss Table. Image courtesy Carlos Peralta and Alex Driver; **193** Moss Table. Picture by Liliana Rodriguez; **194** Moss Table. Image courtesy Carlos Peralta and Alex Driver; **195** Biodigital Chair. All images courtesy Alberto T. Estévez; **196–201** Bioluminescent Devices. All images courtesy Eduardo Mayoral Gonzalez; **202–6** Bioencryption. All images courtesy the Chinese University of Hong Kong 2010 iGEM Team: http://2010.igem.org/Team:Hong_Kong-CUHK; (for all images) **207–9** Algal Filter Machine. All images courtesy Nathan William Smith.

CHAPTER 3

210 Symbiosis. Image courtesy Jelte van Abbema; **211** Victimless Leather. Image courtesy of the Tissue Culture and Art Project; **212** Victimless Leather. Original perfusion

system. Image developed by professor Arunasalam Dharmarajan, School of Anatomy & Human Biology, University of Western Australia; **213–14** Victimless Leather. Image courtesy of the Tissue Culture and Art Project; **215** The Tissue Culture and Art Project. Image courtesy of the Tissue Culture and Art Project; **216–20** Living Watch. All images courtesy Dr Oliver Medvedik; **221–22** Carnivorous Domestic Robots. Image courtesy Marcus Gaab Studio; **223–33** Carnivorous Domestic Robots. All images courtesy James Auger and Jimmy Loizeau; **234** Carnivorous Domestic Robots. Image courtesy Marcus Gaab Studio; **235** Carnivorous Domestic Robots. Image courtesy James Auger and Jimmy Loizeau; **236–38** Halflife Lamp. All images courtesy Joris Laarman; **239–48** Symbiosis. All images courtesy Jelte van Abbema; **249–57** Contagion Advertisement. All images courtesy Glen D'Souza, Lowe Roche; **258–59** Bacterioptica. MADLAB, LLC; **260–63** Bioluminescent Toys. All images courtesy Bruce Bryan, MD; **264** Green Map. Photo by Katarina Stuebe, 2010; **265–67** Green Map. Photo © Troika 2010; **268–70** Green Map. Photo by Katarina Stuebe, 2010; **271** Pigeon d'Or. Image courtesy Tuur Van Balen; **272–73** Pigeon d'Or. Image courtesy Pieter Baert; **274–78** Life Support. All images courtesy Revital Cohen; **279** E. Chromi. Image courtesy Alexandra Daisy Ginsburg; **280** E. Chromi. Image courtesy Alexandra Daisy Ginsburg and James King; **281–87** Synthetic Kingdom. All images courtesy Alexandra Daisy Ginsburg; **288–91** Biological Atelier. Photography by www.2shooters.com; **292–302** Design Fictions. All images courtesy Natsai-Audrey Chieza; **303–5** Plant Fiction. Photo © Troika 2010; **306–11** Prospect Resort. All images courtesy Sascha Pohflepp; **312–15** Growth Assembly. All images courtesy Sascha Pohflepp and Alexandra Daisy Ginsburg. Illustrations by Sion Al Tomas; **316–18** Googol Puddles. All images courtesy Mike Robitz; **319–21** Blood Lamp. All images courtesy Mike Thompson; **322–24** Latro. All images courtesy Mike Thompson.

CHAPTER 4

325 Exploring the Invisible. Image courtesy Anne Brodie; **326–31** Natural History of the Enigma. All images courtesy Eduardo Kac. Transgenic work, 2003–8; **332** Natural History of the Enigma. Eduardo Kac, Edunia Seed Pack Studies I–VI (from the Natural History of the Enigma series), 22 x 30" (55.9 x 76.2 cm) each, lithographs, 2006. Edition of 15. Collection Weisman Art Museum, Minneapolis; **333**

Natural History of the Enigma. Eduardo Kac, Edunia Seed Packs, hand-made paper objects with Edunia seeds and magnets, 4 x 8 inches (10.16 x 20.32 cm), 2009. Collection Weisman Art Museum, Minneapolis; **334** Photo of Limax maximus, the Great Grey Slug. Courtesy Steven N. Severinghaus; **335–39** Egg and Slug. Photography by Béatrice de Géa. Installation at the Museum of Modern Art, New York. All images courtesy Paula Hayes; **340** Objectivity. Image courtesy Professor Eshel Ben Jacob, School of Physics and Astronomy, Tel Aviv University; **341** The Seed of Narcisscus. Courtesy Tomáš Libertiny; **342–43** The Seed of Narcisscus. Photograph courtesy Francesco Allegretto, **344** Courtesy Tomáš Libertiny; **345** Vessel #2 from the Vessel Series. Courtesy Tomáš Libertiny; **346–47** The Honeycomb Vase. Courtesy Tomáš Libertiny; Photograph courtesy Raoul Kramer; **348–52** Algaebra. All images courtesy Nancy O. Photography; **353–56** Genetic Heirloom Series. All photos by Gary Hamill; **357–64** Genetic Heirloom Series. All images courtesy Revital Cohen; **365–68** Cook Me— Black Bile. All images courtesy Tuur Van Balen; **369** Co-Existence. Image courtesy Julia Lohmann Studio; **370** Co-Existence. Image courtesy The Wellcome Trust; **371** Co-Existence. Image courtesy Julia Lohmann Studio; **372** Growth Pattern. Image courtesy Kristof Vrancken/Z33; **373** Growth Pattern. Image courtesy Allison Kudla; **374–75** Growth Pattern. Image courtesy Kristof Vrancken/Z33; **376–77** Growth Pattern. Image courtesy Allison Kudla; **378–81** Contaminant. All images courtesy Steve Pike; **382** Specimens of Unnatural History. Image courtesy Liam Young; **383–85** Specimens of Unnatural History. Photographed by Jamie Kingman; **386** Specimens of Unnatural History. Image courtesy Liam Young; **387** Specimens of Unnatural History. Photographed by Jamie Kingman; **388** Specimens of Unnatural History. Image courtesy Liam Young; **389–99** Pathogen Hunter. All images courtesy Susana Soares & Mikael Metthey; **400–4** Growing Pains. All images courtesy Mike Thompson; **405–7** The Vision Splendid. Photo: Patrick Bolger, with retouching by Alicia King; **408–13** Autoinducer_PH-1. All images courtesy Andy Gracie; **414–18** Exploring the Invisible. All images courtesy Anne Brodie.

CHAPTER 5

419 Branching Morphogenesis. Sabin+Jones LabStudio. Image courtesy Sabin+Jones LabStudio; **420** iGEM. Image courtesy International Genetically Engineered Machine competition (iGEM) and Justin Knight; **421**

Genspace. Image courtesy Dan Grushkin; **422** Pigeon d'Or. Image courtesy courtesy Pieter Baert; **423** BioConcrete. Image courtesy Henk Jonkers; **424–27** ONE Lab. All images courtesy Maria Aiolova and The ONE Lab School for Urban Ecology; **428–30** CASE. All image courtesy CASE, the Center for Architecture Science and Technology at RPI; **431–33** BioBE Center. All images courtesy Jessica Green and Tim O'Conner and the Biology and the Built Environment Center (BioBE); **434–36** Sabin+Jones LabStudio. All images courtesy Sabin+Jones LabStudio; **437–39** iGEM. All images courtesy International Genetically Engineered Machine competition (iGEM) and Justin Knight; **440–42** Genspace. All images courtesy Dan Grushkin and Genspace; **443–46** Royal College of Art Design Interactions Department. All images courtesy Anthony Dunne and the RCA Design Interactions Department; **447–48** Synthetic Aesthetics. All images courtesy Alexandra Daisy Ginsberg; **449** SymbioticA. Image courtesy of SymbioticA; **450** The Tissue Culture and Art Project. Image courtesy of the Tissue Culture and Art Project; **451** Victimless Leather. Image courtesy of the Tissue Culture and Art Project; **452–53** BioProcessing. All images courtesy David Benjamin and Fernan Federici; **454–55** Arts Catalyst. All images courtesy The Arts Catalyst; **456** Exploring the Invisible. Image courtesy Anne Brodie.

INTERVIEWS

457 Microbial Home. Image courtesy Philips Design; **458** David Benjamin. Image courtesy David Benjamin; **459** Ginger Krieg Dosier. Image courtesy Ginger Krieg Dosier; **460** Sean Quinn. Image courtesy Sean Quinn; **461** Jessica Green. Image courtesy Jessica Green; **462** Dan Grushkin. Image courtesy Dan Grushkin; **463** Marin Sawa. Image courtesy Marin Sawa; **464** Eduardo Kac. Photo by Mario Llorca; **465** Oron Catts. Image courtesy Oron Catts; **466** Maria Aiolova. Image courtesy Maria Aiolova.

INDEX

CITATIONS

PAGE 21

T. Friedman, *Hot, Flat and Crowded: Why We Need a Green Revolution—and How it can Renew America* (New York: Farrar, Straus & Giroux, 2008) pp. 241–66.

PAGE 62

Z. Adeel et al., *Overcoming One of the Greatest Environmental Challenges of Our Times: Re-thinking Policies to Cope with Desertification* (Ontario: United Nations University, 2007) pp. 2–25.

PAGE 76

Rob Carlson, *Biology is Technology: The Promise, Peril, and New Business of Engineering Life* (Cambridge, MA: Harvard University Press, 2010) pp. 1-19.

PAGE 76

Heidi Ledford, *Nature*, October 7, 2010: 467 651–652.

PAGE 77

Paola Antonelli, *Design and the Elastic Mind* (New York: Museum of Modern Art, 2008) pp. 14-24.

PAGE 83

D'Arcy Wentworth Thompson, *On Growth and Form* (Cambridge: Cambridge University Press, 1917) pp. 670–718.

PAGE 124

C. Bancroft, 'Long-term storage of information in DNA,' *Science*, September 7, 2001: 293(5536) 1763–1765.

PAGE 246

Alex Driver, Carlos Peralta and James Moultrie, 'Exploring how industrial designers can contribute to scientific research,' *International Journal of Design*, April 30, 2011: 5(1) 17–28.

ACKNOWLEDGMENTS

This book came to life in large part thanks to the early and persistent encouragement of Lucas Dietrich of Thames & Hudson as well as the cooperation and generosity of the architects, designers, scientists, professors, writers, and artists who agreed to participate.

For the variety and quality of the content presented here I am thankful for the enthusiastic support of my close collaborators Andrew Gardner and Barbara Eldredge who assisted in virtually every aspect of content collection, organization and development. Special thanks are also due to Alice Twemlow for her tireless advocacy on behalf of her students and for having the combination of vision and tenacity to establish the MFA Design Criticism program at the School of Visual Arts (SVA) in New York. I am also indebted to Paola Antonelli, Senior Curator of Design at the Museum of Modern Art, New York, for her foreword to this volume, her camaraderie and sincere encouragement, and for her field-defining series of exhibitions and essays, many of which shaped the research that became the foundation of this book. Thanks are also in order to Kate Boothby and the team at T&H who tamed unruly contents and shepherded this book toward concision and clarity. The development of the research paper from which this book emerged was supported and guided by Andrea Codrington Lippke at the SVA as well as Andy Rumbach who consistently challenged me to achieve excellence. For helping to provide access to the people, facilities, and research that were essential for completing this project I am grateful to Dan Grushkin, Oliver Medvedik, David Benjamin, and Maria Aiolova. For granting me my first curatorial experience and teaching me the steps necessary for producing a museum catalogue I will forever be indebted to Matilda McQuaid and Andrea Lipps of the Cooper-Hewitt, National Design Museum, New York.

This book is also partly the product of the inaugural class of the Design Criticism program at SVA. If not for their collaboration and feedback; for their patience in hearing yet again about biology and design; for their support; and for their combined brilliance I would certainly not have had this opportunity – I am indebted to all: Hala Abdumalak, Amelia Black, John Cantwell, Frederico Duarte, Chappell Ellison, Laura Forde, Sarah Froelich, Kathryn Henderson, Emily Leibin, Mike Neal, Becky Quintal, Alan Rapp, Angela Riechers, and Jim Wegener.

I am also thankful for the mentorship of MoMA's Ruth Shapiro, from whom I learned more than can be listed here, but above all how to plan strategically and think as a leader. Of course I am also deeply grateful to Christine Myers for giving me the imagination to write and to Stuart Myers III for teaching me the courage to pursue publishing. Finally, this book was possible thanks only to the encouragement, editing skills, and suggestions to nap of Sunshine Daly, my partner in everything important. She and her band of friends from Reed College, most notably Peter Jordan and Rachel Relph, have helped me to find my voice. They are hereby entitled to endless homemade bread and mead.